THE PAINTER

The shocking true story of a south london
hitman and his brush with the art world

As told to
Dean Cavanagh

About the writer: Dean Cavanagh is an award-winning screenwriter. He co-wrote the Emmy award winning TV series Crime for ITV, Wedding Belles for C4 and the feature film Creation Stories with Irvine Welsh. He is also the co-writer of two theatre plays with Irvine Welsh: Performers and Babylon Heights.

The Author remains anonymous.

A work of art should be like a well-planned crime.

Charles Baudelaire

At the turn of the 20th century, Friedrich Nietzsche proclaimed that God is dead and that man had killed him. This created an arrogance with man that he himself was God. But as God, all he could seem to produce was disaster.

South London boy, David Bowie 2002

Preface

I am The Writer of this book but The Author will remain anonymous for obvious reasons. I can neither confirm nor deny any of the stories and revelations in this book, but it doesn't take a genius to work out what is true and what isn't in these pages. With even just some cursory research and discernment, it is easy to see where fiction gives way to fact and vice versa. With that in mind, this book can be called true crime *and* faction, *fiction/fact*, for want of a better word, and the names have been changed to protect the guilty.

This book has been over twenty years in the research and writing of, and the actual process involved was like nothing I've ever experienced before. I am, nowadays, predominantly a screenwriter, though I have written novels, theatre plays and newspaper articles in my time. In the writing of this book, I had to employ all the skills I have learnt over all these disciplines, but the skill I had to employ more than any other was being a good listener, because absolutely nothing in note form was written down and handed to me, other than a couple of PDFs, but not, I stress, from The Author himself.

I don't know the 'real' name of The Author, what he looks like, where he lives, or his motivations for these confessions. The Author is receiving no financial reward or even credit for his story. I have never met him face to face and my only contact with him has been through hundreds of hours of phone conversations. *His* numbers are always blocked.

Initially I was very sceptical about this whole enterprise and thought it might be a wind up. As time went on though, I started researching these stories and confessions, and I was faced with the fact, that if this was indeed a wind up it was a very elaborate one, and I couldn't understand why. What was the motivation behind it? *What* was to gain? *Who* would gain? *Why* are these stories being told? If it was a prank, why did I have to, on many occasions, do the chasing to keep the stories coming? And I suppose my biggest question was, am I dealing with a real psychopath and what does he actually know about *me*?

I didn't *have* to write this book. I make a living writing for film and television and I have purposefully gone with a small publisher to put these confessions in print, essentially because I didn't fancy having to negotiate and explain the material herein with people who have absolutely no understanding of how the criminal underworld really operates. The Author has always stressed that he finds the mainstream representations of *his world* inauthentic and filtered through the prism of what the chattering classes *believe it to be*, without ever having actually experienced it themselves.

It was at an after-hours drinking club called Gary's in East London where my friend, we'll call him 'Johnny', first started telling me stories about The Author. This was the in the early 2000s. Gary's attracted a strange brew of characters and there was always a buzz around the place. I always drank in places like The Colony, Gerry's, The Groucho, The Coach & Horses and the St Moritz in Soho. You got a better class of character in these places, so to speak.

I started regularly visiting London thirty years ago when I was involved in the music business. It was through the music business that I made the transition into the film and television business. Through Johnny I was introduced to many people who can only be politely called *well known villains*. When Johnny said he had a story and asked if I would I like to hear it, I was all ears. I'm a writer. Why wouldn't I?

At the time I was researching for a TV series we were about to pitch to HBO in the US. It was a story about a group of investors in a restaurant chain who find they are in business with a gangster, and in the story a hitman character has a prominent role.

I met Johnny in The Ship on Wardour Street the day after the night before. The hangover was alleviated by Johnny's tales about this mysterious figure, who he simply referred to as T. Johnny admitted that neither him, nor his extremely well-connected father knew T. Nobody did. He was like some kind of urban legend, a bogeyman that even the criminals who procured his services knew nothing about. Who Johnny and his father *did* know, or rather, *knew*, was the brother of the man who got this hitman into the game, mentored him and looked after all the contracts that were tendered to kill people. Johnny said he'd send me an email.

Johnny told me to read the attached PDF and we would talk when I was back down. He added that this was a leaked document and I should keep it to myself. This was all getting a bit too *Tinker, Tailor, Soldier, Spy* for my liking.

The PDF was an official report about police corruption and establishment links to organized crime. There was nothing in it that I hadn't already heard whispers about, so I just put it to one side. I arranged to meet Johnny and his Dad, 'Senior', the week after at a place on his old manor. Senior was the 'real deal' as far as reputations went, and a great raconteur. Talk eventually got around to this mysterious T. What followed was a very convoluted tale about a very powerful and internationally connected 'Chap' who had told Senior all his secrets when he was on his death bed. This 'Chap's' younger brother, who will become known as 'Uncle', was even more powerful, respected and successful, and this is where the focus was.

It was reiterated that this 'hitman' was an ultra-secretive, almost ghostly figure and that nobody knew who he really was. I asked Senior if this mysterious character even wanted his story telling. Senior replied that according to this 'Chap' he did. I politely asked father and son why they thought he would to tell such a story. Senior hazarded a guess: *maybe he wants to atone for his sins.* Johnny didn't agree: *ego,* he said. We left it with Senior telling me he was going to contact this hitman and ask if he would like to talk to me. That was it.

A fortnight later I got a call at home from Johnny and he sounded excited, "You need to get hold of a burner."

"A what?"

"A burner, a prepaid mobile. You send me the number; it'll get it passed on and you'll get a buzz from him."

"From this ..."

"Yeah, the geezer we've been talking about. The old man's sorted it. Schtum."

"Uh ... I don't know, Johnny."

"Fucksake! What's your problem? It's just a phone call! Have a listen to him at least. There might be something in it."

I dutifully bought a burner, passed Johnny the number and ... *nothing.* I heard nothing for about three months. I never chased Johnny up and figured that it all been forgotten about. It didn't bother me, and I simply put the burner in my drawer and forgot about it.

One day I was going through my drawer and I noticed I had

a missed withheld call on the burner. It could only have been Johnny. I called him and asked him what he wanted. He said he hadn't called the burner, so it could only have been the mystery man. Johnny said he would make it known that I wanted him to call me again. I didn't really expect him to.

The first call with T lasted over three and a half hours. He came across as quite articulate and straight to the point. He reeled off a list of his terms: no face-to-face contact, *ever*, no addresses, no voice recordings, the notes I made of the conversations would have to be burned once I had memorized them, I was to tell nobody that I was speaking to him (whoever *he* was) and that after every conversation we had, I would destroy the burner and go and buy a new one in preparation for the next call.

T said he was a big reader and he had considered writing down his stories, but couldn't in case he was suddenly 'pinched' and the incriminating confessions were found and used against him. He said he liked the idea of readers doing their own research and finding out exactly who he was talking about in his confessions.

T told me he thought his story would be very interesting for true crime readers and that he also wanted it to act as a guide to those who might feel that they would like to make murder their profession. I had to laugh at this, and I told him that it was highly unlikely *many* people were queueing up to become professional hitmen, and they probably weren't waiting for a book to come out to help guide them into it.

T made it be known that he was tired of reading fantastical tales about how the criminal underworld in the UK operates, and he wanted to see something out there that was authentic, "All the stuff they write about contract killings is a load o' bollocks. It's nothing like they say it is. Believe me, I been doing this a long time. I ain't seen nothing saying how it really is."

A week later I asked T to give me some something 'concrete'. When I explained what I meant about giving me something concrete, he said, "All right. Don't do this on your computer or anything, go to a library, get on one of them search engines and type in *blah, blah, blah*, then delete the history thing."

I did exactly as he told me to do and up came an article on an unsolved murder in London decades past. When he called again a few days later, I asked him how this archived news article was concrete evidence of his claims of being a professional hitman. I actually shuddered when he gave me details. They made perfect sense about this particular murder, and only someone who was involved in the killing, or someone who was pathologically obsessed about the killing could ever come up with.

I asked him straight out if I was being set up. He asked what I could be being 'set up' *for*, "All you're doing is writing my stories down."

"Like a court stenographer?"

"Well, no, I mean, I want you to write it proper. Make it readable."

As of this day, *29th of May, 2023*, I cannot confirm whether T is dead or alive. The last time I spoke to him was nine weeks ago when I read him the galleys of this book in a marathon six-hour call. He had very few suggestions, and only asked that I change a couple of pseudonyms because it was far too obvious who he was referring to. T asked me to run through the galleys with Johnny and Senior to make sure that he had disguised the characters enough. Johnny and Senior said that they believed he had. Senior remarked, "You've got *all* the blessings."

I neither condone nor condemn most of the stories and

confessions in this book. I am simply telling you what I have been told.

I don't know whether I will ever get to meet 'T' in the flesh. I very much doubt it though. The intention was always to simply get this story down on paper, and that is what we have done. There are only a couple of people who know that I have been working on this story for all these years, and I am sure they will be interested in finding out exactly why I kept going back to it. The reason, I hope they agree, is in these pages.

This book could have stretched to double its size, but I have only included stories that were I thought were plausible from the research I carried out.

Dean Cavanagh 2023

ONE

*All the information I have about myself
is from forged documents.*

Vladimir Nabokov

We're strolling along Waterloo bridge towards the South Bank and it's heaving with tourists as per usual. London bridges have always been our *go to's* for a face to face. They can be surveyed by cameras, obviously, but there's not a chance you could get audio surveillance to catch a chinwag on a London bridge.

All around us people are yapping in their native tongues and pointing their phones and cameras at anything and everything. I've never understood the urge to visit somewhere and spend most of your time looking at it through a screen, but then, I've not got a tourist mindset. I see places and spaces as potential opportunities to practice my craft.

Tonight, I'll turn up in Shoreditch at an art gallery and I'll be wearing a baseball cap and dark shades and I'll be giving any photographers a swerve. Even if I were to get 'papped', it's highly unlikely that anyone from back in the day would see the photo in print or online. They're not the kind of punters for trendy magazines or society columns. And besides, even if they thought they recognized me they'd be thrown off by the scent of the moody name I've adopted since I got into the art racket. I am an artist, that goes without saying, but I practice my craft in the really fucking *dark* arts and my greatest hits are usually only seen by Old Bill and paramedics before they're scraped off the floor into a meat wagon: *Mm, I can see what he's done with the gun there. I can see what he's trying to say … it's a commentary on society. Those shades of red are really quite bold.*

I'll keep my head down at the art gallery, and come across as a right grumpy cunt, which I truly am when surrounded by these muppets. I play the tortured artist, which again, I *am* tortured, but not by worrying about slapping paint on canvasses. No, what tortures me is my kills, specifically: *did I do everything professionally and minimize the prospect of getting pinched.*

Uncle is by my side as we stroll across Waterloo bridge. As he talks, he constantly strums the tip of his nose with the tip of his thumb, leaving his hand to hover over his cakehole in case there's any lip readers zooming in on him, "I told 'em, I said *you don't wanna get one o' them Swedes to do it.* I said, *they use that EncroChat n' it's only a matter o' time before Old Bill n' the security forces crack it, n' when they do, fuckin' heads are gonna roll. It'll be a bloodbath, blue bleedin' murders* I says. N' I know I'm right. Think about it! Every cunt'll be turning on each other, but we're in clover, son. We ain't left no trails nowhere. Not one bleedin' crumb, all these years, we've always cleaned up … so, I says to the big fella, I gives it, *S'all well n' good mixing it up a bit every now n' then, putting even more distance out, I understand that, but sometimes you just gotta stick to the tried n' tested method.* He listens to me; I've got his ear. He knows we're the best in the business."

Uncle don't have to tell me any of this and I'm a bit uncomfy with it to be honest. It used to be simple. He would just give me the details of the contract, and after the planning I'd go out and do the piece of work. I think Uncle's finally being infected by the mounting paranoia rampant in the serious crime underworld. Surveillance technology *not* armed Old Bill is the villain's real nemesis nowadays, and Uncle – as intelligent and careful as he is – has to listen to the people who offer up the contracts, and it's the arseholes of these villainous powerbrokers that are twitching in the face of this *all-seeing* technology.

Me and Uncle pride ourselves on the work we've done, and a good reputation in this game means everything. Sometimes though, you're only as good as the man who's given you the contract. A couple of years ago a London based multi-millionaire financial fraudster hired a hitman from Marseille to snuff one of his business partners in Paris. Apparently, the hit went down kosher, but this fraudster were paranoid that the Marseille bloke might one day get pinched and offer up his name as one of his customers. This paranoid fucking fraudster set in motion a chain of events that would have made a great comedy film. Saying that, it would be so silly, it's doubtful many people would have sat through its extremely far-fetched plot.

You've heard that old poem: *there was an old lady who swallowed a dog to catch the cat to catch the bird etc.* This fraudster were fretting so much, he hired another hitman to take out the one he was shitting himself about being pinched. Obviously, this leaves him with another hitman he's gonna worry about eventually. So … I don't know how long this caper went on, but rumour has it that three hitmen ended up jam because of this nervous cunt. As stupid as it sounds though, it kind of makes sense. If you're in the market for hiring assassins you're already in a strange fucking world.

There are things you're gonna read in this book that on the face of it might sound fantastical, but what you've gotta remember is that extremely pressurised situations make people do strange things sometimes, and what might sound fucking potty to reasonable people is bread and butter for those facing life and death choices in pursuit of their daily dough.

The contract that Uncle were referring to was pretty straightforward in the scheme of things. Bloke from West London who owned a string of car washes needed clipping. He was to be left where he fell so it were obviously meant to be a message to others. I took the contract and set about the planning. Uncle had worked for this client on some other graft and knew him pretty well, so there were no worries about getting wedged off once the work were done. One this particular piece of work, Uncle would be charging the client £100,000 and he'd been parcelled off with 50k as a deposit and that was his to keep. Prices fluctuate and so does Uncle's cut.

Once the Car Wash King had been snuffed the client would purchase one of my, so called 'paintings' from the art gallery in the West End, usually with cash, and my art dealer would take her 20 percent straight off the top. A couple of days later she would make a bank transfer and I'd end up with £40,000 in a limited company business account. I'm not a director or secretary in the limited company, merely a signatory on the bank account, so I can pull whatever I like out at any given time.

If – *or when* – it comes on top for me, it's a simple click of a mouse or a phone call and the balance of the account gets transferred to a private bank account in France. I have a moody passport, id, birth certificate and driving license stashed in France so I would be sweet, as long as I'd managed to get on my toes fast enough to cross the channel without being pinched of course.

In the art gallery that night I'm surrounded by cunts. To a man, pretentious, hypocritical, soulless cunts who have never done a proper day's work in their lives. I detest 'em all and it gives me a buzz knowing that I'm having their trousers down. There's a couple in here that have paid 40k each to own my 'artwork' and I have nothing but contempt for them.

They are fucking mugs of the highest order and deserve all they get in their pursuit of trying to look trendy, vital and intelligent. They wouldn't know a proper work of art if it jumped up and chinned 'em. These are not people who have paid for me to kill people. They're just idiots who've bought the manufactured hype and think I'm a real artist.

There's loads of 'well known celebrity faces' from the world of 'entertainment' in attendance, whose names I can't even be bothered dropping. My art dealer's doing the rounds and I'm shuffling about trying to avoid eye contact and – *God forbid* – falling into a conversation with any of 'em. I'm supposed to be this shy, awkward, temperamental, publicity hating 'artiste' anyway, so nobody really bothers me. I just keep my head down and sup my orange juice, keeping an eye on my kettle and waiting 'til I've done the obligatory hour so I can fuck off home.

The only person I do talk to, very briefly, is Sebastian Horsley. He's a flamboyant artist from a wealthy family but he used to knock about with Jimmy Boyle, a notorious Glasgow villain back in the day. The couple of times I've spoken to Sebastian he's slagged off the artworld, so I like him. I also think he somehow knows I'm having peoples pants down, but he's definitely not on to what my real occupation is. Sebastian comes out with a few scathing putdowns and shuffles off. Five minutes later and the hour's up. I grab my helmet and I'm away on my Ducati Desert X back home to South London.

All that's on my mind now is the Car Wash King, his imminent demise and my payday. I were glad I would be leaving him where he fell. I'm not a disposal expert and the few times I've been called upon to do it I've not felt confident, though conversely, I once went through a period when I worried about who were cleaning up after me. I had no control over how professional they were, and if they'd been nabbed in the act of disposing of the corpses I'd created, there were always the chance of them blabbing and me getting pinched. Uncle always reassured with, "Even if they wanted to, they couldn't put the finger on you, son. They can't even put it on me! I told ya, it's all compartmentalized."

After all these years I've only ever met one of the people who've had to tidy up after me when I've done some wetwork, and it were a fucking horrific experience. I used think about 'em and I reckon they sometimes think about me. We're bound to, aren't we? I reckon they think, "why don't he tidy up after his 'self n' earn more dough? Just as I think, "why don't they learn to kill *and* tidy up n' earn more dough."

What I've learned is that most assassins, going way back, weren't that clever at cleaning up their hits for some unknown reason, and a disposal expert were often needed to make the bodies disappear. To me it's always felt a little bit like hiring a plumber to come and fix your khazi, but paying someone else to pull the chain to flush the shit away, but there you go. The standards are the standards.

I once brought it up with Uncle. He gives it, "Nah, some people don't have a problem lugging a dead body about, but they get squeamish if it's them that's got to pull the trigger. Their arris's goes. There's not a lot of men can do what you do, son."

Of all my hits I've only ever had to get rid of a handful of bodies, and that's because it made perfect sense to do so and were already factored into the planning from the off. You'll read about 'em later and I think you'll be impressed. The people who paid me were definitely impressed, because as of today those bodies still remain buried and nobody's even had so much as a tug about their disappearances. I later heard that a piece of my wetwork saved someone at least five million nicker. I got hundred large for it, mustn't grumble though, it's just the game and that's that.

So yeah, Uncle loves saying that word: *compartmentalized.* He's a bit of a scholar of the JFK assassination (*seen that flick a dozen times I have, son. Read all the books*) and he's impressed with the compartmentalized way the perpetrators pulled it off. On his recommendation I read a book called *Crossfire* about the JFK job, and it's hard to disagree with Uncle that the complexity of the planning involved were indeed a real work of (dark) art. One day he told me had known one of the actual hitmen who took the contract on Kennedy. He even reeled off a few foreign names, dates and places. I listened, but at the time I thought he were fannying me: just trying to impress his apprentice. I couldn't have been more wrong.

So, yeah, the snuffing of the Car Wash King will gather a few headlines in the London papers and might make the national news, but there won't be any films made or hundreds of books written about it. He'll just be another statistic in a long line of 'gangland hits' stretching back to Dickensian times.

As I'm riding home that night, I'm not thinking about the impact my next piece of work is gonna have on the family, friends, employees, debtors, creditors and enemies of this bloke. All I'm thinking about is putting a bullet in his napper in the safest, most efficient way possible and not getting pinched for it. My meticulous – and some might say, *obsessive –* planning will focus my mind on the run up to the act itself and block out the 'human' aspect from factoring in. I don't care what he's done or supposed to have done. It's not my concern and I'm really not interested in finding out. All I care about is doing my job professionally. I mind my own business.

All Uncle gives me about Mr. Car Wash is his name, age, address, the location of 10 car washes that he owns, the registration number, the make of motor he drives and a recent photo of him. It takes me a couple of minutes to memorize the info, then I tear into it little pieces and drop it in the Thames. I say *ta ta* to Uncle and I'm off. My first port of call is the leafy street in West London where the Car Wash king lives.

As I'm riding down his street, I immediately clock that his four-storey terrace house faces the rear grounds of a private school. Tick. There's speed bumps on the street. Tick. He parks his motor outside his gaff. Tick.

I then go and have a look at the 10 car washes he owns. This takes me a good eight hours and I'm doing it well into the evening. The washes are spread all over London: Brompton, Ealing, Pimlico, Custom House, Brixton, Kensal Rise, Brent Cross, Hounslow, Kilburn, Clapham. I find the one that would be perfect to do the hit, and it's on a side street not too far from his drum.

The next day I go and check out his street again. The private school grounds have a got 10 ft high wall around the perimeter and there are some beautiful tall trees lining it. The entrance into the grounds is through the front – which is a no no – but there's a narrow gate that allows access about twelve doors down from my mark's gaff. I immediately start calculating whether I could get my bike through it.

By 5am the next morning I'm on the street where he lives. I ride up to the gate and it's open. It's a tight squeeze but I get my Ducati through, park it and climb a tree. I'm about 13ft up it and wedged in between a couple of its sturdy branches. Through the leaves I can see his gaff. I'm well camouflaged and happy to stay put for as long as it takes to get my first eyeball on him. I'm there just over 2 hours.

At 7.10 am he comes out and gets into his very nice motor. I'm down the tree in a breath, on my bike and out of the gates on to the road. I tail him all the way to Hounslow. I keep about 4 cars back, but when it's obvious which one of his businesses he's going to, I overtake a couple of times and take a shortcut to where I now know he's heading.

For the next three weeks I repeat this MO and I eventually find the pattern. On Mondays he's go to Hounslow stays until about 10am, from there he goes to Kensal Rise and stays at the wash until around 1pm. From there he heads to a local restaurant, stays until 3pm and then goes home. Tuesdays he goes to the gym at 10 am and then at 11.30 am – noonish, he pops in at his Custom House, Brixton and Clapham branches. The rest of the week follows a similar pattern but it's his Kensal Rise plot that I focus on.

After having done a couple of reconnaissance's of the car wash and environs, I decide that it's the one for me, meaning it will be a Monday morning around 10.45 am when it goes down. I'm happy with that and run through the possible hiccups that might bubble up. Other than someone else being with him at the time of the hit there's nothing else I can identify.

Directly behind the car wash is a quiet street with old, small, graffiti smeared, lock up garages stretching along it. It's a through street that leads to a main road a couple of hundred meters along. It's perfect. Of course, there's always the possibility of some cunt turning up to one of the garages at the crucial moment, but in three weeks I've not seen a soul. *Fucking tumbleweed and the theme from a Fistful of Dollars.*

The fateful day comes and I set off to Kensal Rise at 9am. I've stuck a moody license plate over mine on the bike. I say 'mine', it's registered to someone, somewhere, who's got the same make and model of motorbike as mine. I ride very conscientiously, get to the street behind the car wash and park up. There's a section of the wall that's dilapidated and I climb over it. From there I shoot down towards the portacabin office. At the back of it there's an 6ft gap between the wall. I pick up a half brick that I'd dropped over the wall a couple of days back and smash the glass of the portacabin window with it. It's a tight squeeze but I manage to climb through it.

There's not much in the portacabin: a desk, landline phone, battered old filing cabinet, a dart board on the wall, a few plastic tubs of detergent and a bale of chamois leathers, hence no security alarm. I immediately draw my Glock and point it towards the door. A lot of people piss and moan about Glock's jamming, but I've never had a problem with 'em. Horses for courses.

My aim will remain trained until he unlocks the door and enters. I'm about 5ft away from it, to the left of it opening. It feels like about ten minutes pass before I hear his motor pull up. I take a swift look out of the grilled-up front window. It's him and he's alone. Sigh of relief.

The key goes in the door and I hear him whistling merrily on the other side of it. It opens, he steps inside, turns around and is about to close it. I step forward and the nose of the silencer is about 12 inches from his temple. Pfft and he falls over to the right. I step over him and quickly shut and lock the door. He's jam, but I put two more in his napper to make sure. I drop the Glock and climb back out of the window. It's clean (first time fired) and the serial number's been scrubbed and this is a 'show off' hit. It's always nice when you can leave the piece with the corpse. You don't have to worry about get pinched on your get-away. I do, however, unscrew the silencer and shove it down the side of my boots. For some reason, quality silencers for Glock's are getting hard to find nowadays. I heard it's something to do with the male to female 14mm adaptors, but who knows.

I poke my head out from behind the portacabin to check the coast, then scurry back over the wall to the street and my bike. Up in the distance I can see a black kid yapping on his mobile, but he's got his back to me and he's far too wrapped up in his convo to take any notice, *I hope.* He definitely don't clock me coming over the wall or being parked up so I'm sweet.

I get a real buzz when I turn the ignition and hear the friendly growl of the engine. I go via the Harrow Road and I'm back at my flat within the half hour. I wrap the silencer up and hide it behind a brick I've chiselled out of the wall in the communal bin shed of the flats. No cunt in their right mind would go sniffing round in that dark cesspit.

The door on my flat's triple locked and I strip down. Every piece of clobber, even socks and skivvies are shoved into the washing machine and given the highest temperature treatment. I run my leather gloves under the hot tap with plenty of fairy liquid and then do the same with my boots. I forensically clean my helmet with wet wipes. There's very little claret washed back from Mr. Car Wash's head. I flush the wet wipes down the toilet and go get in the shower. I'm scrubbing away for a good 10 minutes and there's no hot water left in the tank by the time I step out.

I shove the boots, gloves, helmet and freshly cleaned clobber into a large laundry bag and zip it up. Later that night I'll put on my recently purchased new gloves, boots and *white* helmet, ride down to a quiet spot on The Thames, sling the bag in and watch it sink.

Overly cautious you might think? Nah, there's no such thing in this game. You might give it, *why not just run the helmet under the tap as well?* The answer is it's hard to see blood on a black helmet and some of it could have splashed inside when I pulled the trigger. *And,* you might also ask why I wash everything I were wearing at the time of the hit if it's only gonna end up in the Thames? Again, if I'm pinched on my way to The Thames and I'm searched and found with the forensic minefield of clobber, well, I might as well have hired a billboard at Piccadilly Circus advertising that I'd snuffed Mr. Car Wash in Kensal Rise that morning.

I'm too pumped up to sleep after coming back from my visit to the dirty old river. I watch a couple of films on Blu-ray. I don't have a TV subscription, not even BBC or ITV, and just use the telly to watch my films on. I've got a two thousand plus collection that takes up a whole wall of the living room. On the other side I've got a wall of books.

It gets to about 2am and the day's events start replaying. I'm obsessing about what I could have done better or more efficiently. I start thinking about the black kid on his mobile phone. I'm positive he never turned around. *If* he did and he even saw me coming over the wall, all he really had was a bloke on a Ducati motorbike and even then … blah, blah, bleeding blah.

Over and over it goes: intrusive questions that have already been answered a thousand times. I have to go through it though. Have to suffer it, because, well, if I didn't, I wouldn't be a pro', I'd be a fucking amateur, and amateurs in this graft, dead *or* alive, aren't worth a toss to anyone.

TWO

Anonymity is a shield from the tyranny of the majority.

John Paul Stevens

Reality is the ever-present consequence of personal choices. Delusion is the ever-present consequence of blaming others for your choices. There's no cunt to blame but me for the life I choose to live. A life that's realistic, authentic and free from the trappings of modernity and so-called progression. I have no axe to grind with society. How can I? I don't consider myself a part of it and have absolutely no intention of ever fucking joining it.

I have no passport, no National Insurance number, no bank account, no phones, no utility bills, no rent agreements in my name. I'm not registered with a doctor or dentist. If I need their services, it will be arranged for me and they will treat me under a moody name. I'm not registered to vote or to pay council tax. I can proudly say that if you were to Google my given name it would yield zero results. I can also *very* proudly state that I have never once logged onto a social media site, nor is my 'real' name ever mentioned on any of them.

I do, however, have a driving license. The photo id on it is of some cunt who looks like me, but is 5 years older and has an unpronounceable Polish surname. It's a clean licence and cost me seven grand from an enterprising individual working at the DVLA in Swansea. I've only ever had to produce it once. Motorcyclists are rarely pulled over by plod in London, unless of course they are young tearaways on mopeds scouting for marks to mug.

My neighbours in the block of flats I live in don't know me. If they *have* caught a sight of me, they would never be able to recognise my face. Every time I enter or exit the flats I'm wearing a full-face motorcycle helmet. I stride past them and never make eye contact. I never receive post nor do I accept parcels from couriers who've been unable to deliver to my neighbours. I'm not so much anti-social as anti-present. If one of my neighbours were in need of my assistance, they would be out of luck. They could be bleeding to death and still my reinforced door would stay firmly triple bolted. If *I* were to be found dead inside my flat, the authorities would have a real mystery on their hands. A fucking army of Miss Marples' would be flummoxed as to the identity of the stiff.

They would not be able to put a name to my corpse through fingerprints, dental records or DNA. They would have to photograph the face of the corpse to show people and ask if they recognised it because no other photo exists of me. Even then, the couple of people who know me would never admit to knowing me. They have become adept at 'not knowing' me and having any connection to me whatsoever, however tenuous. In my tiny circle we've mastered the art of compartmentalization. My circle knows only two things about me. When they employ me, they know that I'll get the job done, and that if I were to be pinched for doing the job nothing could be proved that they had employed me to do it.

You can quite reasonably ask why I'm telling my story if I'm so obviously obsessed with anonymity. The simple answer is I want this to be a cautionary tale, but not in any moral respect. I want this to be a cautionary tale for would be hitmen – for it is *always* men who enter the profession – to learn by a few mistakes I made along the way. I'm receiving no financial compensation for this tale and you can analyse my words until the cows come home, but the casual reader will never identify me or my associates.

There will be a few people who read this account, put two and two together and suss out which hits I'm talking about. The thing is, those people already know what went down, and if they know what went down, trust me, they are gonna keep schtum in case they put themselves in the mix.

Opportunities in my line of work are bigger than you could ever imagine. I can quite confidently look forward to at least 3 contracts per year. Not all UK based though. I've worked in Belgium, France, Spain, Luxembourg and Holland over the years, I do, however class myself as first and foremost a UK contractor. To be honest I don't really like stepping on the toes of native workers. In an ideal world I believe hitmen should work in their own territories.

Think about this: someone is reported missing every 90 seconds in the UK. Even if the majority of those reported turn up safe and sound, you're still looking at hundreds of thousands who simply vanish off the face of the earth. Unless it's a high-profile missing person or a case that's sparked media attention, to think Old Bill in the UK have the resources or manpower to find or find out what happened to these unfortunate people is fucking ridiculous. Most plod nowadays are too busy on Sensitivity Training Courses, making bunting for their annual Gay Pride marches or bollocking keyboard warriors and Trolls for misgendering people on Twitter.

I am in the missing people business, and the person I once was is also on the missing persons list. Out of those thousands of lost souls who end up on the list every year, you can be sure that at least a dozen have vanished at the hands of people like me. By the occult nature of my chosen profession, you can never be statistical, but when you figure the size of the organised criminal economy and how its human resource departments work, you can be confident that at least a dozen employees are *terminated* every year. These terminations are obviously existential and will never make it to an industrial tribunal hearing.

I'm never fully privy as to *why* these people have ended up on my *things to do list*. I'm assuming it's because they've dangerously transgressed in their jobs, but I don't know for certain. It don't make sense that I am paid good money to deliver their P45's from the barrel of a gun unless they've screwed up epically, but I don't discount that personal transgressions often merit a visit from me. Maybe some cunt fucked someone they shouldn't have, simply spoke out of turn or forgot to invite some other cunt to their daughter's wedding.

Who knows? Who fucking cares? I suppose I can justify what I do by the fact that most of these names on the *to do list* are clearly associating with dangerous people and guilty of making terrible choices. If I've ever sent a truly innocent person spinning off this mortal coil it's a shame, but unlike the venal fucks who ordered the long drawn out and tortuous hit on the one and only truly innocent, Jesus Christ, at least my dispatch of them could be claimed as collateral damage or 'goes with the territory' and free of any religious, political, dogmatic or superstitious hypocrisy. And let's face it, the people I snuff from existence are unlikely to be possible saviours of mankind. They're more likely to be greedy fucking scrotes or incompetent cunts.

Like all jobs, in theory, you get better at it the more you do it. Practice makes perfect as they say, though I'd argue 'perfection' in this line of work is impossible. No matter how good your hit, there's always something you could have done better. In the post-match analysis with myself, which I take very fucking seriously, I relive every second of the execution. It borders on the obsessive I suppose, but then again, how can obsession have borders? The whole point of obsession is the limitless and unfettered focus on something. In my case it all stems from my first killing.

Logically It couldn't have been anything but amateurish, but that don't stop me from revisiting it and chastising myself for not being more prepared. I shouldn't have chosen a grate near Tooting Broadway to dispose of the crowbar, and I certainly shouldn't have let myself be seen by a pissed-up passer-by.

When I relive my hits, I enter a kind of out of body state. I relive my hits dispassionately and measured and most importantly, critically. I lay on my bed and stare at the ceiling for hours. My visual skills are virtually 3D and I've got an amazing ability to recall every instance during the run up to the hit. It's this almost autistic study of detail that fascinates me more than the actual execution.

I take pleasure in knowing that I'm the only cunt on earth who gets to appreciate or criticise my performance. There's something sacred in knowing that a work of art is only witnessed by the creator themselves. God, it goes without saying, didn't have an audience. In my opinion, if you need an audience to validate your work of art, it's not a work of art, but rather a commercial and profane ego trip. Unlike most people nowadays, I don't need my existence or art to be mediated by cunts to be satisfied by it.

I'm ahead of the curve. In the future it'll be anonymity rather than fame that's craved. When every cunt is a close circuit TV facial recognition biometric surveyed superstar, the anonymous shall inherit the earth.

My nightmares are not so much recurring as they are fucking serialised. They're, unsurprisingly, centred around me being cornered and usually climax with me being shot in the fucking nut by Kevlar clad Old Bill. Believe me when I say that I'm unafraid of dying. What terrifies me is the insult of being pinched. It negates all the seconds, minutes, hours, days, weeks, months, years and decades that I have spent mastering my craft. Getting caught *is* the fucking sin.

To be caught and killed or sent to what remains of my life doing bird means I had gotten sloppy, taken my eye off the ball, messed up and made a mockery of the art of assassination. Being good at what I do is more important to me than the dough I earn from doing it. There's very few people who can truly say this, and those that *can* usually keep their cakehole's shut because they don't care about impressing *any* cunt.

Uncle's always maintained that if you know the name of a serious criminal, villain, gangster whatever, it can only mean one of the three things. A: they're very successful 2: shit at their jobs or C: pretending to be gangsters. Uncle only deals with those who are *very* successful and thereby clearly good at their jobs.

Uncle once had a hero: a mild-mannered chap who lived into his eighties without ever so much as picking up a parking ticket. He'd never engaged in fisticuffs or any kind of affray; nobody had a bad word to say about the cunt and he were a pillar of his community in an idyllic country village. He paid his taxes, contributed to charity, raised five lovely children, rarely drank, never smoked, gambled or cheated on his missus, and when he died he left a ten-million-pound fortune to his family.

He owned a dozen florists and would wash the cash he stole from his part time job as a peterman (safe cracker) through the flower shops.

Uncle were The Florist's only contact in the criminal underworld and Uncle would fence the tom that The Florist extracted from safes he'd blown. The Florist recoiled at ever having to deal with fellow criminals and Uncle were paid handsomely for being his broker. Besides Uncle, nobody knew that The Florist were arguably the most successful peterman in the country. The Florist were pragmatic though and realised that the loot he'd masterfully nicked could be put to work and bring in some good dividends. Through Uncle, the Florist financed a major importation of Heroin into the UK in the mid 1980s.

The Florist laid out two million for the enterprise and was consequently cut out of the deal by the gangster cunts behind it. Uncle had to break the bad news to the old chap. Much to Uncle's surprise, the quaint Florist took it on the chin when everything had been explained and proven to him. It were a simple case of greed and there were absolutely fuck all Uncle or The Florist could do about it. The Florist told Uncle not to worry about it. Uncle couldn't believe The Florist's sanguine attitude. It seemed too good to be true. If something looks too good be true, 99.99 times out of 100 it is.

A year after the costly incident Uncle heard that the fearsome leader of the drug smuggling gang had vanished. Rumours started circulating. Fanciful and often absurd Chinese whispers are the lingua franca of the serious crime underworld and all kinds of nonsense were flying around. Uncle assumed the gangster had simply been snuffed out by one of the many people whose toes he'd stepped on over the years.

As Uncle said, "I gets a call. The phone goes n' it's this Florist.

He says to me, he says he wants to show me summink. I say 'what is it you wanna show me' N' he says 'you'll like it.' That's all he says. He asks me down to his gaff in the countryside, down Kent it is, to see this thing. It's a nice pile. Garden of England, Kent. I've been before ain't I. So, I think what's he wanna show me. I ain't got a clue. All I knows is this cunt's got summink to show me. So, I heads down there and all the way down in the motor I'm thinkin'; what's he wanna show me. I mean, I knew him, well I thought I did, so I'm not thinkin' there's any hank panky going on. There's no beef 'tween us. He got scalped on the deal and he knew it were fuck all to do with me. N' besides he's not the type I'd be wary of anyway. He weren't a tough guy, or so's I think. Far as I know he was just a very good tea leaf. Probably the best peterman around in his day. I'm not thinkin' there's anything queer going on am I ... so anyway, I gets to his gaff in Kent. I bowl up and he's the same old gent he'd always been. He's bending over to make me feel welcome ain't he. All over me he is. I like him. He's a decent cunt and I'm obviously intrigued like. We sit down n' have a cuppa."

"He don't bring up the smuggling stuff so neither do I. I mean I'd already apologised and he knew I'd lost out as well. What I'm sayin' is it were amicable. Yeah, *very* amicable. Very pleasant indeed. He shows me some photos of his Great Grandson who'd just been born. Really proud he was. Made up ... I asks him what it was he wanted to show me. I knew it weren't just photos of a new-born teapot. So, he goes *come into the library*. We're in there and there's this telly. He gets this video cassette out and shoves it in the player. I'm thinkin'; *the fucks he up to? He can't have brought me all the way down here to show me a porno or summink, can he?* Anyway, all's I can say is that I've seen some things in my time but this, *this* took the bleedin' biscuit. This is off the bleedin' scale what he's showing me! Can't believe my eyes can I."

"So, here I am sat in the library of this little old tea leaf who wouldn't say boo to a fuckin' goose and he's showin' me a bleedin' video of some cunt bein' tortured! ... it took me a while to work out who was bein' tortured. There were blood and sick and shit all over the mush of this poor cunt. Unrecognizable he was. So, the Florist gives it; *don't you recognize him?* N' I'm like, no, no, not the foggiest. N' let me tell you summink. When you see one o' these things you know they're real. There's none o' that special effects bollocks and you instantly know. Sends a bleedin' shiver right down your spine it does. There's no faking this kind o' caper. No, you want to look away it's so real. It's beyond real really. It's ... I can't think o' the word. It's bleedin' scary is what it is. I mean you're used to seein' people havin' a knees-up or on their hols when you see summink filmed on a video recorder don't 'cha? I mean ... streuth!"

"There's this cunt tied up on a chair. You can make out it's a barn or a stable or summink and slap bang in the middle of it this poor cunt's being took apart from breakfast to arsehole! Stone me! Whoever's torturing him's pulling out all the stops. It's fuckin' medieval! Sickening! Not natural. Turnin' my bleedin' stomach it is, only I can't look away. No. It's fascinating. I mean, you know me, son, I ain't no shrinkin' violet n' I've seen some naughty things in my time, but this ... I looks over at The Florist and the cunt's got this big cheesy grin on his mush as he watches. He's lovin' it ain't he? I'm lost for words, I mean; *the fuck has this cunt done to deserve this? Is he a nonce or summink?* I'm baffled I am ... the fucking Florist gives it; *don't you recognize him?* I'm like, *no. No. Not a fuckin' dolly blue.* He gives it *look closer*, so I gets a better look, I'm squinting I am. I'm right up to the telly now and then it clicks. I recognize this poor cunt. It's only the bloke who fucked over The Florist on the smuggling job ain't it!"

"Now this bloke's a proper piece o' work. A real hardcase, naughty fucker! But he ain't so naughty now is he! No. He's tied to this chair screaming like a baby. He's pissed his pants. Shat himself he has, and I don't blame him. His knees have been smashed to smithereens! He's had cigs put out on him! His eyes look like he's gone 15 rounds with Tyson with his hands tied behind his back! He looks like the bleedin' Elephant Man on a bad day! Christ they've even set his pubes alight and his old man's burnt to a crisp! Like a bleedin' overcooked chipolata it is! You ain't seen nothin' like it ... this is fuckin' awful but I can't stop watching can I. I mean, this is just ... anyway this torturer sets about the poor cunt's fingers and toenails."

"It's like the bleedin' Marathon Man or summink. Straight out the pictures only this ain't no actin', this is proper. The cameraman zooms in and it's horrible ... pincers! All his nails! Off they come, one by one. And the screaming! You ain't heard nothin' like it let me tell ya. Bleedin' barbaric it is. I've had enough I have n' I tells The Florist. I tells him I've seen enough n' he's still got this big cheesy grin on his mush. Cunt's lovin' it he is! He tells me to keep watchin'. He says there's a *good bit comin' up*. I'm feelin' a bit nauseous I am. I tells him I've seen enough so he fast forwards the tape a bit don't he ... fucksake! It's only *him*, The Florist who's been doin' the torturing ain't it! I mean he's got a couple o' goons with him but it's all The Florist's handiwork."

"I can't fuckin' believe it! I mean, this cunt's the nicest cunt you could ever meet! Never in a million years would I have had him down as a torturer. *No way Jose! Not on your nelly!* This cunt would o' give Mengele a run for his money! ... so, this tape gets near the end and this drug smuggler's screaming at The Florist. He's beggin' him to stop but The Florist's not havin' any of it.

I stand up at this point. I've seen enough and I tell this mad cunt. I tell him, I say *it's doin' me crust in.* He presses pause and giggles. He gives it, *that's what you call a real video nasty, eh?* ... I mean, f'godsake! I'm speechless. You think you know people, eh! I wouldn't have had this Florist down to hurt a bleedin' fly but here is takin' a proper naughty cunt apart, bit by bit. He chirps up and gives it *I know you weren't part of it. He admitted it. It were just him and his brothers who robbed me."*

"Listen, I knew I were innocent but it were nice to hear that the poor cunt hadn't roped me in. I'm obviously lookin' this Florist in a new light now. I mean I knew he'd been a good peter-man in his day so he had some bottle, but I'd never have had him down as sadistic cunt. This were first division violence this were! The stuff you only hear about in old fishwife's tales and silly rumours. I don't mind admittin' my arse were goin' a bit. I think it were the fact that this Florist cunt had a glint in his eye. He were proud o' what he'd done!"

"Look, son, you know how many things I've been involved in over the years, but it's one thing takin' some cunt out n' it's another torturing 'em to death. All the years I been in this game I ain't ever seen anythin' like it ... this Florist weren't gonna get the dough back n' he knew it had probably been spunked so this bit o' theatre were purely for pleasure. His *own* pleasure ... mad cunt! ... I obviously kept schtum about what I'd watched and I never heard from The Florist again."

"I'd heard he'd popped his clogs a couple o' years later. He never tried getting in touch again, not that I wanted him to. Fuck that! I'd have politely swerved the cunt ... what I couldn't figure out, afterwards, what I couldn't understand is what he got out of it, this fuckin' Florist. I mean it's not like it were an ego thing. He couldn't go round showin' this video to his mates or the Village

Green Preservation Society or summink could he. He even told me I were the only other cunt besides him and his Goons that had seen it. He said he wanted to show me 'cos I'd lost a few bob in the caper as well n' thought I'd like to see this cunt get his just desserts ... this Florist were my hero up to that point on account of him never bein' pinched, keepin' his head down 'n never fraternizing with other villains, but now ... well, turns out he were a fuckin' psychopath. Just goes to show ... you can never really know *any* cunt."

THREE

Crimes lead into one another. They who are capable of being forgers, are capable of being incendiaries.

Edmund Burke

Uncle's right. If you can never really know some cunt, how can you possibly ever trust *any* cunt? Uncle's my 'associate' and I *have* to trust him to a certain degree or I couldn't function in the life I've chosen. Would Uncle take a bullet for me? No, and I wouldn't take one for him either. We both know this. We're both parasites feeding off of each other. We know that if there were any betrayal it would be mutually assured destruction. We both know *exactly* where the bodies are buried, even if those bodies have now decomposed.

Me and Uncle are blessed really. Our relationship works. There's countless relationships in the criminal underworld that are dysfunctional and a cunt hair away from becoming corrupted. There's no such thing as honour amongst thieves or criminals in general, especially successful criminals. It's bollocks. No, the bigger the stakes the smaller the odds on someone being thrown under the bus. There's more backstabbers in this racket than there were in ancient Rome. Some people have this romantic rose-tinted image of a time when there were a code of behaviour amongst villains. *Double* bollocks with a cherry on top.

Even that old chestnut: *no women and children harmed*, is poppycock. You've only to look at the case of 'celebrity gangster' Ronnie Kray to see that sexually abusing young boys were allowed to happen amongst these so called 'rough diamonds with hearts of gold'. There's also countless tales of women being horrifically brutalized by these cheeky chappy 'modern day Robin Hood's'. There's one particularly gruesome – *and true* – story about a young Richard from Canning Town.

The unfortunate young lady were going steady – *this were the 1960s* – with a notoriously violent gangster. One day he sees her innocently chatting to a Persian bloke in the pub. The Persian's stabbed up and the young lady's dragged from the boozer by her barnet to his flat. Once there he beats her to a pulp, carves 'wog meat' into her chest with his blade and then for the *pièce de resistance*, the nasty cunt raped her with a champagne bottle, both fucking holes.

She suffered horrific internal injuries and after being released from hospital ended up in a psychiatric ward from the trauma. Her 'boyfriend' went on the lam until his fellow gangsters had done some damage limitation. They threatened witnesses to the stabbing in the pub and then threatened the girlfriend that they'd kill her and her family if she grassed him up. Within a few weeks the 'boyfriend' were back on the manor as if nothing had happened.

I keep this in mind when I'm handed a contract on someone. The kind of people who hand me – or rather Uncle – the contracts don't usually do business with 'nice ordinary people'. I'm not cheap, either. Nowadays I can get paid up to 100 large for a 'drop' and 120 for a 'clean'. A 'drop' is where I simply kill the mark and a 'clean' is where I dispose of the body. Sometimes Uncle might take a commission of up to 50%, sometimes as little as 10%. I don't argue, he's got his reasons and I don't really care. It's all still good coin.

I figure that if I'm being paid this kind of dough my marks have been up to some shenanigans that warrants 'em being snuffed in the eyes of my clients. I'm pretty confident that the majority of my marks have transgressed by being greedy little piggies and ripped some cunt higher up the trough chain. Nine times out of ten it comes down to dough, and the sort of people Uncle deals with are big hitters and serious wedge is going through their hands. These are not 'street' people 'anymore'. You've more chance of bumping into 'em at the fucking opera than The Old Bull & Bush.

Having said that, I do know I once snuffed someone who'd been slipping one to the wife of a powerful gangster. This sort were a dirty cow who, allegedly, weren't happy at the wife swapping party 'til her face resembled a plasterers radio. Her hubby didn't mind her getting fucked when he were watching but took umbrage to her doing it behind his back. That particular hit was a 'show off' indicating that the gangster wanted it to be known to any prospective wife fuckers out there that *his* wife were off the menu, unless he could watch, obviously. I didn't feel bad taking out Loverboy. I reasoned that someone so daft as to poke the wife of such a powerful perv were no great loss to the gene pool. If Loverboy didn't know the power of the bloke he were cuckolding, well, tough titties. He should have done a bit of research before he stuck his old chap in her.

If there's one thing that gets my goat it's people who are too lazy to learn the form on their adversaries. There's no excuse in this day and age. You can get the basic info on nearly every cunt nowadays, can't you? A few clicks and voila! I use the internet to gather info on my marks but I'm very careful how I do it.

Like I said, I don't own a phone or computer but it don't stop me using them every now and then. I'm not a fucking Luddite. I use libraries – where they don't require you to have a library card to access their tech – or electrical superstores that have computers on display so that you can test drive them a bit. After I've quickly pulled up and memorized the images and info I need, I completely delete the browser history.

I don't have to research every mark on every hit. I only do it when I feel I ain't been given enough background by Uncle or sometimes his man, 'Billy'. I'm not gonna lie, sometimes I do it out of morbid curiosity, but as a rule it's to gather possible locations my marks frequent: a golf club or perhaps a gym, even a fucking stamp collecting association if that's what tickles their fancy. You never know. And obviously the more location points you can establish, the more possibilities you've got to hit 'em.

I once spent an agonising week internally debating at which one of six possible locations, I could take my mark out. It's very rare that you are offered so many choices, and for a perfectionist like me it were fucking torture.

Sometimes you're offered no choices at all. I once found myself at a dogging site out in Hertfordshire as the last and only resort to make bones of the mark. The pervy fucker I pinged died with his cock in his hand as he sat in his motor watching some skanky old bird getting two'ed up on the bonnet of an old Mercedes.

His window were rolled slightly, so it were a simple case of sneaking up and poking the silencer through the gap. Potential witnesses were too busy watching Mucky Maureen's fat arse panel beating the Merc's bonnet to notice my ninja like execution. When it came out in the news, the kill was put down to a possible sexual jealousy scenario or something. There were no mention of any criminal Underworld connections, which was a bonus for me but I can't speak for my client as this was a 'drop'. My client could have potentially wanted the kill to be a message, but I got paid and work didn't dry up, so who cares. No point crying over spilt blood, eh.

That is all bollocks of course – totally made up, *Jackanory*, pulling your strides. One, I wanted to lighten the mood a little and two, I wanted to see if you were paying attention. I would never, *never* whack some cunt with so many potential witnesses about, even if they *were* concentrating on watching humans rutting like pigs.

I were, truthfully, offered this piece of work though, but it would have been impossible to carry out successfully. The bloke was indeed a voyeur at dogging sites, but unfortunately that's about *all* he was. He never left his drum other than to go watch other people spunk up. His wife or girlfriend did *all* the errands in that household.

So, it was to be the dogging site, see, but every time I tailed him to his favourite alfresco fuck fest I were always surrounded by traffic, so the chance of a moving hit, or even a pull up hit were out the question. This obviously weren't some masterstroke on his behalf, he obviously didn't know he were being stalked for death, but you've got to believe me, the lucky cunt managed to pick times to go for his communal wank that shielded him from my bullets.

I heard later that somebody else took the contract and hit the jackpot by ploughing the cunt down with a stolen 4 x 4 motor in Stevenage, making it look like a hit and run. What he were doing in Stevenage is still a mystery to me. I would have loved to have found out, because all the cunt ever did when I had the contract was have me go back and forth to that sweaty arsed woodland carpark to try kill him.

What my clients get from me that they don't get from other contract killers, I like to think, is a forensic attention to detail and extremely high plausible deniability warranty. If, and it's a big if, they were ever to be connected to me or the contract, the Crown Prosecution would have an easier time trying to prove that a rocking horse had broken into a house and intentionally shat on an expensive rug. My compartmentalization process is forensic. I don't know the clients and the clients don't know me. Even if I were to have a sudden revelation and wanted to atone for my sins and start pointing the finger, I couldn't. It would be impossible. I don't know these people.

I've heard you can contract a killer for as little as 10 grand nowadays, but as the old saying goes, you pay peanuts, you get cock eyed, inbred Albanians. If you want to skimp on hiring someone to commit murder, I would suggest you're either a moron, a pathologically cheap cunt or you're so desperate for the victim to die that you should save your pennies, get tooled up and have a go at some DIY.

It's bleeding insulting expecting someone to risk a life of porridge for a poxy few grand, and this lack of respect tells me everything I really need to know about the cunts who will only pay this kind of dough. Fucking mugs. If they really think an Albanian or some other East European fresh off the dinghy won't serve them up if they get pinched, well ...

No, you can't skimp on assassinations. At a push, I reckon you could get a competent Hitman contracted for around 30 large, but then it all comes down to weighing up the odds of a potential fuck up. I'm not saying I'm infallible, far from it, but I take great pride in the planning of my assassinations. Your common or garden Hitman would usually – I'd hazard a guess – spend a few days planning the piece of work. You pay for what you get.

My rule of thumb is that the least amount of planning I'll put into a hit is just under two weeks, this weren't always the case. I done a couple of hits in the past at short notice, but I don't *contract* nowadays unless I'm given at least a fortnight for planning. I've turned down numerous and very generous offers to take people out quickly. I once turned down a cool two hundred large to take out a bloke in Sandbank's, Dorset, within a week. It were a 'clean' and it blew up in the face of the bloke who'd put the contract out a couple of years later when the body turned up. I've not had *one* ghost float to the surface in my career. Don't take that as arrogance or me being a cocky cunt. It's just a fact.

I'm meticulous in my execution and disposal methods, but I've had a few fuck ups in the past that you'll get to hear about. A couple where it really looked like it were gonna come on top. The thing about me though is I'm a glass half empty man. I approach every job thinking I'm gonna get pinched. It's healthy. I look at every angle in the process where there's a potential weak link and I prepare accordingly.

Shit happens in this game, and when it does it can have terrible consequences. The proverbial don't so much hit the fan, it becomes a fucking stinking tsunami and the pong can linger for years, even decades.

You may remember the cold-blooded murder of popular TV presenter Jill Dando. To any cunt who knows the score it were without doubt a professional hit. You'd have bet your last ten bob on it. This were a very audacious, very calculated, meticulously planned hit that could have only been carried out by a seasoned professional. Having said all that, there were one fatal flaw in the performance that immediately negates all the work that went into the run up of it. Nobody knew this at the time though. Even the Hitman.

Miss Dando worked for the BBC and fronted *Crimewatch*, a program that appealed for info from the public to pinch criminals. In 1999 the 37-year-old was snuffed on her doorstep. The public were rightly appalled and the cry for justice were deafening. Nobody could understand why such a lovely young woman were executed. It didn't make sense, but obviously you couldn't discount the fact that she had pissed off many a villain on her show.

All kinds of theories started to circulate about who had put out the contract. Some theories were potty, others seemed plausible. The thing is, they were all wrong. Nobody posited that Jill Dando could have been taken out in a case of mistaken identity. If they had, they would have been bang on the dough.

The hunt for Miss Dando's killer were instantly fired up and went on to become the biggest criminal investigation since the hunt for that Yorkshire Ripper cunt. The Media were all over it like a rash. One of their own had been snuffed. The papers and the radio and telly told us that the masses were screaming for justice and MPs were quick to jump on the wagon and promise *anything* it would take to bring Jill Dando's killer to book. There were 'questions asked in the house' which translates to 'Oi, Old Bill! Pull your fingers out and get a result. Fucking sharpish!' Every media outlet in the UK were braying for the blood of the cunt who'd popped their lovely TV Presenter.

What weren't news or public domain at the time were that it turned out Jill Dando was hit because she looked similar to another BBC journalist: both in their 30's, blonde, similar facial features, same height and stature. That might sound implausible, but trust me, one day the truth will out and it will become a matter of public record.

Uncle shook his head and breathed a sigh of genuine

sympathy when he filled me in, "You see. What happens is, this other bird, another reporter at the BBC, well she were in the middle of exposing this Italian cunt. Fashion designer or sum-mink. Cunt's been abusing models or whatever and this BBC bird who looks like this Dando bird, well she's investigated n' she's gonna put this dirty wop cunt *right* in it, ain't she … from what I've been told it weren't the Hitman's fault. He were just doing his job. One of these eye-tie mugs that worked for this Fashion ponce had gotten fuckin' sloppy n' give the Hitman the wrong mark to snuff … what a fuckin' cock up, eh … poor gal. Thank fuck she wouldn't have seen it coming. The Hitman's good, clearly: broad daylight, busy street, quick, proficient, makes off on his toes, takes some nerve that does, eh. He's got balls on him; I'll give him that … he's more than likely one of those working out o' Marseille. Poor French cunt wouldn't o' been too happy finding out he's snuffed the wrong bird though. It's not right. It's a fuckin' balls up and it brings the whole game in to disrepute."

Old Bill did indeed get a result on their Dando investigation, but it were a dodgy result in my mind, even before the finer de-tails came out. Plod served up a fruitcake called Barry Michael George, a fantasist with a fondness for using the real names of famous pop stars to go about his silly business.

This Barry cunt used a string of other moody names as well, and was, even from early reports, quite clearly a sandwich short of a picnic. He were instantly tagged as a stalker. He weren't right in the head, but to anyone who knows anything about street ex-ecutions it were blindingly obvious that Barry were fitted up by an impatient and under pressure Old Bill.

The hit on Miss Dando were professional and clearly this Barry George Michael were existentially amateurish. Barry were in a constant battle with reality and spent most of his time imagining he were alternately a pair of pop stars: Gary Glitter and Freddie Mercury, f'fucksake.

Old Bill were hell bent on banging the cunt up though, and somehow, they managed to persuade the CPS to get lively. After Old Bill claimed they couldn't find a motive and they turned up nothing about a conspiracy to kill Miss Dando they went all out, shit or bust on simpleton Barry. The poor bastard was sent down by non-circumstantial ballistics. A speck of firearm discharge were found on him that matched the ammo used in the hit. He was lifed-off but the conviction were judged unsafe 7 years later.

After a retrial in 2008 he were acquitted and became free to carry on acting the cunt in society, living in his own little fantasy land, happy as Larry. The poor fucker's claim for compensation were kicked out but he managed to get a few bob from The Tabloids on account of them slagging him off over the years.

This weren't a miscarriage of justice. It were a fucking abortion of justice, and you've got to feel pity for Jill Dando's friends and loved ones having to watch the Keystone fucking cops make such a mess in the pursuit of justice for her.

I don't know what happened the real killer of Jill Dando or the fate of the 'Italian fashion ponce', all I know is that neither of them have been pinched in connection with the pitiful piece of work. They'll probably be dead or senile by the time the truth comes out.

Uncle gives it, "See, you could argue that if this bird – this Richard who were the real mark on the contract – really had some sauce on this Fashion Cunt she'd have put it out by now, exposed the cunt for being a sex pest, rapist, whatever, right. But then you got to look at it another way. I mean, she sees Dando get rubbed out and her arse goes. She's put two n' two together n' realized the hit on Jill were mistaken identity. The bullet were intended for her. I reckon after that she thinks; *fuck it! This Italian Fashion Cunt's gonna have me done in as well if I carry on exposing him. I'm jacking it in.*"

Like I say, crime, by its very nature, is occult. If it weren't hidden it couldn't possibly be crime in the real sense. Like all forms of occultism, crime's hierarchical, but it don't always figure that those with the biggest bag of marbles are the top dogs. Pavement Artists (armed robbers) were for many years, especially in the 1970s, classed as the elite. These were the balls out bandits who had the bottle to walk into a bank, casino, shop or post office, climb over the jump and say *gimme*. When The Beaks started handing out very long stretches of bird for these offences the shine started to wear off for these sawn-off Sundance Kids.

Add to this a burgeoning security culture, and an infestation of rats who'd turn in their grannies at the drop of a hat, and pavement artistry quickly became a dying craft. Many of these 'Chaps' used the notoriety they'd earned from the stick-ups and heists to diversify within the crime employment market. They were generally feared, and quite rightly so, and many transitioned seamlessly into the nascent drugs trade. A few chose to be contract killers though. They knew their way around shooters, still had bottle, contacts and organizational skills, so they understandably figured they could make a decent living popping people. The problem here though comes down to simply one thing and that thing is – wait for it … patience. Some people say it's a virtue. I don't know if I agree with them, but what I do know is that if you wanna be a hitman you need fucking loads of patience.

These Chaps were used to performing on a stage with other performers. Being a hitman is like one man play without an audience. A play you've rehearsed over and over to the point of obsession. It's the difference between being in a one-man Samuel Beckett play at poxy arts centre in the middle of nowhere and being in the chorus of Mama Mia in the West End.

These Chaps were used to the high octane, adrenalin pumping, arris twitching, sheer life affirming fuckery of turning over a bank or jacking an armoured truck. That's not to say they didn't do their homework or recces of the places where they were gonna do their robberies, of course they did, but what they weren't intentionally going out to do were make some cunt cease to exist, they were going out to scare people into handing over the dough.

Pavement Artists would only use their shooters if they had to. The difference between hitmen and armed robbers is self-evident. I don't reckon a hitman would make a successful armed robber, but I *know* for a fact that a few armed robbers made terrible hitmen. Comical even.

FOUR

*A success is anyone who is deliberately doing a
predetermined job because that's what he set out
to do deliberately. Only one in 20 do that.*

Earl Nightingale, The Strangest Secret

I know there's rumours, whispers and hot air circulating about
my true identity in the upper echelons of the European organized criminal fraternity, Scotland Yard and Interpol. Uncle
tells me my handiwork's been attributed to all sorts: ex-military
Serbians, Russians, Cartel Mexicans and even Irish paramilitar-
ies from both sides of the religious divide. More power to the
gossips I say. They help muddy the waters and long may they
continue talking bollocks.

I had mixed feelings when an amateurish old 'hitman' from
Bethnal Green were pinched for one of my jobs in the late 90s.
I were obviously happy that some poor cunt had been fingered,
proving Old Bill were a million miles off the scent off of the truth,
but I were a little annoyed they thought this mug from Bethnal
Green could have been the artist of such an intricately planned
hit. Plod really can be silly sausages sometimes.

I know it's a cliché, but you can't buy experience. I've been
a killer since I were 18 and I've just turned sixty. My first 'hit'

37

weren't professional. No dough changed hands, though lots of it were 'saved' from the consequences of my first kill. No, I carried it out as a favour to my neighbourhood and particularly my mother.

I were raised in South London on a council estate (housing project if you happen to be a septic tank reading this) in the 70's and 80s. It were no worse than any other council estate in the country at that time. It did, though, have a disproportionately large number of women whose husbands or boyfriends were banged up. Dozens of kids on our estate had Dads who were 'away' and it were down to the Mums to raise them as best they could. I never noticed a marked difference between kids of my own age with Dads doing bird, than those who had Dads at home. It weren't a big thing and hardly ever talked about.

I didn't have a Dad that were 'away', I had a Dad that was home, and that were the fucking problem. My Dad weren't a villain. My Dad was nothing. He never got off his arse to provide for me and my Mum and younger sister, which is cuntish on its own, but when you add to it an entitled attitude and a superiority complex you really do have a Dad that was about as much use as a spare hole on a nun. He wouldn't even get off his arse to go down the Labour Exchange and sign on for work and get some dole money. No, it were all beneath him.

He weren't physically violent, but he were extremely violent with his tongue and clever with it to boot. Looking back, I wish he *had* been psychically violent. Bruises and cuts eventually fade away but some of the things that cunt said will always haunt me.

My Mum worked her socks off to try and give us a decent life. She worked shifts at a factory packing envelopes in boxes and at the weekend worked behind the bar at the local working men's club or the pub. On top of this she fenced a few knock-off goods round the estate, usually clobber that had been hoisted from department stores in the West End. She knew a lot of tea leaf's and they trusted her to move their low yield goods on. She can't have been making much out of the enterprise, but I think she saw it as providing a service to the community.

Mum were very community orientated and sometimes this fucked me off. From an early age I realised that she were something of a soft touch, and this were consequently one of the reasons why she were still putting up with my Dad's diarrhoea. I really wanted her to toughen up, but it were never gonna happen. She were simply a good-hearted soul and there were nothing could be done about it. Leopards changing their spots and all that. Anyway, even with all her jobs she were still finding it hard to make ends meet. Mum always made sure we ate well though.

Food were something she was absolutely unwilling to skimp on. No matter what shit she were facing she managed to feed us decent nosh. We had meat with nearly every meal and a plate of her 'Full English' could have fed the proverbial five thousand. How me and my Sis' didn't end being fat cunts is a mystery.

I suppose I inherited cynicism from my Dad. It's the *only* fucking thing I inherited from him, mind. My coldness definitely comes from him but thank God I never inherited his trait of poncing off people. The cunt – as far as I were aware – had never worked a day (honestly or dishonestly) in his life, and miraculously managed to survive by putting the bite on other people, especially my Mum. This were no mean feat in the community we lived in. Men – if they weren't in The Scrubs or HMP Wandsworth – were supposed to be out working or grafting or simply pilfering to support their families. My Dad were an anomaly.

He were having *none* of it, no. It were like he had an aversion to actually earning a crust. Some weird, twisted notion that getting your hands dirty or working up a sweat to earn a wage were beneath him. If poncing were an art form this cunt were Michelangelo. I refer to my Dad as a 'cunt' because that's what most people called him. They usually prefixed it with 'clever' though. My Dad were known as 'that clever cunt, Ronnie.' Growing up, I had trouble sussing out whether this were a dig or a compliment, and I believe that most of those who used the sobriquet didn't know either. People couldn't work him out. Inscrutable cunt.

Looking back now, I truly believe that my Dad had something of the black magician about him. A slight pong of sulphur masked by Old Spice aftershave and Brylcreem. When I got older, I read a book called *The Master and Margarita* by a Russian writer called Mikhail Bulgakov. It's a cracking read and I were enthralled by it, not least because the main character is supposed to be a representation of The Devil incarnated, roaming the streets of 1930s Moscow and having every cunt's strides down.

Reading about this character I couldn't help but find similarities between him and my Dad: the way they manipulated people to do their bidding through clever language and confidence. I don't know, maybe I'm giving my old man too much diabolic credit, but it still don't change the fact I recognized him – to a certain degree – in the novel.

My Dad was a ponce. Simple as. He'd borrow money off Tom to pay Dick back then borrow off Harry to start the cycle all over again. It were a kind of Ponzi scheme, or rather a *poncy scheme*. It weren't that he had balls, he didn't, but neither did he have any shame, and that were handy for a sponger of his calibre. He'd pontificate about his beloved Marxism but would exploit working men and women by borrowing their hard-earned cash and creating a right old palaver when he had to pay 'em back. He had many a beating but managed to avoid many more by using that silver tongue he had, and he were careful never to put the bite on *really* heavy men.

I remember once being in the tiny kitchen of our flat when two blokes burst in. I were about 9 or 10. They made straight for the ponce demanding he cough up their dough, but Mum jumped in and threw a pan of boiling hot Heinz tomato soup is this poor bloke's boat. He screamed like a bastard and Dad scurried out like the rat he was. Neither of them laid a finger on my Mum and I respected them for that. I remember wishing she hadn't stepped up and that they'd have been allowed to give him a good fucking hiding, maybe knock some sense into the cunt.

When Dad ran out of people to tap up, he would turn his attention to our very humble possessions. I lost count of the times he pawned the furniture, Mums' best clothes or anything else he could get his mitts on. My Mum had bought me a Chopper bicycle for my 12th birthday on the never-never from The Catalogue. Words can't really describe how much I loved that bike. She'd only made two payments on it before the cunt had flogged it and pissed the proceeds up the wall. It's one of the few times that Mum really lost it with him. She asked her Old Man and Mum if it would be OK if she moved back home and brought me and my little sister with her. My Grandad told her that she'd made her bed and she'd have to lie in it.

If there were nothing tangible left to flog, the cunt would turn his attention to our gas, electric and TV meters. These meters had to be fed with 50p pieces to keep us in light, heat and entertainment. You would often hear the shout go out in our flat, "The 'lectrics gone! The gas has gone! The telly's gone" and this would be the starting pistol to scurry around trying to find 50p pieces to feed the greedy bastard meters.

Dad didn't give a fuck about all this though, he spent most of his time down the local pub anyway, so it were no skin off his arse if we were suddenly plunged into darkness, freezing our knackers off or left wondering how *Randall and Hopkirk Deceased* had finished. It were bad enough that we were deemed so poor we couldn't get credit from utilities companies or buy a TV of our own instead of renting it, but to know that your Dad is spunking the money for essentials down the boozer were just fucking humiliating. I lost count of the times they had to come and replace the meters he'd crowed open for beer money. Mum were forever having to report moody break-ins down the Old Bill Shop to cover for the cunt.

It weren't like Dad was an alcoholic. He weren't even what you'd class as a big drinker. He just always had to have an audience and the boozer were the only stage he had. He'd be there for early doors, come home for an argument and/or a kip in the afternoon and then head back when it opened for the evening. He would buy drinks for people so that they'd listen to the claptrap that came out of his cakehole. Fucking Karl Marx this and fucking Karl Marx that and up the workers this and up the workers that. He didn't have the money to be a champagne socialist, but he were definitely a pale ale and stout socialist. A fucking hypocrite of the highest order like the majority of so-called socialists.

I later realized why he spouted this guff all the time after reading a biography of Karl Marx. Marx were a fucking ponce too. Never worked a day in his life, borrowed without ever intending to pay people back, treated his servants – when he could afford them – like shit on his shoes and kept his wife and kids in abject poverty even when he had a few quid. And by all accounts, Marx was also a fucking nasty cunt with the verbals as well.

No wonder my Dad were so enamoured by the scruffy old German fucker. It all became clear after reading the book. Dad used the cover of Marxism to justify his extreme laziness and superiority complex. I remember the cunt once arrogantly proclaiming, "why would I get a job and be exploited to make a rich capitalist pig even richer! I'm an intelligent man!"

It's easy to ask "why didn't she just divorce the cunt?" I obviously wish Mum had, but these were different times. Very rarely did you hear of divorces in our neck of the woods. It weren't the done thing and besides we were already in a small flat. There were no way the cunt would leave *us*. He were on too much of a good thing. I know Mum were terrified that if she left the cunt, we'd be on a long waiting list for council housing. I could be wrong though. She might have actually loved him. Maybe the cunt had put a spell on her. Maybe he really was a magician.

Who knows really? All I know for sure is that back then, you wouldn't sit down with your Mum and ask her why she was still with your dad. She would have given me a clump and told me to mind my own bleeding business.

One thing the cunt never managed to pawn were Mum's record player and her records, but that's only because she used her nous and hid it whenever she sensed he were about to go scavenging. Mum's music was quickly salted away in Ethel and Bert's flat next door if she got even a whiff of his desperation. Mum loved music. It were her big passion and I think she once had dreams of being a singer. Problem was she had a terrible singing voice. Tone deaf really, but me and my Sis' loved watching her sing along to her precious records and we never pissed on her parade.

She would put her heart and soul into it as she bopped about singing into a hair brush, imagining she were performing at The

Palladium or somewhere. I think the music were a great escape for her from the realization that she were married to a fucking deadbeat. She seemed to be a different person when she had her records on. She came alive, bless her, and the weight of having a rotting, stinking albatross around her neck was temporarily lifted.

Windmills of Your Mind by Noel Harrison, Concrete and Clay by Unit 4 + 2, Where Do You Go to My Lovely by Peter Sarstedt, The Last Waltz by Engelbert Humperdink and Jesamine by The Casuals, she belted these out and me and my sister knew them by heart, and we loved 'em even more because Dad claimed he hated 'em. He reckoned he were into 'classical music', though I never heard the cunt listen to any. Another pose from a ponce I suppose.

FIVE

The criminal is the creative artist; the detective only the critic.

Gilbert K. Chesterton

Dad were the reason I became a hitman, because, without his disgraceful fucking attitude towards money, Dennis would never have come into my life. If Dad were my enemy, Dennis were my arch-enemy, my nemesis and ultimately the reason why you happen to be reading this, because without him I would never have become a professional killer. I popped my cherry with Dennis and in doing so realized I were actually good at something.

Dennis were the loan shark on our estate. He had the unofficial franchise, as he did on a couple of neighbouring estates in South London. Dennis' brother-in-law were a notorious, six feet 3, 20 stone hard man called Keith. Keith were a bully and allegedly very dangerous. He worked for a few small-time villains extorting and collecting debts for them. In exchange for doing gratis dirty work for them, Keith and Dennis were allowed to loan shark on a few lucrative patches.

Dennis were at one time an accountant and doing well for himself. Something dodgy happened and he were struck off and told he couldn't practice legit accounting anymore. He already had a few bob in the bank and owned a few drums that

45

he rented out in Tooting. He weren't short of money but, being human and susceptible to greed, he got into the loan sharking business.

Dennis were the 'respectable' face of the unregulated and illegal financial service sector on the council estates around us. You would only see Keith when someone refused to pay Dennis back or their repayment schedule got really behind and they needed a good talking to you. Rarely did Keith need to show his ugly mug. Most of Dennis' clients coughed up every Friday night when he did his rounds.

There *was*, however, the case of a big Irish navvy called Eammon who once got fed up of paying Dennis the extortionate vig (interest rate) on his 50 quid loan and took a stand. He gave Dennis the 50 quid back and told him, that he weren't paying the cunt another penny.

Eammon explained to Dennis that he'd already paid back 140 quid in interest on the loan without chipping anything off the capital. Dennis' interest rates weren't tied to the Nasdaq or anything, the cunt made 'em up as he went along, and he thought this thick paddy Eammon wouldn't have the nous to understand this. So, Dennis threatens Eammon with a visit from Keith and Eammon shrugs, "Do what you gotta do. I told you. You're not getting another penny."

I've never had a toe-to-toe fight in my life – which might surprise you – but I've seen plenty, and the fight I saw between Eammon and Keith were the most brutal and fascinating display of violence you could ever wish to witness. People still talk about the fight decades later, but most of them weren't there. They're just repeating and embellishing the legend. It's like that tale about all them people claiming they saw The Sex Pistols play at a dive in Manchester in their early days. The place would have had to have been the size of the fucking Albert Hall to fit 'em all in.

There were only fifteen people who got to witness Eammon versus Keith, and I was one of 'em. In remembering it I can't help but feel it were something of a psychedelic experience. I were 11 at the time and it imprinted itself on my memory. I often had flashbacks to it as I were growing up.

It was the day of the Queens Silver Jubilee, 11ᵗʰ of June 1977, which kind of kicked off the oddness: union jacks and bunting everywhere and a big party with tables laid out in the street piled high with sausage rolls, sandwiches and all kinds of crap impaled on little cocktail sticks. The parents were getting royally pissed up and the kids were guzzling fizzy pop and initiating food fights, but round the back of the flats a mighty showdown were taking place.

Dennis had brought Keith and a couple of his mates round to hopefully knock seven bells out of Eammon. Keith asked for a toe to toe with Eammon and Eammon were game, so they took their shirts off and squared up on the area where people hung out their washing. I just happened to be knocking about there with a couple of mates. One of them had recorded that week's Top 40 off the radio and we were listening to it. A few adults watched and no doubt a few side bets got laid.

Keith would have been about 30 at the time I reckon. Eammon, I'd say, late 40s. They were both big lumps but Keith had more of a physique and were a good few inch taller.

The light were strange that day. It were hazy sunshine but the sky had a burnt orange tinge; the type you usually get during twilight in English summers. Also, everything seemed to be in really sharp focus. I don't know if this were because I was witnessing a real live fight right in front of me, and it were the excitement heightening everything, but it were unusual. It felt almost *too* real but not real at all, like I were watching a film.

So, it were ding ding and from the off Keith landed a few decent jabs on Eammon's chin to absolutely no reaction from Eammon, not even a flinch. Keith throws a haymaker and catches Eammon on the temple, but again, Eammon's not the slightest bit fazed. Keith comes in with an upper cut but Eammon's steadfast. Eammon hasn't thrown yet and Keith's clearly now getting riled. Eammon's now letting Keith hit his body with a flurry of shots but Eammon's got a grin on his mush and he's egging Keith on: *come on, son. You can do better than that.*

Keith's losing his rag now. He grabs Eammon around the back of his neck, pulls him in and head butts him clean on the hooter. We all hear the crack and we wince. Eammon's nose splits open. He's caught him right on the bridge and blood pisses out. Keith steps back and breathlessly asks, *have you had enough?* Eammon grinningly shakes his head, dukes still up.

Keith is now fucking furious and steams in with a volley of shots aimed at Eammon's head. Eammon's parrying the blows now though and not one of them gets through. This cunt Keith's losing his puff. He backs off and looks over at Dennis and his mates as if to say, *fuck me, this mick's tough!*

Dennis gives it, "finish him, Keith." Keith takes a deep breath and rolls in again. His blows are connecting on Eammon's arms and torso but the cunt might as well be tickling him for all the effect it's having. Eammon spits a big glob of blood and starts stretching his mitts out, getting Keith's measure, but he's still to throw a punch and that grin is really getting on Keith's tits.

It's not unusual for some fighters to let their opponents wear themselves out, but this were ridiculous. Me and my mates were now screaming at Eammon to fight back and you could see on Dennis' boat that this weren't what he'd pictured for his guard dog. The beautiful lovers rock reggae song, 'Sideshow' by Barry Briggs were playing on the tape and it seemed fitting.

Keith can't let this go on. He's being made a mug of by this grinning paddy cunt. He closes in and puts the nut on Eammon again. Thud! Right in the middle of his forehead. A thin seam of blood spreads across Eammon's napper, but again, Eammon's still standing and simply wipes the blood from his eyes. Keith's really out of puff now and again he asks – hopefully – if Eammon's had enough.

Eamon shakes his head and beckons Keith back into the fray with his fingers. Eammon's now badly cut up, his eyes are swelling and bruises on his body are appearing. Keith looks at Dennis but Dennis just shrugs at Keith. Keith starts calling Eammon a mad bastard but Eammon's just grinning at him with his hands up. Keith slips his hand into his pocket and when it comes out there's a brass duster across his knuckles. This is bang out of order, but Keith is now clearly desperate. Eammon didn't even raise an objection to Keith now being armed, which made it all even more surreal.

Keith bops about a bit and then shoots in with a windmill and catches Eammon around about the temple. This knocks Eammon on his arse but his lights are still on. Keith pauses as he stands over him, but Eammon's just looking up at him with that sinister fucking grin.

This really pushes Keith over the edge. He drops to his knees and wraps his laughing tackle around Eammon's ear, breathlessly warning Eammon that he's about to take his lug off. Suddenly Eammon flips Keith over and he's on top of him. Eammon instantly shoves both his thumbs deep into Keith's sockets and pops his eyes out. I don't know if you've ever seen someone have their eyes plucked out, but let me tell you if you haven't, it's something you never forget. They do literally dangle on a thin rope of nerves.

Keith puts his hands over his detached eyeballs and screams like a banshee bitch. Keith's mates and Dennis are flapping about like headless chickens. Eammon gets to his feet and asks Dennis and the others if they fancy a go. They shit themselves, quickly throw the now hysterical Keith in the motor and speed off. Eammon grabs his shirt, takes out a packet of fags and lights one up. Silence. Deafening silence from the spectators.

This is broken when some cunt politely tells Eammon he should go up the hospital. Eammon says he's OK and heads to his flat like he's just returning from taking the bins out.

Nobody said nish until the inevitable: *Did you fucking see that!* Went up. Within minutes it were all around the estate what had happened whilst most of the residents had been celebrating her Majesty's jubilee. Of course, everyone had their own interpretation of what had happened, especially those who hadn't witnessed it. I felt privileged to have witnessed such a display of violence. I weren't being ghoulish, far from it. Even at that young age I realized I had just seen something quite poetic. Eammon – without even throwing a punch – had seen off a brute who was feared all over South London. This were dirty fighting *par excellence*, and taught me that to win in life you just have to be willing to do something your opponent won't.

You see, biting Eammon's ear off were obviously OK with Keith, but Eammon used the opportunity to go one step further and take Keith's mince pies out. I don't fully understand the etiquette of dirty fighting, but I'm imagining it's OK to feast on a lug, but popping some cunts eyes out is frowned upon. It's obvious that Eammon were a seriously tough fucker after having let Keith pummel him, but he topped the performance off with a curtesy of pure fucking brutality. Eammon proved that no matter how big you are, how hard you are or what reputation you have, you can always come unstuck with a cunt who's willing to go that extra mile.

Apparently, the doctors managed to pop one of Keith's eyes back in so it weren't all bad news for him. I would have loved to have heard how he explained to the doctors what had happened. It goes without saying that Old Bill never got a whiff of it, officially at least. They would have picked up on the gossip but knew they'd never get anyone who'd witnessed the bloodbath to talk about it on the record. It's called fair play. Those that know ain't talkin', n' those that are talkin' don't know.

The code of the street is far purer and has more integrity than the code amongst successful villains. On the street you have nothing to gain and everything to lose if you yap to Old Bill. In the monied, high stakes villainy arena it's inverted. If something seriously comes on top you have everything to gain and nothing to lose if you yap, because you'll be offered protection or a lighter stretch of bird for doing it. If you don't keep your gob shut on the street you instantly become a rat and it's open season on you. Well, it used to be at least.

It's naïve to think that villains that come up from the street will carry the code with 'em when big money becomes involved. They really don't. It's a cliché, but it really is the self-preservation society after a certain earning level in my experience. The streets are a quaint, distant memory.

After the Royal Jubilee rumble, Keith decided to hang up his brass knuckle and stay indoors polishing his glass eye. Dennis had to bring in a new enforcer. He went a little bit exotic this time and hired a big Turkish lad called Sevket. Dennis continued his extortionate practice and it were like nothing had ever happened. Business as usual. Dennis still did his rounds but always swerved Eammon.

I had to deal with Dennis every Friday night. Mum were one of his customers and would take out 30 quid loans on a regular basis. For this she had to pay a tenner a week and she would leave it for me to hand over to him. She worked at the pub on a Friday night so I would babysit my sister because my cunt of a Dad were nowhere to be seen. I were 11 and my sister was 6. Paying for a babysitter would have been daft, I were perfectly capable of looking after us both. Mum would buy us pop and crisps before she left for the night and me and my sister would watch the telly, safe in the knowledge that we had plenty of 50p pieces at hand in case any of the greedy meters needed feeding.

Dennis would turn up at around 8pm. I'd open the door and he would step inside and I'd hand over the tenner. He always had his little black book with him and he'd enter the payment in a column with a little bookies pen. Once the transaction were through, he'd ruffle my hair, wink at me and leave. It were over in seconds and we only ever talked if Mum hadn't been able to leave the tenner that week. I would have to repeat the mantra, "She can't pay this week. Is it all right?"

He never grumbled because it were more than "all right" for Dennis. It meant he could add default interest at God knows what rate he were charging, and he were clearly happy to let my Mum sink further into debt.

At that time, I didn't really have a fixed opinion on Dennis. He were just something that existed. A part of the furniture, a regular fixture of my reality and I knew that there were dozens of others on the estate whose doors he knocked. I only started feeling shame when I got to around 15 and realized there were no escape from him unless Mum died, we did a bunk, won the football pools or *spot the ball* or came into an unexpected and ridiculously implausible inheritance. Actually, I doubt her dying would have changed the situation. I were positive that Dennis would have hounded me and my little sister for the dough Mum had died owing him.

So yeah, from around 17 onwards I harboured a hatred of Dennis. This took shape in the intrusive thoughts of him being killed in the most horrific ways imaginable. *Hammer House of Horror* films were often played on the telly around that time and I would fantasize about Dennis meeting the same fates of these hammy actors. There were one of them Hammer films where Vincent Price offs Robert Morley by making him eat his own dog. I liked that one. It occurred to me that if Dennis were to get the scripted ending he deserved, somebody were gonna have to step up and write it.

I were 14 when I finally jacked school in for good. I could read and write and add up and that's all I reckoned I needed. I had never attended much and Mum were often threatened by the Education Board that she would be in trouble if I didn't start showing up. It weren't hard to overcome this. I would attend registration, get my mark and then skedaddle with a few other rascals. I got a job working full time at a local scrapyard a month after my 15th birthday.

It were illegal as I didn't have a national insurance number but the Old Man who owned the yard didn't give a monkey's. I worked from 8am to 6pm Monday to Friday and from 8am until noon on a Saturday. For these 54 hours a week I was paid 30 quid in cash. It were only a little over 50 pence an hour but I didn't mind at all. Working in the yard were far more interesting than going to school, and 30 quid a week were a lot more than others at my age were earning.

The job entailed making endless cups of tea for the boss and whoever popped into the yard, running errands, sorting salvage-able car parts, emptying old engines of their oil and generally doing anything the boss told me to do. It were a lot of heavy and usually dangerous lifting but I just got on with it. I looked at it as paid exercise that were building my body up. More important than this though, the job taught me how to shoot.

The scrapyard were plagued by rats. Big fuckers. Behind the yard were a large bakery and obviously the vermin were attracted to it. This meant that the cheeky little bastards used to go scav-enging through the bins and skips of the bakery, but then come and have a kip in the scrapyard amongst the car wrecks. There were nowhere at the back of the bakery for them to get their heads down, and the scrapyard proved to be a perfect doss house for them after their hearty dough-based meals.

The old man were sick of seeing the cunts scurrying about and his dogs were too slow to catch 'em. Instead of bringing in poison, a few cats or an air rifle into the yard to kill them though, he brought a real pistol and a real rifle in. He proudly admitted he had loads of firearms and ammo at home, *why* he had an arse-nal he never explained, but within a few weeks he had taught me how to very efficiently use a Browning High Power L9A1 pistol and a 7.62mm L42A1 rifle.

Work now became not so much a chore as a joy. I were over the fucking moon. I reckon I would have paid *him* 30 quid a week just to let me come and kill the rats. I could only shoot 'em when the baler or big reciprocating saw were being used to drown out the snap n' cracks, and obviously I couldn't shoot when there were any customers in the yard, but there were lots of rats and we had lots of bullets. Nothing up to that point in my life had given me a bigger kick. I had found something that gave me real satisfaction.

I would give my Mum a tenner out of my wages and salt away the twenty. I never bought fags or cans of beer or went to the pictures or the football or bought clobber like most of my peers. I used to hide my dough under a floorboard in the bathroom. I had saved 160 nicker after a couple of months but then my Dad found it and pocketed it. He'd obviously tippled I'd been saving up and as I didn't have no bank account he quite rightly figured it were somewhere in the tiny flat.

When Mum and me confronted him, he denied it, swore on mine and my sisters' lives, even though he were supposed to be an atheist Marxist. Mum found out that on the day my savings went AWOL the cunt had been in the boozer flashing the cash and buying every other cunt drinks. In a few hours he'd done in what had taken me a couple of months of hard, dirty work to save. Still, he denied it and gave not a fuck about what he'd done. Other than swear revenge in my mind, there were not a lot I could do. I just got my head down and started hiding my savings at the scrapyard. Mum refused to continuing taking the tenner a week I used to give her. I insisted but she weren't having any of it.

On my seventeenth birthday the gaffer gave me a pay rise. My two years of hard work and never having a day off sick had paid off. He bumped me up to 60 quid a week. Doubled my wage bless him. I had a national insurance number now but it were strictly cash in hand at the scrapyard so I were never taxed. I liked the idea that the government didn't know what I were up to. It's stayed with me.

As a bit of a celebration, I decided to spend a few quid and pay for me, my Mum and Sis' to go on holiday for a week at Butlins in Bognor Regis. It cost me 80 quid for the one chalet and a further tenner for the coach tickets. Your food were thrown in and all the entertainment were free for the week. Mum borrowed 50 bar off Dennis for our spending money. It were the first time we'd been on holiday together and my little sister were so excited that Mum was on the verge of shoving one of her Valium down her Gregory. My Sis' didn't sleep for two nights before we were set to leave.

We had a fantastic time at Butlins and when we got home, we got the good news that my cunt of a dad had been poorly. Unfortunately, He hadn't kicked the bucket but he were in pain. We walked in on him sat in the room with his foot on chair, a pillow underneath it. The cunt had gout – a very painful inflammation brought about by consuming rich food and alcohol usually – and his big toe were swollen and bright red. He were in agony and couldn't move and I couldn't have been happier … at first.

After a few days of him not being able to fuck off to the pub it became apparent that this weren't a good situation. He'd sit in the chair and piss and moan and slag this and that off until it got to the point me, Mum and Sis' spent most of our time in the kitchen so we didn't have to listen to him. He was out of pub duty for a couple of weeks but it felt like a lifetime. I had prayed every night that the gout would kill him or it got better and he could fuck off back to the boozer and put us out of our collective misery.

It were during his time of gout that I had my very first thought about actually killing him. I reckoned it wouldn't it be too much of a stretch to borrow the pistol from the scrapyard and shoot the cunt. A pipe dream of course: *how could I do it without my Mum and Sis' finding out, and how would I dispose of the body.* I used to conjure up all kinds of elaborate scenarios in my mind just before I fell asleep every night. My dreams often revolved around me pumping the cunt with lead and chopping up his body, sticking it in plastic bags and lobbing it in The Thames. One recurring dream I had was of putting him into the baler at the yard and watching him being crushed to death. His screams often woke me up and I would be pissed off that the dream had ended with him still, barely, but *still* alive.

So, there I was at 17, obsessed with murdering my Dad and Dennis the fucking Menace loan shark. Other lads at my age – I'd imagine – were thinking about girls and getting their end away and going down the road that eventually leads to them settling down and procreating. I were only interested in going down the road that leads to death. I knew it weren't healthy, but I weren't in a healthy environment anyway, so it didn't bother me too much. It was what it was and it really didn't worry me. Killing Dad would be problematic, sure, for obvious reasons, but it had to be done. Dennis were gonna be easier to snuff so I decided I would do him first.

I were 18 and I was gonna lose my cherry popping the local loan shark. It felt like a mission, a quest, something admirable. I'd be doing the community a service. I mean, I knew a lot of people on the estate relied on Dennis' financial services to help them survive, but I also knew that another shark would surface as soon as this cunt had been taken out.

What I were thinking was: *at least their debts to this particular cunt get wiped clean.* At least the debt cycle could be reset. Sure, the next parasitic cunt would be just as bad, but it were unlikely he'd have access to Dennis' little ledger book of outstanding debts. I would make sure that the book vanished when I snuffed him, which meant I would have to hit him at just the right time. A Friday. Collection day. In all honesty I never gave it a thought that he would have a big wad of cash on him when I struck. I weren't mugging the cunt. I had a higher calling.

I made a fatal error from the off by confiding in my mate what I was gonna do to Dennis. Fatal at the time, but as it turned out, essential in me becoming what I am today. He didn't believe me at first. Why would he? When I told him about my planning, he started to take me a bit more seriously, but I know he never thought I'd really go through with it. It were ridiculous.

It were through this mate and what I'd confided in him that I met Uncle. Uncle was my mate's actual uncle. He were a dapper, handsome, well-built 45-year-old South Londoner. He drove a plum-coloured Daimler and when he visited the estate a few people would come out and look at his motor in admiration. You didn't get too many Daimlers on the estate and I were surprised it were left alone. When my mate told me who Uncle really was, I weren't surprised his motor never got touched.

Uncle was, on paper, a bookmaker – or Turf accountant as many liked to grandiosely call themselves – but he were more involved in 'fixing' for a well-known South London crime family. It took me a few years to find out what 'fixing' entailed, but basically it means he were involved in the organizing of crimes and the raising of funds to commit them. If the crimes turned into a result, Uncle would be in charge of the handling and distribution of the loot, be it cash, tom, merchandise or whatever. I'd be lying if I told you about all the capers he were involved in, because I don't know, but I do know he were on good terms with some of the biggest organized villains in the UK and Europe, and he were clearly making a shit load of dough from his grafts.

Uncle lived up North London, Golders Green to be precise, but he grew up in Bermondsey, South London and had never lost the accent. He'd started out flogging stuff that had fallen off the backs of lorries and then got a job chalking up for a local bookie near the Elephant and Castle. He started his own racing book and from there he graduated into his role as 'fixer' and became very wealthy from it. Uncle were quick witted and had excellent communication and organizational skills. He could talk the birds down from the trees as they used to say. His charm and intelligence were always on display and he had plenty of patience. Nobody on the estate knew what he really did, but it were known that he were 'connected' and it meant he were treated with respect and seen as something of a local hero in having done so well for himself.

I couldn't shake the thought of killing Dennis, but eventually came to my senses and realized I were such an amateur I'd be caught and spend the next 25 years over the wall. Besides, I were doing all right for myself. The Old Man at the scrapyard were now paying me a decent wage: 200 readies a week. I now operated the baler and saws and he brought in another young urchin to do the dirty jobs. I still kept my position as rat killer though. I were becoming something of a marksman and I loved nothing more than practising my shooting on the varmints.

Out of my 200 I gave Mum 70 and my little sister a tenner pocket money. I put ninety away – that I kept buried in a safe box at the scrapyard – and had 30 nicker left over for bits and bobs, petrol, oil and that. I paid for us to get a phone in the house and had a few sovs down with my mate to decorate the flat and give it a spruce up. Mum was made up and able to pack in her part time job at the pub because of the seventy nicker I were coughing up.

I were doing sixty-five hours a week at the yard but didn't mind because I weren't bothered about having a social life. Pubs or clubs never interested me and I couldn't care less about finding a bird to go out with. I'm straight and enjoy sex, but I really couldn't picture myself in a relationship. This could well have been because I'd seen the fucked-up relationship my Mum and

Dad had, but I don't know, after my first professional kill, it became obvious that having a relationship would have been impossible with the career I'd chosen.

I'd salted away just over a grand when I decided to confront Mum about Dennis. I asked her what she owed him exactly. She replied she didn't know, but thought it were around 400. I said, *fine, we'll pay him off once and for all.* Mum pulled out some scraps of paper and borrowed my sister's calculator to try work out an exact settlement amount.

She reckoned the vig Dennis had been historically charging were around 80%. So, on a loan of 30 quid, she'd be paying him back 24 quid. This were all vig/interest though and nothing off the 30 quid capital were being reduced. This meant that if over the year she borrowed, say, £360 in £30 increments and paid a tenner a week back to him he would pocket £520 in pure interest, but fucking zilch were being chipped off the £360. So, for the 7 years she had been a customer, Dennis were toting up the capital still be to paid off.

Mum had never really sat down to do the sums. When it dawned that it were gonna cost over two and half grand to get Dennis the Menace off her back, she were beside herself. Fucking mortified. She broke down and blamed herself for being an idiot and told me to forget about paying him off. 2 and a half K was more dough than she'd ever seen in her life, and no way were she gonna allow me to bail her out of the shit. No, she were gonna continue paying Dennis and I were told to forget about it all.

She did, however, finally admit that her biggest mistake in life and been meeting my cunt of a Dad and letting him get away with murder in his responsibilities. She said she wished he were dead and I suppose from that moment on the die were cast. I were gonna do in Dennis and then do in my cunt of a Dad.

SIX

But I wondered, how would I feel about killing someone? Now I know. It's no big deal.

Chris Kyle

I bought a 3rd hand Yamaha FS1e motorbike off one of my mates for 90 nicker. He had discovered the joys of heroin, like many others on the estate, and he were learning how to service an increasingly bad habit. I could have probably got it for seventy but bartering would have been pathetic.

The Yamaha 'Fizzer' were a much sought-after little bike at the time. It had a 50cc engine that had a restrictor in the exhaust pipe that stopped it going over 30 mph, but it were a doddle to take it off and get 60 mph out of it. I didn't have a licence to ride it and I never paid any road tax or insurance. If I ever got pulled over by plod, I just gave the name of the smackhead who flogged it me. I'd give him a fiver for a bag of brown and he'd go into the station and produce his license. South London Old Bill had a lot more to worry about than minor traffic offences in the mid 1980s.

It were because of my purchase of The Fizzer I got my first hiding. The older brother of The Smackhead I'd bought it from had a bee in his bonnet about the sale. He thought I'd taken advantage of his dopey sibling and wanted me to cough up another 40 quid. I produced the black book price but Big Brother were having none of it and demanded the dosh. I told him it weren't gonna happen and he chinned me. I hit the deck and he put the slipper in. I had a shiner and a bust lip but I'd saved 40 nicker so it were a result in my eyes.

Up until that point I had miraculously managed to avoid being beat up or pulled into a fight. The majority of the lads on the estate grew up scrapping on a regular basis. It were something you had to do to be accepted, but I had somehow swerved the convention. I can only assume it were because I kept my trap shut and never got lippy with anyone. I know a lot of the lads thought I were 'soft' and could have easily taken a liberty, but they left me alone and never bullied me. A lot of this was to do with the fact that my best mate was one of the naughtiest lads on the estate and when I did hang about, he were always around. I were charmed I suppose.

When my mate found out I'd be chinned he immediately offered to avenge it. I told him I didn't want him to but I'm sure he had a word of warning for my assailant to make sure he didn't take another liberty. He ripped the piss out of me as well, *how the fuck you gonna kill some cunt if you can't even have a row?* I explained that I didn't *hate* The Smackhead's brother, but I sure as hell hated Dennis. I had stupidly confided in him that I was planning on popping Dennis. He thought it were hilarious.

One Friday, out of the blue, Mum plucked up courage and asked Dennis exactly how much she owed him. She were trembling a little bit when she posed the hypothetical question: *uh, Dennis. If I were to say, settle up with you, y'know, pay you everything I owe you … uh, what would it be?*

Dennis looked a little surprised, *where you gonna get that kind o' money, love?* He snorted, smiled and left. Mum stepped out after him and pleaded, *can you get me a figure?*

She asked him again the week after and again he snorted and just pissed off back on his rounds. That were it for me. That same night I stalked him around the estate. It were a good bit of surveillance work and I really enjoyed it. It turned out that after doing his collection he would nip into a boozer on the high street and have a few jars. At kicking out time, quarter past 11, he'd go get in his motor and drive off – presumably – home.

I stalked him again the week after and he followed the same MO, only this time I waited on my motorbike and found out where he lived in Tooting. I kept a couple of cars behind and were made up with my surveillance skills. He kept to the speed limit and drove carefully, as most drivers who'd had a skin full back then did, and he led me right to his doorstep. I left it about 10 minutes before I rode slowly past and got a closer peek at his house. It were a smart semi with a garage and two large hedgerows at each side.

I rode around to the avenue behind his house and had a gander at the garden of the house that backed onto his. I couldn't get a good view in the dark so nipped back down the day after and rode along the street pretending to be looking for an address. This time I saw that the house behind's Dennis' only had a 6ft wooden fence separating the gardens. Just after that I scouted around for any alleyways or wooded areas nearby. I found a small tree lined passage that led to another avenue from the two I'd seen. Perfect, I thought.

For the next four Fridays I would stalk Dennis doing his rounds. He never deviated. Rounds, boozer, home. You could have set your kettle by the cunt. I started riding back and forth to Tooting in the evenings just to get in the right frame of mind.

I would always ride past Dennis' gaff, go to the bottom of the avenue, swing a left up to the next avenue and go back in the direction I'd come down in. I never noticed anyone giving me a second glance and my confidence were growing.

I thought about using the pistol from the scrapyard as my weapon. The problem would be the loud, clacking report and echo of the pistol when it fired. If I'd known how to source a silencer at the time, I would definitely have used the pistol. As it was, my weapon of choice were a crowbar. You can't go wrong with a good old crowbar, and if I were pulled on my way down to Tooting in possession of one, the only thing they could have possibly pinched me for was sus of going tooled up for a spot of breaking and entering. As I said, even back then for me, it were all about planning and being able to deal with any eventuality.

I ran the mantra through my head for weeks: *gloves, crowbar, tinted full face helmet, carrier bag, dark clobber, change of clobber, wet rag, tin of lighter fuel, box of matches, stolen licence plate.*

The big day came, this was it, shit or bust. All day at the scrapyard I were picturing the scenario that was gonna play out that night. Were I nervous? Shaking like a shiteing dog. The old gaffer noticed I weren't myself and asked me – for possibly the first time in all the years I'd been working for him – if I was all right. I told him I had a dicky tummy, which were true. I were never off the fucking khazi. I managed to put in a half decent days' work at the yard and fucked off home at 6.30 pm.

I couldn't face the Shepherd's pie, chips and veg Mum had rustled up. She were a bit miffed and shoved it in the oven on low in case I got my appetite back later. I couldn't tell her there were more chance of Shergar turning up safe and sound than that. I went and sat in my bedroom for an hour and tried to read a book. Obviously, I couldn't concentrate. The words looked like a mixture of Double Dutch and Egyptian hieroglyphics. At around 8 I heard Dennis' knock at the door. I went to *my* door, cracked it a little and listened. I couldn't believe what I heard.

The cunt had only come up with a settlement figure hadn't he! Today of all fucking days! I thought I were hearing things, hallucinating maybe. Dennis tells Mum that he'll settle on her coughing up 3 and half a grand. He knew she was never gonna come up with that kind of dough and he had almost giggled when he said it. Mum told him she though it would be more like 2 grand. Dennis gives it, "Why? You got 2 grand have ya?"

"Uh, no, not right now, but –

"Well, if you ain't got two grand, how you gonna manage paying me back the 3 'n a half, love?"

The cunt were toying with her. She were relatively young and he knew he could keep ploughing her for exorbitant vig for many moons to come. Dennis, like all loan sharks, *never* wants his prey to pay off the capital, unless, of course, they fall so far back with payments it's becoming a ball ache collecting from 'em.

Mum were a good customer though. The cunt knew she was still ripe for harvesting regular cash. And do the sums. She had already paid him the capital back a dozen times over. Loan sharks aren't dummies. If she'd kicked the bucket, he would have just pestered me and possibly my little sister for the dough. He knew my Dad were a deadbeat, so there were no chance he'd get hassled for it.

I came out of my bedroom when Dennis had gone. Mum told me what I'd already heard. She said that she'd never get rid of Dennis and her debt. I kept my trap shut. I didn't want her getting a whiff of what I was gonna do to him that night.

I rode to the pub and got there at a 10.45, knowing Dennis

would be leaving in a half hour or so. I pulled up outside the parade of shops. There were a Chinese takeaway that stayed open 'til midnight and there were plenty of customers coming in and out. A girl I knew from the estate was eating chips and I chatted with her for a bit. She asked me what I was doing there and I told her I was waiting for someone. She got on her toes after a couple of minutes and I spied Dennis coming out the boozer and going to his motor.

I followed him for a half mile or so and then overtook him. My heart were beating like a bastard and my guts were turning over. At one point I thought I was gonna literally shit myself, but I kept motoring on and got to the avenue behind Dennis'. I checked that the lights were out at the house I was gonna use to gain access to Dennis' Garden. They were, so I went and parked the Fizzer up in the tree lined passageway just round the corner. I had my full-face tinted helmet on and the crowbar under my jacket. I left the carrier bag hanging from the handlebar of the bike, had a good look around to make sure the coast were clear then ran down the avenue.

I went down the path to the garden and effortlessly climbed over the fence. I were now in the enemy's garden and I paused for a second, *how the fuck was I was gonna explain if someone caught me?* I'd run the scenario through my head hundreds of times but I'd forgotten the answer, but I were here and it was now or never and I went and hid behind the back of the house. I crouched down and listened for Dennis' motor to pull up. It were only moments later but it genuinely felt like hours. I swallowed hard and said a silent prayer as I heard the motor shut down and Dennis' size elevens on the gravel.

After a big gulp of night air, I creeped out and caught him just getting his key ready to open his door. I took a few steps forward and then ... freeze! But it weren't Dennis or a vigilant neighbour that brought me to a stop. It were me. It was in my head. I'd completely bottled it, become petrified and watched Dennis simply open his front door and mosey on inside without even noticing me. I rounded and shot back over the fence I'd jumped, back up the path, down the avenue to my parked-up Fizzer and I was on my way back home faster than you could say, *what the fuck was that you bottle-less cunt!*

The nerves gave way to self-loathing. I hated myself. All the planning and Dennis living in my head for all that time, and when it came to it, I'd shat it. I didn't sleep at all that night. I just tossed and turned and pictured the wasted opportunity. I had been a few feet away from him and it had been a golden opportunity. An open goal at the FA Cup final just ready for me to tap in the winner and become a hero. *What a useless cunt!* Maybe I was just like my Dad. Good for nothing. Total waste o' skin and self-delusional with it.

I were knackered at the yard next day. At one point I fell asleep on the forklift and nearly pranged it into the Gaffer's cabin. It pissed it down as well, and I took out the rifle to shoot some rats to make myself feel better. It didn't. When I got home that night I went straight to my kip. My sister sensed something wrong because I'd never, ever, missed an episode of Starsky and Hutch of a Saturday night. She had to watch it on her tod, bless her.

Monday comes around and I'm still feeling shit. My mate – who from now on will be referred to as H – knocks on the door and beckons me out. He's excited and I'm curious, *what's up?*

He whispers, smirking, "D'ya wanna get yer end away?"

"Howd'ya mean?" I asks, looking at him suspiciously, and hoping beyond hope he didn't think I were an iron and he were gonna let me bugger him.

He tells me that he's got some solid intell' that there's a Richard who's just moved to the estate and she's on the game, "She lives with this big spade n' he's pimping her out. She's a right sort! Seen her in the Paki shop n' she's well up for it."

H goes on to feverishly tell me that this newly arrived Brass is a cross between Raquel Welch n' Farah Fawcett Majors, "We can fuck her for a score or a blowjob or it's a tenner if we just want a wank! Let's get in there while she's nice n' clean. I don't fancy sloppy seconds after all the other cunts on the manor."

"No thanks."

"*Fuck off!* We can wear rubber johnny's if it's the spook yer bothered about, n' wait 'til you see her! She's like a page three bird, only sexier!"

"I don't care. I'm not paying for it, H."

"You don't have to. *I'll* pay." And with that he whips out two twenty bills and a pack of rubber johnny's like the magician Ali Bongo.

H was, and I'm sure he still is, one of the most persistent men you could ever meet. He simply won't take no for an answer and after a bit of slather he talked me into going with him. I certainly weren't game but I can't say I weren't a little intrigued and excited. I were a virgin and H knew it. Most of the lads had lost their virginities around 14, 15, so I were a bit of an odd bollock in their eyes. Not that it bothered me. Sex has never been something I gave too much thought about.

So, we get round this flat and H knocks on the door. I'm nervous now but H is positively beaming. The door's opened by Doreen and H is right. She's beautiful. Blonde, petite, huge firm knockers and a really pretty face. She's wearing cropped T-shirt and very tight hotpants. She's got a lovely smile and a sweet Northern accent and she seems really friendly. I reckon she's about mid-twenties.

Me and H step in and we see a lanky black lad sat in a deck-chair watching the telly, eating a pot noodle and washing it down with a can of Red Stripe. They haven't decorated or furnished the flat: bare lightbulb, no carpet or lino on the floor, blankets taped up at the windows instead of curtains, etc.

The black lad turns out to be called Spammy. He's about 30 and talks with a South London Jamaican accent. He's got a deep mars bar running down his left cheek and looks like he can have a row. He's straight to business, casually reels off the price list and holds his mitt out. H don't hesitate and he slaps the two twenties down. Doreen politely asks who wants to go first and H eagerly puts his hand up like he's about to answer a question at school.

Doreen smiles at us both, grabs H's hand and leads him to the bedroom. H is beaming. Spammy's still watching Wogan on the telly and I'm stood there like a spare prick. After a minute I gives it, "Uh ... do I just wait here?"

"Yeah, just sit down, man." Seeing as Spammy is sat in the only deckchair I take it he means I park my arse on the floor. Spammy gives it, "they won't be long."

He were wrong. Terry Wogan's now chinwagging with his main guest and there's no sign of H and Doreen. I'm getting really uncomfortable watching Spammy watching Wogan and chuckling every now and then at the 'light entertainment, re-hearsed answers' Wogan's guests are spieling out. I've had enough so I get up and walk out the front door. Spammy don't say boo.

I wouldn't leave H there on his tod so I wait outside for a good half hour. *What the fuck is he doing in there?* Eventually H comes floating out on a cloud with a big goofy grin on his boat. He's shaking his head and exhaling in wonder as he proclaims that he's just 'officially' had the best fuck in history. *Two* best fucks in history no less, because when it became apparent I'd nashed, he'd had another go on Doreen.

H won't like reading this, but the truth is he became cunt-struck by Doreen and it resulted in an attempted murder that he were very lucky not to be pinched for. H were no mug, but after banging Doreen he unfortunately let his cock rule his brain for a time and made himself look like a right bleeding dolt. You know I love you H but it's an important part of my story.

If memory serves right, it was as we were heading back through the estate that very same night that H declared his un-dying love for Doreen. I gives it, "She's a brass, H!"

"I know she's a fuckin' brass you muppet, but I'm gonna save her ain't I!"

I were hoping that H was suffering from a temporary post-shag elation that would pass, but three days later I bump into him and he's still rabbiting on about Doreen and how she's too good to be on the game and that he reckons she genuinely really likes him, and that he knows if the big coon were out the picture Doreen would fall in his arms and they could start ...

I had to chirp up *again*, "Look, H ... no disrespect, but she's ..."

H was having fucking none of it and tells me, almost proudly, that he's been back to bang Doreen two nights on the trot. He's literally spunked another 40 bar on her. H weren't short of a few bob as he had a job in The Print, but still, a score a shag weren't exactly bargain basement.

It were at that point I knew it were futile trying to make H see sense. If he wanted to spunk his dough away it were up to him. He was a stubborn bleeder and I didn't wanna stick my neb too far in, in case he took umbrage and gave me a clump. H could hold his hands up and I'd never even thrown so much as a shadow punch in all my life.

I were still grappling with the fact I had bottled out of stoving Dennis' head in. I felt like shit. I tried to put it out my mind but the thought kept turning up like a bad penny. I couldn't rest. I knew I were gonna have to have another go at it.

I were in the kitchen the next Friday when Dennis called. I was making a cup of tea and I couldn't look at him. My skin were crawling and I had a weird buzzing in my ear. My Mum coughed up and he pissed off on his merry way. I took the brew into my bedroom and sat on my bed. As I sipped it, I just kept thinking, *now or never, now or never.* In my mind I consolidated that last Friday was a dry run and all I had to do was repeat it, but actually wrap the crowbar around his bonce this time. I took deep breaths and focused. I kept checking my kettle. Minutes were flying by. This was it. Tonight's the night and if my arse goes and I bottle it again, well, that's it. I would have to live with it.

·

SEVEN

He didn't know the right people. That's
all a police record means.

Raymond Chandler

Wallop! The first blow caught him on the top of his napper and it had a bit of a bounce to it. His eyes widened, his gob hung open and he looked at me in horror. The second blow split his forehead open and the claret started flowing. Dennis lets out this pathetic little yelp and he falls to his knees right in front of me, like he were about to suck me off or something. The third blow made a kind of squelch as it opened his head up wider. Dennis is now on all fours and making like he's trying to crawl away.

I go to his arse end and the fourth blow is to the back of his head. It was like I were teeing off on him with the crowbar. Dull thud! The cunt's out for the count, face down, spread eagled. The fifth, sixth and seventh blows are just to make sure he's never waking up again. I crouch down and quickly rifle the inside pocket of his jacket. There's a fat wad of rolled notes and his little black ledger book with all the debts in it. Result.

I'm on my toes and back on my Fizzer in no time. I felt really calm, like a weight had been lifted, and I remember kind of thinking, *well, if I do get nabbed now it'll just be bad luck. Nothing I could have done. Fate.*

I pull up at some lights on Tooting Broadway and look down at a grate. I just thought, *now, do it!* I slip the bloody crowbar out from under my jacket and just drop it down the grate. I'm revving the engine a bit, keen to ride off, when I see a pissed-up bloke on the pavement eating a kebab and I just know he's seen what I've done. He's looking puzzled and he wobbles over and sways above the grate. Green and I'm off like shit on a shovel. The calm's now been replaced not by nerves, but real fear. *The pissed-up kebab muncher saw me. Fuck!*

A quarter of a mile later and I pull into a communal concrete playground. I park up and quickly change clothes. I shove the soiled ones in the plastic bag, put it in a bin, spray the lighter fuel on it and toss it in, light the box of matches and woosh! I sling Dennis' debt ledger in the fire. It burns beautifully and I'm back on The Fizzer and gunning it for the estate.

I am absolutely convinced that this pisshead had reported seeing me ditch the crowbar. I doubt he would have remembered the reg on my motorbike but I couldn't take any chances. I had some spare keys for the locks on the scrapyard gates so I shot home and grabbed 'em. I parked The Fizzer up behind a mountain of old fridges in the yard and then covered it over in tarpaulin. I hid Dennis' roll of cash in an old oil drum where we threw the rats I'd shot. Quite fitting looking back.

I walked home from the yard and kept picturing the crowbar slipping down the grate. In hindsight though, I think it were meant to be that I got eyeballed dropping the crowbar. It gave me something to fret over, other than the fact that I had just taken another human being's life. I thought about going back and torching The Fizzer just to be on the safe side, but – and I know it sounds a bit soft – I truly loved that motorbike. I figured that if it got out on the wind that Old Bill were looking for a yellow Fizzer it wouldn't have taken me ten minutes to crush it at the yard.

I didn't sleep that night. My mind were going ten to the dozen and I got changed into my work clothes five hours before I was due in. Again, strange but true, I weren't contemplating the enormity of what I'd done to Dennis. It were all about silently chastising myself for dropping the murder weapon on a brightly lit Tooting Broadway. *What a cunt!*

I slipped out to work early and walked the long way round to the scrapyard. The Old Man were there already and he asked me why I was bowling in and not on my bike. I muttered something and got straight to work. I kept having flashbacks of Dennis in the crawling position and me teeing off on him, but again, it weren't really what you could call remorse or guilt. It were just an intrusive thought that didn't need analysing. I don't think I said a word to the gaffer that day. Just kept my head down and tried to think happy thoughts.

On the Sunday, H was knocking at the door. I was convinced he was here to tell me Dennis' murder was on every cunt's lip and I was up for being the culprit. H had his own obsession though, "I'm gonna do summink about that black cunt pimp!"

"Eh?"

"Doreen's ponce. I'm gonna do summink."

H paced around on the landing, chaining Benson & Hedges and working himself up into a right lather, "I'm not havin' it. Doreen wants to be with me! She's told me."

H were babbling blue murders about this cunt Spammy. He reckoned that Doreen reckoned that if it hadn't been for her bumping into Spammy when she got off the coach from

Manchester at Victoria, she would have never ended up flogging her fanny. I didn't know how much of it was true or how much of it were wishful thinking, but to be honest, I didn't give a toss. I had just murdered Dennis, and H's strange love life was the least of my worries.

So, H is chuntering on and on about what he's gonna do to Spammy and how Doreen's gonna go straight and shack up with him and everything's gonna come up roses and there'll be a white picket fence and this and that. I'm listening but I'm not there. My mind's on The Fizzer and whether I should torch it or not. I'm thinking of the sentence. I'd be lifed-off and mitigating circumstances wouldn't even get an airing on the stand. H interrupts my train of thought again, *you with me or what?*

"What?"

"I'm gonna scare the spade off. Send him packing back to Brixton."

"You sure about this?"

"Yeah, I got a crossbow. I'm gonna shit him up. Pel and Ginner are up for it. You in or what?"

I paused. I had to be careful. I'm not saying you would ever grass me up, H, not a million years, but I *had* told you what I was gonna do to Dennis and it was about to come out, literally touching cloth, so I couldn't really give you the shoulder in your delusional hour of need could I? I gives it, "I'm in, but I don't know why think you need *me*, H."

H rubs his hands together, "The more the merrier, eh."

It were on this that I had to spill the beans. I would have hated H to hear about it before *I'd* filled him in. He would have thought I were a cunt.

"Come on, let's go for a walk."

We were near the main road and well out of earshot of any

nosey cunt when I told him what I'd done to Dennis. He said I were having a laugh; *I'm not buyin' it! No fuckin' way! What a load of old bollocks! I weren't born on half day closin' you cunt, etc etc etc.* After about ten minutes of this I told him it would be in the papers what I'd done to him, and he could make his mind up then. He told me I were a fanny merchant and weren't having any of it. I shrugged as he flipped it to what the plan was regarding Spammy and the lovely Doreen.

It weren't exactly what you'd call sophisticated. H were gonna knock the door with the crossbow cocked and aimed square at Spammy's boat. Ever the planner, I was straight in with, "What if Doreen answers the door?"

"Well, we just barge in and I shove the bow right in his mug, don't I! He'll shit his strides!"

From there, H went on to explain that he'll give Spammy an ultimatum: *leave Doreen alone and fuck off back to Brixton or you'll get a fucking arrow in your head and then we'll give a proper kicking just for old times' sake.*

"And if he won't?"

"He gets fuckin' marmalized don't he!"

"When you thinkin' o' doing this?"

"Wednesday. It's Doreen's quietest night."

I couldn't help but laugh in my head. Here was H going on this mad fucking romantic crusade to save a damsel in distress, that he knew had a *quiet night* on Wednesdays. A 'quiet night' from fucking, sucking and wanking any cunt who had a score on 'em. It weren't exactly Mills & Boon, but there would have been no point trying to talk H out of it. He were cuntstruck and that's all there was to it.

Come Monday and I'm still fully expecting a knock from Old Bill. I go to work and on my walk home I grab a local paper.

Right there on the front fucking page is the headline: *Tooting Businessman Killed on Doorstep.* My throat instantly dries up and every nerve in my body feels like it's trying to break out of the skin and bone that surrounds it. I stop dead in my tracks and lean back against a wall. I'm staring at the words but they're non-sense, pure gobbledygook in *my* mind. I were obviously expect-ing it to be reported on, but until I actually saw it in print it hadn't known how I would react.

It took me a good five minutes to be able to actually make sense of the words: *vicious, brutal, respected businessman, no motive, massive haemorrhaging, found by his wife, no witnesses, appeal for wit-nesses* all stood out. I re-read it, word for word at least six times. It had now sunk in deeply that I was a murderer. *I. Had. Murdered. Some. Cunt.*

I were walking along the landing to my flat when I sees him. H is stood staring at me. He's holding a copy of the local pa-per and he's – very uncharacteristically – lost for words. As I get closer, he just points at the paper and mouths, *fuck me!* I bundled him inside and lead him into my bedroom. We are whispering but it soon begins to look like H is gonna jump up and start cheering.

He's fucking ecstatic and, it's hard to explain, but looking at me slightly differently. Even the tone of his voice. Some people will understand what I mean by talking to someone with respect, not fawning or arse licking, but a certain tone. To say H were im-pressed would be an understatement. He keeps shaking his head in disbelief and repeating, *fuck me!*

My Mum kept shouting in and reminding me that my T were in the oven. I began thinking H was never gonna leave. He made me promise to meet him up near the shops at 9 that night. When I rolled up, he begged me to talk him through it all. Every little bleeding detail. I did as he asked and then he'd go back to a certain detail and asks questions, like he were fucking Columbo or something. He was loving it though and he told me I were a proper hero and that everyone on the estate who'd had dealings with Dennis owed me. I pointed out that reason I'd done it was so people weren't in debt anymore. He gives it, "y'know what I mean."

The next day at the scrapyard I finally plucked out Dennis' wad and shoved it in my donkey jacket. When I got home, I had a count up in my bedroom. The grand total was £2355. I counted it three times, I don't know why, but probably because I'd never had that kind of dough in my paws all at once before. I knew I couldn't go flashing the cash and raise suspicions, so I wrapped it nice and tight in a couple of carrier bags and took it back to the yard. I buried it under a rusty old RSJ that had been there since Moses played in the under 10's Jerusalem five a side team.

When the Old Man had his afternoon kip, I pulled out The Fizzer from behind the old fridges and I crushed it into small pieces. Like I said, I loved that bike and it hurt me doing it, but it were the only solid piece of evidence linking me to the crowbar – and consequently Dennis' murder – *if* the kebab loving pisshead had reported what he'd seen to Tooting Old Bill. And besides, with Dennis' ill-gotten gains in my possession I'd eventually be able to buy a new bike. Mum and sister asked what had happened to The Fizzer and I told 'em it had been half inched.

There were a couple more pieces in the local paper asking for potential witnesses of Dennis' fatal walloping to come forward, but Old Bill hadn't come asking questions round the estate. My theory were that they suspected him of being a loan shark but nobody would confirm it. Also, I doubt his widow would have given plod any info about the dodgy financial services he provided.

People in South London who knew the score in those times were more likely to talk to lampposts than they would Old Bill.

I kept my head down even more than I had naturally kept it down pre the Dennis job. H started relaying gossip to me about how happy people were that Dennis had his comeuppance. Nobody, as yet, had come round the estate claiming they were taking over the debts. Mum used to worry about this, and it were awful not being able to tell her that I had done Dennis in and torched his little black book, so there were very little chance of it happening. A couple of weeks later H tells me there's a new shark on the prowl. He goes by the name of Melvin and he's signing new customers up at a rapid clip. I didn't care as long as Mum didn't sign up with him.

H never bothered me again about joining his caper to win the hand of the fair maiden Doreen. H, Ginner and Pel went to the council flat knocking shop tooled up one Wednesday night. H did indeed have a crossbow and the other two had a lead pipe and a baseball bat respectively. Obviously, I weren't there, but I know it turned out to be a right old fuck up.

Doreen did indeed open the door and the trio stormed in. H has the crossbow aimed at Spammy – sat in his deckchair as usual – and Ginner and Pel are brandishing their weapons over him. There's shouting and histrionics as H tells Spammy that he's got to let Doreen go so she can be with him. True love, written in the stars and all that.

Allegedly Spammy told the trio that they were messing with the wrong nigger and that he were gonna bring a team over from Brixton to, *mash them up!* The mug should have tried to diffuse the situation rather than inflame it. Doreen's screaming blue murder at this time, telling H and his firm to just leave. H is getting a bit confused. Spammy makes to get out of his deckchair and H shoots an arrow into his chest. This is the cue for Ginner and Pel to start bashing Spammy up with the lead pipe and baseball bat. H joins in and starts smashing Spammy over the head with anything he can get his hands on.

They make a right bleeding mess of poor Spammy; broken jaw and nose, eye socket, smashed ribs and bleeding on the brain, oh, and a little hole in his chest from H's William Tell impression.

They left Spammy in a bloody heap and H tells Doreen to grab her things and leave with him. Much to H's confusion and eventual anger, Doreen gives it that the only place she's going is round to the local plod station to report what's happened. They start arguing and H tells her he thought she loved him. Doreen's having none of it and calling H every name under the sun as she starts attending to her pimp's wounds.

H is looking like a right fucking mug in front of everyone. He eventually snaps and tells Doreen she's a fucking filthy brass and that he never wants to see her again. Poor H's heart were broken. H and his firm get on their toes; salt away the weapons, burn their clobber, have bubble baths and then hit the local boozer, telling the Landlord and customers that if anyone asks, they've been in there since opening doors.

Spammy – fair play to him – never coughed about the attack and got the fuck out of the estate, probably plotting up on another one to sell Doreen's super snatch to all comers waving a score. H, Ginner and Pel were hyped up for months about the possibility of a revenge attack and they armed themselves with little CS gas canisters, brass knuckles, knives, and in the case of Pel, a neat little Derringer pistol. Thankfully there were no revenge attack and H got away with it, *this time.*

EIGHT

What is crime amongst the multitude,
is only vice among the few.

Benjamin Disraeli

Uncle pays me a visit about six months after I'd hit Dennis. To this day I don't know exactly what H had told him about my handiwork, but Uncle assured me that my secret were safe with him. The upshot of this visit were simple: did I wanna work for him. I felt flattered truth be told.

I asked Uncle what it would entail and he gives it, *what do you think?* He asks me if I'd like to go out for a spot of grub with him. So, we gets in his beautiful Daimler and head out of South London towards Kent. When I say Uncle never stopped talking, I mean he didn't even draw breath. He tells me that he works for certain individuals who are always in the market for having certain other individuals taken care of. It were all very matter of fact and unemotional. I liked that he didn't dance around the fact he were a middle man for assassinations. It went unsaid that the reason he felt comfortable in telling me this is that he knew I weren't gonna yap about it.

All the way to Kent, he fills me on someone who he's been working with for a few years who's made a nice packet taking hits

81

on. This 'person' is now about to retire and start a new life somewhere with a nice pillow of dosh to cushion him. According to Uncle this hitman had been really successful and had never had so much as a sniff from Old Bill, let alone a collar. Uncle gives it, *there's a formula. You learn it n' stick to it n' you won't go wrong.* He adds, *it's all about plausible deniability and covering yer tracks in the murder game, son. The bloke I'm talkin' about, guess how many hits he's had?*

I shrug, "Dunno."

"Guess."

"Uh ... I dunno ... five?"

"Double it. Listen, you shown some promise with the hit on that toerag shark. You're a performer, son. I take me hat off t'ya, I do. You can make some serious coin wi' me you can. I'm talkin' life changing amounts ... thing is, we'd have to get you learning how to shoot, o' course. It's not very professional stoving cunts heads in wi' crowbars."

"Uh ... I *can* shoot. Been doin' it for years. Only rats in the scrappers where I work but ..."

Uncle were even more excited, "Really? You know your way around a tool, eh?"

"Yeah."

"Well, listen, you stick wi' me n' you'll be shootin' some real human rats in no time, son."

We had some lovely grub at a village pub in Kent and Uncle knocked back at least eight G & T's and chained at least 15 cigs. He was impressed that I weren't a boozer and didn't smoke. On the way back home, he giggles and hands me a Police warrant card, "have a butchers at that."

I fucking froze and thought the nosh I'd just eaten was gonna suddenly liquify and shoot out my arsehole at supersonic speed.

He were fucking Old Bill! Everything closed in on me. I went drip white and could feel bile bubbling in my throat. I'd been fitted up by H! My best mate had fit me up! What a fucking rotter!

Uncle clocks that my arse has gone and he quickly explains, "It's moody! It's a moody warrant card. Well, it's *real* as it happens, I just use it 'case I get pulled over for drink driving. We've got a few Old Bill on the payroll n' I just have a borrow of it every now 'n then." To say I were relieved would be like saying Michelangelo's mural up the Sistine chapel were a spot of cash in hand, bish-bosh painting and decorating. Understatement of the fucking century! My ticker were going like the clappers. Uncle laughed out loud, "Look at me! Do I look like Old Bill? *Gordon Bennet!*"

I get home and start thinking about Uncle's proposal. *Could I really become a proper hitman?* I had to admit that I weren't feeling bad about snuffing Dennis and were only concerned about getting pulled for it. Uncle had offered to show the ropes and he said he had plenty of potential customers and they had plenty of potential victims.

As anyone who were involved in the organized criminal life of London in the 1980s will attest, gangland assassinations were a regular occurrence. It were a time of transition. The days of pavement artists doing banks, security depots and post offices were coming to an end. Even tie-ups – where a couple of blaggers would go into a posh gaff wielding sawn-offs and tying up whoever was inside and then proceed to rob them – were coming to an end. The sentences being handed down were shocking.

This were the crossover time of wised up villains moving into the importation of drugs. Drugs brought massive profits but they also brought a big headache: total chancers who would flip at the first switch entering the market. Blokes who weren't dyed in the wool crooks, had no allegiances and couldn't stomach the thought of doing serious bird. To paraphrase a popular song: *this were the dawning of the age of the grass.*

Don't get me wrong, other nefarious activities were still going on: protection, blackmail, kidnappings, porn, heists and prostitution were still earners, but the huge profits from the supply of drugs were a game changer, and any cunt who had a spare few hundred grand, a tentative connection and some good old healthy greed could step up. What a lot of these *johnny come lately's* didn't understand was that they would now have to deal with real nasty bastards who wouldn't think twice about killing to protect their coin. Obviously nasty bastards didn't need to put themselves up for the job when they could hire a good hitman to do it properly.

I carried on working at the scrapyard and didn't hear anymore from Uncle. I spoke to H about it and he said, "He's probably waiting for you to get back in touch. You want me to give him a bell?"

"No, no … not yet."

"Fuckin' golden opportunity if you ask me."

"Don't *you* fancy it, H?"

"Me? … never really thought it about it. You reckon I've got the bottle for it?"

"Well, you shot that Spammy."

"Yeah, but that were an arrow, weren't it? It weren't gonna kill the cunt."

"It could have."

"Bollocks. I'd have had to shoot it right up his hooter for it to have done any proper damage."

One wet Thursday afternoon The Old Man keeled over on the khazi at the scrapyard. He were jam by the time the ambulance turned up. He did rather like Elvis Presley, so it might have been a fitting way for him to go like his hero. I were gutted. He were a miserable old cunt but he was a decent bloke and had always seen me right.

I opened up the yard on the Friday and worked as usual, not really knowing what were gonna happen. The Old Man's two sons turn up in the afternoon and tell me to go home. They were closing the yard and selling the land to a developer. I were fucking shocked. They were very matter of fact about it. The yard had been operating for 40 years and they were just flogging it off like it meant nothing. It's obvious that they'd been in the wings just waiting for their old man to peg it so they could get their mitts on his assets.

I were at least expecting a month's pay along with my, *thank you for your service*, but nah, nish, fucking nada. They reckoned because the Old Man used to pay me and the others in readies, they were gonna have to bring in a good accountant to go through the books, and until then they weren't paying anyone nothing. I were pissed off but ready to accept it before it dawned on me.

"So, you got the spare keys for everything?" H asked with a glint in his eye.

"The gates, the alarm, the plant, the shed where we keep the lead n' copper, *everything*." I replied, "N' best thing is, they don't know I've got 'em or they would have asked for 'em back now."

"What we talking? How much you reckon all that stuff's worth."

I gives it, "I dunno ... with the equipment n' scrap, uh ... I reckon you're looking at hundred grand."

H spat his tea out, "*How much!?*"

"Oh yeah, I reckon so."

H set to work and within a couple of days he got back to me. He were roping in a cousin from Rotherhithe on his mother's side. He were a pro according to H and he'd be using a 'big fucking truck', but he'd need me on the caper with his little firm. I said, *no thanks, not my game.*

"But *you* know your way round the yard n' what to pinch."

"I can tell' em what to pinch."

"Nah, you need to be there."

I were hesitant but H and his cousin talked me into it. We had to abandon the idea of stealing the plant machinery, as it were proving impossible to find a truck big enough to handle scrap *and* plant. We would have off with all the precious scrap though, and it should bring in a tidy sum. The slaughter would be split 5 ways between me, H, his cousin and the other two.

We pulled it off without hiccups on a very pleasant Wednesday night a week later. We had to make it look like we'd broken in and after we'd turned the alarm off, we smashed it. It really were a doddle, even though we were there a good four hours loading the truck to overflowing with precious metals. After what I'd done to Dennis, this really did feel like a piece of cake.

As in most of the capers that go down, greed reared its ugly fucking mug and H's cousin insisted we go back and fill up a second time. I really weren't into it but the others were, so after offloading at an empty warehouse in the middle of nowhere, we went back into the yard and grabbed a shit load more.

When weighed in, the two loads brought £79,650 in readies, which should have translated into £15,930 each at the slaughter, a very tidy sum in the 1980s. H's cousin starts toting up his expenses for the caper though. Talk about creative accounting! This cunt could have got a job in The City of London! He were throwing in all kinds of expenses, but none of us had the bottle to challenge him. H's cousin were a few years older than us and what you might call 'a handful'. Anyway, the gang of four walked away with 12 grand each, which was still a huge payday for us nippers.

H blew his cut on buying a couple of nice motors to start him off on a little car sales business that he eventually grew to become a goldmine. One of the lads shot it all up his arm: a pathetic junky, and the other spunked his cut gambling on the horses.

Fuck knows what H's cousin did with his because not long after he simply disappeared. It were rumoured that he had been poking the wife of a very naughty ex Pavement Artist and had paid for it with his life. Some say he just got on his toes and started a new life somewhere because Old Bill were after him for a spate of other robberies. We'll probably never find out. H weren't close to him and didn't seem to give a toss when he turned up missing.

The Old Man's sons never pulled me about the robbery at the scrapyard. They obviously hadn't tippled that I'd had a spare set of keys. I bought a little peter, shoved the cash I'd accumulated in it, and stuck it under my bed. My cunt of a Dad didn't have a clue, and he had picked up emphysema to keep his gout company so he were less prone to scurrying around the drum stealing from his own family now. He hardly ever left the front room anyway. He just sat and drank cans of beer and smoked fags and argued with the telly. Me, Mum and Sis' spent most of our time in the kitchen and I went and bought us a coloured portable telly. We had a giggle in the kitchen whilst that useless cunt rotted away in the front room.

I get a knock from H one morning and he hands me a scrap of paper with a phone number scribbled on it, "Uncle said to give him on a bell on this number. From a phone box he said."

"What's he want?"

"How the bleedin' ell do I know! I'm not a psychiatrist, am I?"
I smirk, "No H, you're definitely not a *psychiatrist.*"

I don't know if you remember but public phone boxes in
the 1980's invariably reeked of piss, shit, vomit, glue and stale
cider, and if you were to find one that hadn't been vandalised
or robbed you were lucky. The dyslexic graffiti always revolved
around sexual acts and football and claims that some wannabe
tough cunt were 'harder' than another wannabe tough cunt.
They weren't these quaint jolly old England red phone boxes
that tourists buy models of on Oxford Street. No, they were more
like toxic crime scenes, and if they still existed today, you'd be
advised to wear a hazmat suit when entering one.

Uncle answers and gives it, "That you, son?"

"Yeah."

"All right, now listen. Memorize this number. Don't leave it
lying about on a piece o' paper or nuffink, you hear?"

"All right."

"Good. We start as we mean to go on. Whenever I want to talk
to you on the dog, H'll nip 'round and tell you, all right? You call
me *as soon as* on this number, right?"

"Yeah, right, right."

"I won't be knocking at your gaff from now on, see? We'll
meet up but never down the estate. So, memorize it and when
I need to have a natter, you'll be contacted. You got that, son?"

"Yeah, definitely."

"And you never say nish to my nephew, H, you hear?"

"Uh, right."

"I love the little berk but he don't need to know anything
from now on, right?"

"Yeah, yeah. Right."

Uncle signs off with, "Good as gold. Toodle pip."

NINE

*The question isn't who is going to let me; the
question is who is going to stop me.*

Ayn Rand

I didn't hear from Uncle again for over three months. I'd got
myself a job driving a forklift at a stone yard in Merton. It were
a bit of a schlep – bus and tube, nearly two hours getting there
and back – but it were half decent cash in hand and the Chief
were a decent chap to work for. There were no rats to shoot, but
it were never boring because a few lads who worked there were
real characters.

There were a 16-year-old gofer who worked there called
Timmy. He were on one of those shit government schemes because he had Down's Syndrome. The other lads constantly ripped
the piss, but Timmy took it on the chin though and gave them a
bit of slather back. One day a lad went a bit too far with Timmy
and got him piping. Timmy were hysterical and went fucking bal-
listic. He grabs a carbide blade hammer and sets about the lad.
Timmy catches him a couple of times on the arm and the lad's
shitting it.

Someone manages to disarm Timmy and calm him down.
From that day on no cunt overstepped the mark or got too saucy

with him. I liked Timmy, but he were fucking useless around the yard and I were always thinking it was just a matter of time before he was involved in, or more likely caused, a nasty accident.

I eventually splashed out on a BMW RS80 G/S on-off road bike. It were a beauty, and even at second hand cost me the better part of eight hundred sovs. It went like the clappers though, and could handle any off-road terrain. The commute to Merton there and back were cut by nearly an hour.

One day the Chief asks me if I want to go on the books. I declined and he gave me a wink. It were the right choice. What sort of cunt *chooses* to pay tax and insurance! Before long he'd upped my wages and I were really happy there.

Merton were a lot quieter and less cutthroat than where I was from, and sometimes I'd join the lads in the boozer after work on a Friday. Not being a drinker and having the bike with me, I never stayed too long into the night. They were all big drinkers and I saw a few tear-ups in there, which were a bit fucking *handbags* compared to the rows I'd seen on the estate.

It were down Merton that I lost my virginity to a Richard about 7 years older than me. She were tidy and took a real shine to me one Friday night. I ended up banging her behind the boozer next to the bins. She took charge because I didn't have a clue what I were doing. A standard knee trembler but very nice all the same. I seen her the week after in the pub with her boyfriend, who were a big lump with a cauliflower ear, so I supped my orange juice and got on my toes sharpish.

One Sunday morning I gets up and Mum tells me a note's come through the door for me. There's a little envelope with my name scribbled on it. I open it and it tersely says, 'Call Uncle today at 1. Get rid." I'm instantly energized and curious. Mum asks what it is and I say it's something about a motorbike for sale or whatever. I dutifully go and go burn the note in the sink. This is all feeling a bit James Bond and truth be told I were well into it.

I head out and find a slightly less minging phone box than the others on the estate and bell him.

Uncle gives it, "I ain't forgot about you, son, see? You still game for that thing we talked about?"

I paused, "Uh, yeah."

"You don't sound too sure."

"No, yeah, yeah, definitely."

"It's not to be taken lightly, son. You sure, you're sure?"

"Sure."

"Smashing. Right, I'm gonna give you some directions. Don't write 'em down, just remember 'em ..."

I met Uncle by the River Ching in Epping Forest one pleasant Saturday afternoon. There were a couple of people walking their dogs but other than that it were quiet. Uncle had a small transistor radio with him as we walked along, and every now and then he would hold it up to his ear and have a listen. It were tuned into the horse racing and he told me had some big money down on a few nags that day.

"You have a flutter on the gee-gee's, son?"

"Me? Nah."

"Well don't! Fucking mugs game! I'd be a multi-millionaire if it weren't for the nags!"

Uncle then tells me the address of a fish and chip shop in Stratford, "Its open every day, 12 'til 12. You go in and you ask for Bernard. Keep your helmet on, don't chat with him or anything. Bernard'll take you out back in the yard n' you'll pick up the tool. You do some practicing with it. Somewhere remote, well out the way, back o' beyond, n' practice with the silencer on. It's a Glock you'll be using. You heard of 'em?"

"No."

"Don't worry. There's an instruction manual. These are brand new. Reliable. There's not many in the country." He lights a Rothman's fag and looks me in the eyes, "When you're happy with your way around it, you bell me. Any day, about two in the aft's preferable … not a dicky bird to H, remember."

"All right."

"Listen, I know I don't need to say it, son, but I'm gonna anyway. Your family … if this goes tits up n' you get pinched, not that you will, but you can never say bleedin' never, right? I'm saying, *if* it did balls up for some reason, and you keep schtum, your family'll be well looked after if you get bird. You go away and do your time n' keep your trap shut and you got nothing to worry about. We'll make sure they're looked after. You know what I'm saying, son?"

I weren't thick. I knew *exactly* what Uncle were saying. He was saying that if I *did* get collared and started blabbing to Old Bill it would be my family that suffered. By 'family' I mean my Mum and sister. Uncle knew I how felt about my cunt of a Dad. I were all right with Uncle reminding it would be my family on the chopping bloke though. It made total sense to me. See, this weren't confidence about *not* getting pinched, it were confidence that I'd *never* grass. This were nothing to do with Uncle knowing I'd done in Dennis either, I just knew I'd never dob him in it. If I got caught it were down to me and nobody else. I take responsibility for my actions. I'm not like my cunt of a Dad.

Years later I found out about some cunt who Uncle had employed to do a hit. This berk bottled it on the job, dropped his piece and ran off like some silly little schoolgirl. He got on his toes and fucked off to Amsterdam or somewhere, knowing Uncle would have the raging hump with him. The mark this mug were supposed to pop also got on his toes knowing he were now a marked man. I heard Uncle made this wannabe hitman's family suffer something rotten until he came back from Amsterdam and accepted whatever punishment Uncle had sentenced him to.

I went to the chippy in Stratford as instructed. Bernard, I presume, took me out to the backyard of the shop and with a pickaxe lifted up a paving stone. He reached down and handed me the gun, ammo and silencer in a rag. I shoved it inside my jacket and headed home. No words were exchanged, which suited me fine.

I gave the Chief a bell on the Monday morning and told him a porky I'd been sick as a dog. He were sweet and told me to take a couple of days off. I headed down to some woods in Mitcham on the bike and had a couple of hours of shooting practice with the Glock. I knew my way around it in no time and could assemble and disassemble it a treat.

Uncle gave me the name, age, height, description, make of motor he drove and address of the mark. No photo, but let's just say he wouldn't be hard to miss. He lived just outside Chipping Ongar in Essex. I scouted him for seven days but couldn't work out a pattern. I tailed him travelling back and forth into Chelmsford on a daily basis: gym, office, boozer, supermarket, but the times were all to cock.

I went back to work at the stone yard on the Monday and told the Chief the bug had mullered me: shits, headaches, fever, the lot. On Wednesday evening I decided I'd get back over to Essex and have a spy on my mark. I pulled into a lay-by not far from his impressive detached drum. I could see his motor parked up from my vantage point. When any traffic went by, I'd pretend to be fixing the bike. I had a couple of spanners in my rucksack with the shooter. On my life, I weren't nervous. Not in the least. I don't know why, this were a fucking monumental thing I were about to do, and even though I didn't know this cunt from Adam, and had no beef with him like I'd had with Dennis, I felt calm. It were a strange feeling actually. Like I'd turned on the auto-pilot or something.

It's getting dark now and I won't be able to pretend I'm fixing the bike for much longer, but a minute or two later my mark comes out, gets in his motor and drives off. I leave it a little bit; this is a fairly long road we're talking about and there's hardly any traffic. The last thing I want is for him to cotton on he's being followed.

I'm keeping a good distance between us. A couple of fucking mugs in Ford Cosworth's speed past, obviously racing, and my mark throws a left down a winding road. I follow him and can see some temporary traffic lights a few hundred meters up ahead. Then it hits me. If we catch a red and he stops, this is the perfect opportunity. Probably the best I'm gonna get. *Never look a gift horse in the mouth and all that.*

The nerves kick in when I see the lights turn to amber. *Fuck! Can it be this simple? Am I really gonna do it? Am I fucking mental?* Adrenaline's tearing through my veins and I can feel my stomach doing cartwheels, and then it comes: the focus. Everything around and between me and my mark becomes one big blur. I adjust my glove and reach into the rucksack just as the lights hit red and my mark stops. I can see him lighting a fag as I pull out the Glock. I rail it and with one hand ride the bike slowly up alongside him, the shooter hanging down by my side. His window's down as he blows smoke out. I stop and he looks over at me, gives a quick shrug as if to say, *fucking traffic lights, eh?*

I aimed straight at his face but in a nanosecond, he must

have turned ever so slightly, because the first shot's sent his head flopping on to his shoulders. The other two shots go into the side of his head. I don't look at the damage they've done. The Glock goes back in the rucksack and the fucking light's still on red. *I could turn around I suppose. I could wait for green. I could cut go through red but possibly smash into a motor coming the other way.* Unbearable! Felt like a fucking eternity and then … green.

I'm down that lane like Meatloaf. Nothing coming the other way. Good. I come to a junction and decide to go further into Essex instead of heading back to London. I've done my homework. I know there's an A-road not too far ahead and once I get on it I've got the option of going a dozen places. My thoughts are now on the rucksack with the Glock in it. I'd completely forgotten what my plan to ditch it were.

I knew I'd worked out where I were gonna get shut but I were hit by a fucking brainstorm. I started to panic. All these scenarios came flooding back. If I'd have snuffed him near the gym, it would have gone down a drain, if I'd done him outside his drum, it would have … fuck! Couldn't think straight. Total fucking confusion. Very frightening, like you imagine you'd feel if you suddenly went mad, and I mean *clinically* mad.

I tried to snap back into sanity. I sped up I think, but I could have slowed down truth be told. You've heard the phrase, *living hell.* It took a minute of pure panic to pass before I started mentally picturing the area I were in. The river I'd clocked on my reccy suddenly came into focus. It were in the other direction. A van overtook me as I slowed down to do a U-turn.

The river can't have been more than a quarter of a mile away and I were gunning 60, but believe me when I tell you that it felt like I were riding through fucking quicksand. The panic had totally skewed my perception. It genuinely felt like I were on a treadmill surrounded by these colossal black walls that were slowly closing in on me.

I reached the bridge over the river and threw the rucksack in like it were a bomb about to go off. My arse had gone, literally, and I could feel hot stinging liquid squirting into my skivvies and forming a pool around my bollocks. I reckon if I'd been able to smell it, it wouldn't have reeked of shite ... it would have reeked of pure liquid fear!

TEN

*Because it is so unbelievable, the Truth
often escapes being known.*

Heraclitus

I went to work as usual on the Thursday, hadn't slept a wink, but didn't feel tired one bit. In fact, it were the opposite, I were energised, physically I felt brand new but my mind were mush. It were like everything was happening behind a screen, really hard to explain, but like I weren't there, weren't really connected to physical reality. Everything felt remote and kind of dull. Obviously, the stone yard *was* pretty dull, nothing to write home about, but that day it were like I were watching it as a black & white film instead of in technicolour.

I managed to get to the weekend and told myself I'd just do nothing but sleep on the Saturday and Sunday. Have a proper fucking marathon kip to recalibrate. I purposefully avoided grabbing a newspaper or watching the news on the telly. I started thinking that if I never heard anything about what I'd done, it meant I hadn't really done it. I know it sounds fucking nonsensical, but that's where my nut was at the time.

Nodding off was proving to be impossible, so I grabbed a couple of Mum's Valium and slung 'em down my Gregory. That were around 5am on the Saturday morning and then the next thing I know it's 6am Monday morning. Mum reckoned she'd try to wake me up a couple of times but thought I'd just picked up some lurgy and let me sleep it off.

I had a stonking headache but popped some Anadin and managed a full day at the yard. It were fucking cats n' dogs that day and I were happy about it. It meant most of the lads were working in the shed and I were left alone on the forklift outside. Daft as it sounds, the pissing down rain brought me back into focus. This weird detached feeling started to lift. I actually started feeling normal again.

Uncle answers the blower and gives it, "You done good, son. Nip over the chippy. There's a nice fish supper waiting for ya. I'll be in touch, ta ta."

I walk into the Stratford chippy and 'Bernard' sees me. He grabs what appears to be a Sun newspaper wrapped order of fish and chips, hands it to me over the display, heater thing they keep the nosh warm in, not a dicky bird from him but I give it, "Thanks very much." I shove the fish supper parcel inside the front of my jacket and take a circuitous route home in case I'm being followed.

I'd never really had a natter with Uncle about how much dough I'd be getting, or if I did, I couldn't remember, so I can't say how much I were expecting exactly. I were probably imagining somewhere around 10 grand, and anything North of that would have been icing.

I shoved a chair against the doorknob on my bedroom door, sat down on my bed and unwrapped the fish supper. Straight off, I knew this were more than ten large. What I didn't expect is that it would be two n' half times that amount.

It looked and felt like a bleeding fortune! £25,000 in used

notes, every denomination, plenty of ladies. I counted it three times and didn't come up for air for hours. This were life changing pie n' mash. Over double what I'd scored on the scrap yard graft. I now had more wedge that what the majority of the others on the estate would ever see in their lives at any one time. This were the early 1980s, remember.

I were now the proud owner of just over 39 grand in readies. I could buy me, Mum and my sister a modest flat to live in and leave my cunt of a Dad wallowing in his own shit and self-pity. I shoved the cash in the peter, put it under the floorboard and went into the kitchen. Mum were watching *Pot Black* on the telly. Snooker's never been my cup of tea but *she* loved it. Big fan of Steve Davis, who was ruling the snooker world and making some serious dough at the time. I obviously weren't in his league but I could understand what drove people to want to clean up when it came to earning. Earning is addictive.

I asked her if she ever fancied moving. She gives it, "What? Off the estate? Leave it out. What's wrong wi' round here? I wouldn't know anyone anywhere else."

"Yeah, but wouldn't you like to plot up somewhere a bit ... I dunno, nicer."

"There's nothing wrong with it round here."

"Yeah, but if you had the bread. If you won the pools or something?"

She paused and thought about it, "I dunno. Not gonna happen is it! I only ever get one or two score draws. Bleedin' useless I am."

"I been saving up you know, Mum. salting a few quid away."

"Yeah, you've got a good head on your shoulders."

I let the conversation tail off. I could never tell her I were sitting on a small fortune for the likes of us. She might have been stupid when it came to putting up with my Dad's shit, but she'd soon suss out I was 'at it' if I told her exactly how much I'd saved up for a rainy day. I decided there and then that I'd surprise her with a nice gesture that wouldn't make her think I were up to no good.

I were feeling a bit shitty about H not knowing what I was up to now. I really wanted to tell him, not out of any of ego or anything, just because he were my best pal, but when I really thought about it, *not* telling him was doing him a favour. Now, don't get me wrong, H would have never in a million years grassed me up, but what he didn't know couldn't hurt him, me or Uncle, and, obviously Uncle didn't want H knowing so, it were a definite no no.

I spruced up the BMW bike, put it in the Exchange & Mart and got 100 quid more for it than I'd paid. I couldn't face riding it again. I'd murdered someone on it and shat myself. It reminded me too much of that night. I had a couple of hundred down on a Honda CB900F. A lad on the estate flogged it me, because, like many others round our way, he'd discovered the joys of smack and needed to service his habit rather than his bike. Bargain.

At the stone yard The Chief gave me another bump. Thirty bar a week extra. He knew my worth. I worked harder than all the others put together and he never got any moaning or slather from me. I hardly ever blobbed either. I turned up rain, shine, sleet or snow and never fucked off home 'til I'd finished what I had to do. Like I say, I weren't a social animal. I didn't drink, I weren't courting a bird and didn't have any hobbies. Sound like a right boring berk, eh? But that's just how it was.

One of the lads from the estate knocks one night and asks if I wanna earn a few quid helping him out. I didn't have a clue what 'helping him out' meant. Had he heard of my extracurricular and wanted to contract me to snuff some cunt? Surely not. Nobody but Uncle knew I were now a gun for hire, so I very much doubted it. He gives it, "I've got a bit o' graft going on. I need someone I can trust. You're about the only honest cunt I can think of round here."

The graft were a piece of piss. Harry had a contract at a colossal carpet distributor up near the Westway somewhere. He were a self-employed delivery driver and moved carpets and rugs all over the south east in his van. He soon tippled that pilfering were rampant and before long he'd realized that by dropping one of the warehouse lads a few quid he could have it away with these really nice, relatively expensive rugs. The warehouse lad would sling dozens of rugs in Harry's van that weren't on the docket. This place were fucking huge and apparently it would take the bosses donkeys to realize their pants were being pulled down.

Weekdays after my slog at the stone yard, I'd jump in Harry's van and we'd tear all over the shop selling these rugs door to door. This were real *Sale of The Century* stuff. Brand new rugs marked up at 80, 90, 100 bar a pop and we're asking tens, fifteens, scores and, at most, 30's. Went like fucking hotcakes they did. Didn't matter where we rolled up, they were getting snapped. Harry did all the talking and selling but we were 50-50 on it, minus a bit of petrol money for the van. Some weeks I were pulling down two and three, sometimes four hundred sovs from the caper. Added to the 240 bar I were earning at the stone yard; I were often clearing 600 a week in readies. This were very good money in anyone's books for the time. And because I spent nish on myself my little nest egg were getting fit to burst.

After a couple of months, I'd managed to stop even thinking about what I'd done at those temporary traffic lights. Curiosity didn't get the better of me either. I never looked up on who I'd rubbed out. I knew it would have made the news, and I could easily have found out, but I figured I'd be just torturing myself by revisiting it. Uncle – who I hadn't heard from since then – would have been proud of me.

ELEVEN

Better to be known as a sinner than a hypocrite.

Proverb

One day I decided to splash out on a fortnight in Benidorm for me, Mum and Sis'. They were made up, first time any of us would be venturing abroad. When I told H he immediately insisted on coming, "You can't go to bleedin' Benidorm with just yer old lady n' your sister, you pillock! It's full o' tarts out there. Wall to wall fanny!"

H bought a seat on our Dan-air flight and said he'd just crash in my room with me. We stayed at the Rio Park hotel in the centre of Benidorm and it were just a skip to the main drag of pubs, discos and cafes. Mum and Sis' did their own thing and I hardly saw 'em. H were a fucking handful though. Soon as we got there, he got popped up on the ridiculously cheap booze and started making a nuisance of himself. Leery, loud and suddenly very patriotic for an England I never knew he even gave a toss about.

On the very first night we're walking back up to the hotel at 4 in the morning. There's this young Scottish couple having a right barney. The bloke's slapping her around a bit but she's giving it back. H starts poking his nose in and I tell him to leave it, but he's giving it, "Hey, you jock cunt! Pick on someone yer own size."

As I'm trying to pull H away, this big Scot bounces over and sticks one straight on him. H wobbles but he's right back in at him and they're wrestling. For a few seconds H is getting the better of him but then the Scottish bird takes her heels off and starts attacking H with one of 'em. She screaming at H to get off her beau, but H is throwing wild windmills now and connecting with a few. I jump in and try to stop her stabbing at H with her sharp heel and she turns around and clocks me right in the mince with it. I were fucking blinded!

I step back and something catches my good eye. Now, I shit you not, this were a sight straight out of a comedy film. There's this humungous cunt wobbling over to the fray. He's about 25 years old and he'd clearly gained a stone for every year of his life. When I say fat, I mean absolutely fucking morbid, like one of those poor cunts you see on the telly that have to be airlifted out their gaffs to go down the hospital. On top of this he's wearing really tight union jack shorts, about three sizes too small, and a T-shirt that stops trying at his crater like belly button. He's also wearing Doc Marten boots. Probably the first and only cunt to ever wear a pair in sunny Benidorm.

If you've ever seen the original video nasty film *Texas Chainsaw Massacre*, think back to when Leatherface makes his first appearance in the doorway: all fat, sweaty, excited, clumsy urgency. Well, that was like this cunt. He were nimble for a whale and straight in to the ruck, swinging like marvellous Marvin Hagler.

Thud! Leatherface smacks the Scot round his lughole. Bang! H gets one in the kisser! Clout! The Scot gets another on his hooter. Bosh! He clips H on the back of the head. Leatherface is loving it, nearly squealing in delight and singing in a proper west country fucking Wurzel's yokel accent, "Torquay aggro, Torquay aggro, hello … hello." The beam on his mush indicated that he were about to cum in his union jack shorts he were enjoying it so much.

I move forward, and not being a fighter, tried to distract him with some verbals. The Scottish bird's now attacking Orca with *both* her heels. She's calling him every cunting thing under the Spanish sun but The Fat Bastard just pulls back and launches one at her. It's bang on the button and she's sparko! I reckon he must have done a bit of boxing fifteen stone ago. It were a sweet KO, even if it was a Richard he chinned.

H has now managed to scramble to his feet and he's bouncing around Leatherface throwing a few kicks at him. Leatherface tries to get his meaty mitts on H but H slips him and throws an upper cut. It connects but nish. He just snorts at H and continues singing his stupid fucking football chant. The Scottish lad picks himself up and gets straight back into Leatherface. He just swots Scotty away and lands a punch on the back of his nut. H dives in with a flurry of blows that make not a jot of difference.

This west country bastard ain't going down, but the Scot goes down again and Leatherface puts the slipper in. H jumps on the beast's back and gives it some reach round punches. Again, useless. This is getting ridiculous now and I were feeling like a right bottling cunt. I looks around for something to hit the cunt with and spy like an ornamental rock on a bit of greenery. Quick as a flash I grab it with both hands. Leatherface is still putting the slipper in on the Scot so I shoot over, rock aloft, and bring it down as hard as I can on his napper.

He's stunned but he's still up. H is still doing the hunchback and he's now got his laughing tackle around Leatherface's lughole. H is biting into it and Wurzel Gummidge is finally yelping. He's trying to shake H off him but H is in for the long haul. I muster up again and repeat the rock treatment. This time he goes down like the titanic, and being such a fat bastard there's no chance of him getting up without a winch. H is throwing well placed kicks to his head and the Scot is trying to revive his still sparko bird. Leatherface is breathlessly asking, "Are you Brentford? Are You Brentford?", presumably asking if we were hooligans from a low league West London football team. *Fucking doolally!*

The rock had opened Leatherface's head up and claret were flowing. A motor rounds the corner and me and H get on our toes lively in case it's *El Ploddo*. As I look over my shoulder, I see the Scot stomping on the beached whale's head.

H were instantly sober but out of puff. We get to the hotel and the spic security guard sees blood on H's white Ocean Pacific T-shirt. He shakes his head and the big window doors stay firmly shut. H gives it some creative effs n' jeffs but it's futile. We climb over a wall to the pool area and kip on sunbeds until the hotel comes alive. H were bashed up a bit and my eye were bloodshot and swollen, but it could have been a lot worse if Leatherface had managed to suck us into his orbit and give us a proper pasting.

We'd sunbathe all day and go out about 10 at night after shovelling down plate fulls of grab at the hotel buffet. There were a disco bar called Jokers and one called Lennon's that we always went in. Jokers were full of Spanish but Lennon's was all Brits and the DJ played cracking soul and funk music. H pulled a different bird every night and would usually slink off about 4am with his pull. I've never had the confidence to chat up birds and were happy just hanging about listening to the music.

On the second week in, H decided that the shops in Benidorm would be a piece of piss to hoist from. I'd never done any shoplifting in my life but H had regularly gone up into the west end with others from the estate to do some pinching. He'd been nabbed a couple of times but just got a bollocking from Old Bill.

I warned H that these spic plod were known to be a lot livelier than *our* beloved constabulary, but he weren't having it, and it turns out he were right to be dismissive. These shops and stores in Benidorm were a lot less security conscious than the ones back in London. No visible security cameras or guards and shop assistants who were so aloof and disinterested that most of their day were spent chaining fags with their faces buried in copies of *Hello*. Or rather, *Hola* to give it its proper Spanish name.

There were some cracking clobber boutiques a couple of streets back from the beach, and H figured that the best time to go hoisting would be just after these dopey shopworkers had returned from their cherished siestas in the late afternoon. I told him straight I weren't lifting anything, but that I'd keep the coast for him as long as we were splitting the booty down the middle.

One afternoon we nipped into a store and H bought a pair of boxer shorts. He'd done it to make himself look like a kosher shopper when we went in the other shops, and he insisted on putting the skivvies in a large carrier bag. We head down the parade and go in a smart, spacious boutique that flogged Fiorucci, Chipie, Lacoste and Martinique gear. The blindingly fit shop senorita was occupied on the blower, laughing and giggling with some lucky cunt.

H gives me the sly wink and heads over to the Lacoste section. There's four rows of Lacoste polo shirts folded immaculately and stacked 12 high. They were all colours and sizes and looked lovely just waiting there to be adopted.

I stood a few feet away from H and blocked him as I looked at some Lois jeans. H, quick as a flash, just scoops a pile of 12 polo's straight into the carrier bag and wanders out, casual as you like. I followed him out about 30 seconds later and the senorita was still (probably) talking dirty to the lucky cunt on the blower. Beyond a piece of piss.

We went back to the hotel and H flogged the lot to some British lads around the pool for 4000 pesetas a pop, 20 nicker in real money, which is half of what the boutique were flogging 'em at. Brits really do love a bargain. Once exchanged back, we'd pulled 120 sovs each for basically doing a jump up on a baby in a pram for its milk money.

The next day H used the same carrier bag to hoist three Armani shirts and two leather belts. He had the lot off to a cockney Landlord of a boozer called fucking *Pride of London* or something for 20,000 pesetas: translated, 100 bar. This Landlord's made up and tells H if he happens to be in the area when another spic lorry sheds some of its load, he's up for buying.

That's all H needed to hear. We spent nearly all the next day nipping in and out of jewellers up and down Benidorm. H finally decided on one, that to me, looked a bit risky.

H gives it, "Nah you weren't paying attention, soppy bollocks! That case with the TAG Heur's in weren't locked. The jeweller just pulled it open and took the kettle out when I asked to have a look at it."

"I don't know, H. Those TAGS are what? Seven, eight hundred a piece in our money? It's not really hoisting, is it?"

"*Not really hoisting?* The fuck's that supposed to mean? Course it is. It's a shop innit? They're watches. I'm gonna lift 'em so it's fucking shoplifting! Ain't you ever read a dictionary or summink?"

"I mean, *high fucking end,* H! You get pinched n' I reckon they'll spank your arse with the book after they've thrown it at ya."

"Stop fucking worrying. *You* killed some cunt. What's a bit of a grab after what you done?"

H were ribbing me, but it got me thinking about Dennis and the Temporary Traffic Light bloke again. I went quiet as H spieled his master plan to lift the timepieces. I felt shit the rest of the day and went to get my nut down back at the hotel.

I caught up with H later that night at Jokers and he were firm with a gang of mixed race Scouser casuals. H were knocking San Miguel bottles and Vodka tumblers back like prohibition were suddenly gonna be declared that night in Spain and he'd been given a heads up.

The Scousers were really good lads. They were from a place called Fazakerley, which really amused H for some reason. H immediately starts taking the piss out of me for their benefit, telling 'em I don't drink because I'm a shirt lifter and that I had AIDS and booze don't mix well with my AIDS medicine. I could tell they were politely humouring H, but were getting a bit bored of his leery loudness and shit jokes, so I got us on our toes to Lennon's, but not before H made a total cunt of himself dancing to 'Mad World' by Tears for Fears on the empty dancefloor.

We'd only been in Lennon's fifteen minutes before he'd pulled a sort from Luton. She were staying at an hotel not far from ours called The Pueblo. H reckons he's gonna come back after he's done the dirty. He were already fucked so I didn't hold any hope out of him returning. I sat outside Lennon's on the patio and soaked up the great music the DJ was playing. Two birds asked if anyone were sitting with me and then joined me.

We finally got talking and turns out they're from Leighton Buzzard. I didn't have a fucking clue where it were. One of them slinks off because she's got a promise on with one of the cheeky chappy touts that littered the pavements, trying desperately to get punters in the pubs and clubs. Fucking pests, they were, and on the second night I'd had to stop H from chinning one of 'em for being a persistent berk.

I'm left with blondie and she's a sort and really pleasant with it. You could tell she weren't no mug and had had a bit of higher education. We're getting on like a barn fire and before long she asks if I wanna go back to her hotel. It's a good job, because I'd have never put it on her toes, being the shy spastic I were when it came to the birds of the species.

We were at it 'til about 9 in the morning. The Spanish sun were poking its nosey fucking beak through the curtains by the time I rolled off her. Sweating like a fucking nonce case at Disneyland I was, so I dived in the shower while she got her head down. We didn't have a shower at home and I made a mental note to get lively about having one installed when we got back.

I pulled a cunt's trick on her when I'd dried off and got dressed. She were snoozing and I could have woke her up to say ta-ta, but I just got on my toes and went back to my hotel. As the day wore on and I'm sat sunning myself round the pool, I'm getting this horrible, fucking grotty feeling in my stomach. I kept picturing her lying there asleep, sweet smile on her boat, all innocent and dreamy and then me ratting out on her without so such as a bye-bye.

This were a bird I could have fallen in love with, or rather, what I thought 'falling in love' were at that age. I couldn't get her out my head and then the thoughts of her started mingling with thoughts about Dennis and Traffic Lights Man and ... I don't mind admitting it, I went back to my room and started piping like a little girl. Fucking sobbing I were, had never cried like that before, even when I were a teapot. As soppy as it sounds, the empathy I had for this bird, who I hardly knew, started consuming me and I were even feeling empathy for all the rotten cunts I'd ever met in my life. And get this, even my cunt of a Dad.

I'm thinking maybe I've got sunstroke or something and manage to pull myself together. I think I'll put H's little ghetto blaster on to ease my mind and I press play. Big fucking mistake. 'William, It Was Really Nothing' by The Smiths starts blasting out and I'm piping again. I usually loved listening to that *Hatful of Hollow* tape, but now it were like it were suddenly speaking to me and dragging me down into its miserabilism. I were in a right two n' eight and decided I needed to get out pronto. I blew my hooter, wiped the tears and heeled it.

I went for a walk and plopped my arris down in a park up the road from the hotel. I sat on a bench and just stared into the unfocused distance for what seemed like donkeys, it couldn't have been more than half an hour though. This strange empathy invasion were choking me.

A memory kept coming up: me and my sister when we were younger, outside a cakeshop on the main road, me coppering up to try and buy a vanilla slice she wanted, and being 5 pence short and not having the bottle to try and strike a deal with the woman behind the till. The look of disappointment on my sister's boat and now, now I'm thinking how I'd feel if my sister had been treated like I'd treated the bird from last night, just walking out on her.

I know I hadn't done anything really offside to the bird, but in my mixed-up fucking nut at the time it felt like I had, and I were choking on a steady stream of black bile that was bubbling up from my gut. It really were shocking.

I shot back to the hotel room. H were snoring like a pig and I quickly pulled on my swimming shorts. I dived in the pool and spent the next couple of hours bobbing my head up and down in the chlorine, baptizing myself over and over, trying to get this horrible, alien, invasive empathy washed away.

I'd got myself thinking straight by the time the evening buffet was laid out, but I couldn't eat fuck all. H more than made up for my lack of appetite and stuffed enough grub down his Gregory to feed a village in Ethiopia. H were on a good screw. He'd only paid for a flight and was top to tailing with me, but spending most of his nights in the hotel rooms of bints he were banging.

H didn't seem to have a care in the world, and I suppose I envied him. Not that I were worrying about anything on a regular day to day level, but these irregular, panicky invasive thoughts were shitting me up. It was that night that I decided I could never kill another human being, ever again, no matter what. It weren't worth it.

All that night H were in my ear about how we was gonna turn over the jewellers the next day. He reckoned he could lift 5 of the TAG's no sweat. At between 8 and 900 bar – English – a piece that were 4 and a quarter large. If we laid them off at halves that means we would have cleared over a grand each, but H weren't having any of it. He reckoned he was gonna ask the cockney Landlord for 6 hundred each, meaning we'd be pocketing 1500 each.

I weren't into it anyway and asked him why he were being greedy. Did five hundred bar make that much of a difference? H got the hump and threw it in my face that it was *him* doing the hoisting, I were just coasting, so he could *bleedin' well ask what he wanted for the kettles.* I didn't bother arguing. Pointless.

I didn't bump into the bird from Leighton Buzzard that night and I weren't sorry. I didn't wanna face her after the meltdown I'd had earlier that day, sparked by tip toeing out on her.

We did hit Lennon's again and had a good crack with some lads from Deptford. I turned it in about 3am as H sidled up to some sort from *godknowswhere*. I can say all this about H because I know his long-suffering missus, B, knew he were a fucking hound dog before he settled down with her.

H had planned to swipe the watches on our second to last day, which made sense, but before that he lifted some Lladro ornaments from a shop. These weren't for flogging though, they were a present for his Mum. The ease in which he just strolled out with the three hundred quids worth of ceramics only emboldened him for the upcoming big score.

The day comes and I goes in the tom shop and engage the owner about a silver chain I were pretending to be quite partial to. This is down the other end of the jump, obviously. I'm asking this spic tom dealer all sorts o' silly questions about this chain when in bowls H. He heads straight down to the end of the counter. There's a few punters in which made good cover and H deftly dips his hand under the glass display and manages to grab six TAG's.

H is in and out in a breath. I'm still blabbing with the owner about this silver chain and the poor cunt's telling me he'll knock 10,000 pesetas off. I give him a big smile, feign I've left my wallet back at the hotel, ask him to keep it for me and promise I'll be back in ten. *Adios amigo* and I'm on my toes. I look down the drag and can see H well up in the distance jogging away before slipping down a side street. I hang a left and keeping walking in the direction of the hotel. When I get there, H is already in the room looking like the cat that's got the pricey kettles. He wraps 'em carefully in a towel and shoves 'em under the mattress.

We walk in to Benidorm Old Town knowing that there's a

high-end tom shop there. H wants to price the pieces up because there's no tickets on the ones he's pilfered. After he
squints inside the window for ten minutes and does some mental calculations, he snaps round to me and hisses, "Fuckin', get
in! Result!"

Two of the kettles are priced up, English, for 2 large apiece,
3 are 1800's and one's just over one large. Bingo: 9400 Great
British Pounds! We fence 'em at half's and that's £2350 each
for another piece of piss caper. H dives straight into a bar and
I follow him. He orders a celebratory bevvy and starts planning
his next move. He's gonna off load 'em to the cockney Landlord
but he's gonna wait until tomorrow, a few hours before we're
due to head to the airport for the skip and jump back to dear
old Blighty. I'm impressed and think myself blessed that I've got
a china like H.

It's our last night and H is riding to the state called Paralytic.
He were knocking 'em back like the fucking Queen Mother,
while I kept trying to engage him in chat to stop him guzzling so
much. I kept pointing out Richard's to him, hoping he'd click on
and go fuck one of *them* instead of fucking his liver. 10 minutes
later he's eating the face off a big brunette unit with massive
knockers from Norwich, so I know I can stop babysitting him
now. I go outside and sit on the patio watching the Benidorm
wildlife in all its lairy glory. Something catches my eye. It's the
bird from Leighton Buzzard sat on the wall with her mate, de-
molishing cocktails the size of kitchen pans. I don't know why,
but I mustered up and went over to her.

I'm stood in front of her and I find myself saying, politely and
genuinely remorseful, "Hi, Uh, I ... uh, sorry about the other
day. I should o' woke you up, but, uh ..."

"No problem." She cheerily gives it.

"Yeah, what it is, I had to get to back to …"

She hurriedly smiles, "Yeah, don't worry about it. See ya." Translated as "Fuck off!"

Two tanned, tall, Brummy berks instantly appear holding two cocktail refills apiece in their paws. They hand the Leighton Buzzard birds theirs and they all start clinking glasses, *fucking cheers!* They all just ignore me like I'm one of those fucking touts or something. I'm blushing, feeling like the biggest cunt on the Costa Blanca. I'm dumbstruck as I very slowly back up and away, thinking that every set of mince pies on the drag are honed in on me. I slunk back to the hotel to Mum and Sis' and we watched a terrible Freddie Starr impersonator perform round the pool for the guests. I was glad it were the last night.

A couple of hours before the coach were due to take us to Alicante Airport, me and H go round to see the cockney Landlord at *The Pride of London* or *God Save The Queen*, or whatever the fuck his joint were called. He takes us out back and gives the watches a good looking over. He's clearly very interested.

"Nice", he gives it, "What you lookin' at?" stroking his chin.

"Retail back home, we're talkin' nine n' half large. We'll take five." spitting in his palm and holding out it for Cockney to shake.

Cockney comes back with a snort, "Five? You got no chance, sunshine."

"You can easy put a couple o' ton on each kettle. That's twelve hundred in yer bin for nothin', chief."

"Nah, I'd wanna pass 'em on at half price. So, I'm looking at … what? Three grand for the lot? Readies."

What followed was a mind numbingly stupid haggle that went on for over a quarter of an hour. The Landlord were giving H the right hump by telling him that he'd never get the kettles through customs at the other end because there were no stamp duty or there *were* stamp duty or some other baloney. In other words, he were saying to H, *you best flog me this loot at what I'm offering or you're fucked.*

H weren't having any of it though. He kept asking the Landlord to explain exactly what he meant about Spanish/ English Import/Export law and the conversation were getting fucking absurd. These two weren't exactly the best legal minds in the business. I'm telling H that we better fuck off or we'll miss the coach, but H is getting right up in the Landlord's mush now.

The Landlord made a fatal error by putting up a few 'names' who he reckoned he were pals with back home.

H laughed in his face, "Are you fuckin' seriously droppin' names in *my* lugholes, you cunt! I don't care if you've got Mister T, Rocky Balboa n' fuckin' Al Capone on the firm you spunk-bubble! We ain't in the fuckin' Mile End now you cunt!"

With that, H set about the Landlord with one of those hard plastic crates that they deliver those Schweppes tonic waters in. Hard plastic is a fucker, as anyone who's ever stood on a piece of Lego barefoot will attest, and H battered him all over the back-yard with it. I just watched and wished he'd hurry up.

Landlord's arris went AWOL and he crawled up in a ball on the gravel. He were wearing a gold chain that you could have towed a truck with, so H reached down and ripped it off his Gregory, "*I'll* have that you timewasting cunt!" not pausing to recognize the great wordplay he'd just come out with it.

I were half expecting we'd get a tug as we started going through the gate at Alicante, I wouldn't have put it past that plastic gangster Landlord to have dobbed us in it, but like all the other spics we'd encountered, the airport mob looked like they were half asleep or nodding off on smack. No agg at Gatwick either. Within hours of being back on the estate, H had been on the blower and had offloaded all the TAGs and we were both 2 large richer than when we'd set off. The other bit of hoisting, the Lacoste, Armani and the Ronker chain that H took off the silly bollocks Landlord, had more or less paid for our holidays as well. All in all, it were a cracking holiday, but it were unlikely Judith Chalmers would be featuring it on her popular *Wish You Here* TV holiday show anytime soon.

TWELVE

Freedom: To ask nothing. To expect
nothing. To depend on nothing.

Ayn Rand

I were straight back to the stone yard after the Spanish jolly. Something weren't right though. The Chief weren't his usual self. One day he calls us all in his office and looks like he's on the verge of piping. He tells us, apologetically, that he's owed a big cheque by a customer and it looks like it's not gonna turn up anytime soon. He's genuinely rattled as he tells us that it's so serious, he might have to close the yard. His operating costs are fucking him and he's hovering on declaring the business bankrupt.

We're all fucking gutted, especially the lads that weren't 'at it' on other graft and relied on the yard for their daily dough. I were pissed off but more for them than me. I were now sat on over 45 large and it would last me donkeys, and I knew I'd find another job because I'd not let myself idle under any circumstances. I hadn't heard from Uncle but I were determined that I'd not be taking up any more wetwork for him.

I gets talking to the Chief on the quiet, condolences and all that, and I ask him how much he actually needs to keep the yard operating. He gives me a despondent look and gives it, *it don't matter. I can't raise it.*

I were about to make a big fucking mistake, I reply, *I might be able to help out.*

He smiles and snorts, "Thanks, son, but I doubt it. It's big dough."

I continue opening my big fucking stupid cakehole, "How big, Chief? What we talking?"

"Thirty grand. Might as well be thirty million though. I'm fucked. This company have had me over right n' proper. They reckon they can have it to me in three weeks but the yard'll be under water by then. Nah, I'm just gonna have to throw the fucking towel in n' swallow it."

The Chief decided we'd make the next day our last at the yard before he called The Receivers in. Everyone were gutted, even Timmy, who didn't really have a fucking clue what was going on. He just clocked all our miserable boats and copied us.

That night I thought about all the lads at the yard that were relying on it staying in business. Like I said earlier, these were good blokes, and the Chief – so I thought – were a decent chap who'd just happened to hit a major fucking dam with his cash flow. I thought about my stash. It were just there, under the floorboard, in the portable peter, doing fuck all. I got it out and had a count. I actually had £46650. Over sixteen hundred more than I thought I had.

The next day I goes in the Chief's office, close the door behind me and lock it. He's looking like death warmed up. He's obviously hit the liquor the night before and would have fucking combusted if he'd gone near a naked flame. His eyes were like piss holes in the artic and he had that rank, sweaty booze pong wafting off him. I'd never seen him in this state before.

I took the cash out of my donkey jacket and put it down on his desk. He looks up, wide eyed, "What's this?"

"The thirty large you need. I got left it by my granddad when he kicked the bucket." I lied.

"Fucking hell!"

"It'll keep the yard open until you get sorted, eh?"

He's made up and gives me a hug, promises I'll get it back in a month and offers to give me some interest on it. I told him I don't want any. I added that I'd appreciate it if he didn't tell anyone about it. He were fucking cock-a-hoop and all the misery and anxiety on his boat disappeared.

So, the yard carries on as usual, the Chief tells the lads that he's sorted something out and it looks like we're all safe in our jobs. It were obviously a huge relief. I obviously kept schtum about it all and just got my head down.

A month comes and goes and I quietly ask the Chief one day whether there were any news on my loan. He said it'd only be a few more days before he expected the cheque to land and that everything were sweet. I had no reason to doubt him.

It's six weeks now and he's still telling me the cheque's about to land. One day at the yard he shoots off in his motor. About half an hour later Two Heavies turn up asking after him. Nobody let on they'd seen him that day and said they didn't expect him popping in. The Heavies probably clicked they were being fucked off, but said that if we did see him, we were to tell him he had to call someone called Tony.

I had a bad feeling in my gut. I got home that night and thought about calling Uncle to see if he had any advice for me. When I turns up at the yard the next day, the lads were huddled outside. The gates were locked and there were no sign of the fucking Chief. *Fuck!*

I didn't need to ask Uncle's advice about getting my 30 large back. Fucking pointless. The Chief had sucked on the exhaust pipe of his Ford Capri in his garage at home. He were jam, leaving his wife and kids destroyed and boracic. It turns out he were a fucking hopeless gambler and had built up debts all over the shop with bookies, casinos and loan sharks. He'd remortaged his family drum, took charges against the stone yard, owed suppliers from John O Groats to Lands End and put the bite on family and friends for tens of thousands. And, more importantly, the cunt had turned *me* over for thirty thousand!

So, there I was, 30 large lighter and out of work. If I'd had a shooter at the time, I'd have turned it on myself for being such a fucking idiot. I started questioning my sanity for offering to lend him the dough. He wouldn't have done the same for me. I marked myself down as a full weight cunt. I should have called Uncle and asked his advice. It then dawned on me that if I had told Uncle he'd think I were a totally fucking mug and would have never wanted anything to do with me ever again.

I could tell absolutely nobody in the world that I'd been had over. I had to deal with it myself. For a few weeks I skulked about the flat alternately feeling sorry for myself and getting angry at the cunt who'd had my pants down. One day I just pulled myself together and went out looking for a job. I found one at a pallet yard in Kennington. The pay was shit and the hours were long but it were cash in hand, so.

I'd heard about pallet yards where they were a bit of graft going on, but this weren't one of them. No cunt were on the fiddle, very straight bunch of lads. I loaded and offloaded pallets all day with the forkilft and sometimes had to repair pallets that had slats missing. The Gaffer were a bit of a cunt and he'd bollock me if I had the flatbeds waiting longer than 5 minutes to get sorted out. I was tearing around that yard like Ayrton fuck-ing Senna!

The Gaffer were a lanky streak of piss and not much older than me, but you could tell he fancied himself as a bit of a tough nut. I'd heard him a few times telling the more gullible that he'd 'done' so and so and he was gonna 'do' so and so. Mugs that talk like that, in my experience, can never really hold their hands up. I never bit when he bollocked me. Head down, trap shut. This didn't stop from me fantasising about wrapping a fucking crow-bar around his napper though.

One day he stretched my patience right up to the bleeding edge. The forklift's ran on gas and we used Calorgas bottles to power them. We gets in one morning and find that we'd run out of gas refills. This cunt starts screaming and shouting at me for not telling him the bottles were running low. He's giving me it in front of everyone and getting in my face, spits flying out his gob and he's pointing and calling me every name under the sun. When he's finished I calmly give it, "Go look in your office. I put a note in there yesterday morning telling you we was low."

I never got an apology and I wanted to string the cunt up, but I kept my cool. It did go through my mind that I would give him the Dennis treatment one dark night, but I had sworn to myself that I would never kill anybody ever again.

I tried getting cash in hand work at various firms but jobs were getting harder to come by. H offered me some work buying and selling motors with him, but I were no salesman and I knew fuck all about motors. I bit my lip and stayed at the pallet yard. I still had over 10 large salted away but it were dwindling pretty sharpish. Mum had always wanted to learn to drive, so I paid for lessons and bought a little Mini Cooper for her from H. I paid for my Sis' to go to France on a school trip and finally got us a shower installed. The flat were looking nice now, but we still had that fucking eyesore littering up the front room.

My cunt of a Dad were suffering from all sorts of illnesses and I were counting the days until he snuffed it, but it felt like he'd outlive us all. It had got to point where I didn't even disguise my hatred of him and completely blanked him whenever he tried to speak to me, which, thankfully weren't that often.

My hours were cut at the pallet yard to three days a week and I was now down to 7 grand in my piggy bank. *7 left from nearly 50!* I squirmed whenever the 30 grand debacle invaded my thoughts. 7 large were still a tidy sum for a lad my age back then, but it were rapidly going South. I had a word with a few lads on the estate to see if there were some lower league graft going on I could get involved in, but it were a bit of a barren time and nothing much was happening.

Uncle hadn't been in touch for ages and I thought about trying to make contact and seeing if he had anything – other than killing people – I could get my teeth into. I bottled out of calling though. What the fuck was I going to say? *I don't wanna do any dirty work for you anymore, Uncle, but have you got anything I could earn good dough on?* Nah, he'd have thought I were pathetic.

Work at the pallet yard dried up for me. The lanky cunt Gaffer had it in for from the off so I weren't surprised. A couple of weeks sat on my arse and my head were about to explode. I gets a knock one day from a right herbet called Tex. He'd heard I were at a loose end and asked if I wanted to help him out in a little business he'd set up. Tex were about 30 at the time and he'd be doing bird since he were a kid. His claim to fame was that he had once broken out of Borstal and managed to stay on the lam for a year. This led to him being featured in a Thames

TV documentary about kids behind bars or something. Why he was called Tex I haven't a fucking clue.

Tex tells me he's set up this flyposting graft with an old bloke that used to work up Wapping in the print. They were printing and sticking up those big posters you used to see everywhere, advertising gigs at venues and festivals and what have you. Tex had a van and, under cover of night, would go out and splash the posters all over the place. It weren't rocket science. You just dipped your brush in a bucket of paste and blitzed anywhere you could.

Me, being the ever-fucking naïve mug I was at the time, thought I'll *have some of this.* Tex gave me a score a night to work from 12 midnight to 5am, and we'd hit sites all over London on weeknights. It were better than nothing, and there were no way I were gonna sign on the dole like a lot of other lads on the estate who were in schtuck.

I'd been on the flyposting caper for a couple of weeks and everything seemed to be all right. We had to swerve plod if they showed up, but the most they could have pinched us for was littering or something, otherwise it were a doddle. What Tex hadn't told me is that flyposting in London at that time was being controlled by a gang of nutcases from North London. They'd had the graft stitched up for years, but Tex being a clueless cunt thought he'd just set up in healthy competition with them. *Free enterprise innit! Thatcher n' all that.*

We were grafting one night when I pointed out to Tex that the posters we'd slung up the night before had already been covered with posters for other gigs. The posters of ours that hadn't been covered had had 'cancelled' pasted across them. Tex just told me not to worry about it.

A few nights later we were sticking up posters for a Scritti Politti gig near Kings Cross, when all of a sudden this fucking Ford Sierra comes screeching round the corner with four big lumps crammed into it. Soon as Tex sees it, he's running to the van and screaming at me to do the same. The van were already moving when I climbed into the passenger seat and Tex is flooring it. The Sierra slams on and starts reversing in our path. Tex, fair play to him, swerves and we head towards the Grays Inn Road at a fair clip. It's 4 am so the roads are pretty clear and for a minute it looks like we've lost the Cauliflower Lug Brigade, but then suddenly they're right up our arse. I'm yelling at Tex, asking him what the fuck's going on, but he's concentrating on trying to lose The Sierra.

Tex jumped at least four sets of lights and nearly drove us straight into the side of a Spar Supermarket articulated. After a spot of nifty driving though it looks like we've lost the cunts, but no, The Sierra is side by side with us now and one of the Lumps is pointing a sawn-off shotgun at me from the passenger seat.

I ducked down and closed my eyes and heard the bang and ping as the sawn-off scattered hot metal into the door. Thankfully none of it pierced through but I kept my head down, trembling and cursing Tex. We must have gone on to and off the A5200 at some point because I were thrown around like a rag doll a couple of times.

I didn't dare look up until we'd got to Borough Market and Tex gives it, "I think we've lost 'em."

"What the fuck's going on, Tex?" I yelled.

"Just a bit of a misunderstanding. I'll square it."

Fair play to Tex, he did have the bottle to go and meet with the North London flyposting firm and promised he would never step on their toes again and that he'd hung up his paste bucket and was retiring from the game. They'd already found the screen-printing place where Tex was getting them manufactured and had smashed it to bits. They let Tex off a hiding as long as he coughed up a 3 large tax to them for all the trouble he'd caused. Tex promised he'd pay the tax when they showed him the correct address of his Mum on a piece of paper.

Tex didn't have 3 large but he somehow managed to scrape together 1200 of it. He were scared to death and even thought about going to Old Bill, but I managed to talk some sense into him. Tex tried borrowing the 1800 shortfall off of H, but H laughed in his face and told him to fuck off, unhelpfully adding, that he'd better find it soon because this North London mob were known to be absolutely garrity.

Tex broke down one night and told me were considering topping his self. I obviously tried to talk him out of it. He actually seemed like he were gonna through with it. I didn't know Tex that well, but I could see he were definitely not shitting me.

Around that time in the 80s, it felt like some people had a licence to print money. I were feeling like I had a licence to fucking *lose* money. I'd had my pants pulled down by that cunt from the stone yard and now I was gonna bail Tex out with the 1800 shortfall. At least Tex were being honest with me though.

We worked out a payment plan before I handed it over to him. He promised to give me 300 a month for six months. I trusted him because I knew he feared H and his family. He said he were gonna go into knocking smack out on the estate to get his finances in shape. I told him I didn't give a fuck how he got it as long as I got my dough back. He told me there'd be a drink in it for seeing him right, but I weren't bothered as long I got my 1800 back.

That old saying, *it never rains, but it pours.* The envelope factory where Mum worked went tits up. The receivers were brought in and it were gonna be a fight for any of the workers who would have been due some redundancy to even get a penny. Mum were gutted but got on her toes and went looking for another job, to no avail unfortunately.

For the first time in her life, she had the indignity of signing on. She said we should sell the Mini Cooper, but before we had a chance, she hit some black ice one night and crashed it up the arse end of a Vauxhall. Mum had no insurance on the motor, but luckily the prang happened on the estate and H were able to persuade the Vauxhall owner not to get plod involved. The Mini were a write off and I had to cough up 200 to Mr. Vauxhall to get his arse end repaired.

My Sis' found my cunt of a Dad dead in his chair one morning. It were a stroke, and in my mind a stroke of good fucking luck. Mum cried but me and my Sis' just went quiet. I were glad at the time, but I weren't gonna show it in front of Mum. Not long after they'd carted his corpse off, I dragged his chair down to the communal area and set fire to it. I'd have happily left his corpse in the chair and done the cremation there and then.

It would have saved me even more dough. The cunt didn't have life insurance or a funeral policy with the Co-op like normal people had back then, so it were up to fucking muggings here to stump up for the disposal. We went for the cheapest possible, but it still cost me 700 sovs. Mum said she'd pay me back, but she were now even more potless than usual and I would never have took a farthing off her anyway.

Me, Mum and Sis' now had the living room back and we got rid of any traces of him. We didn't need any reminders of the cunt's passive aggressive occupation. I even bought us a new set of furniture, new telly and a VHS video recorder, that replaced the Betamax video recorder that I'd bought off a smackhead who'd pinched it from a local school.

I were now down to my last grand in the piggy peter. Tex were servicing his debt but that was just covering bills, rent and food. I knew how much Mum hated signing on so I told her to stop. The few quid weren't worth the indignity. Sis' got a paper round and me and Mum were made up. It meant she hadn't inherited any of the dead Cunt's traits.

I were really getting the hump with trips to the Jobcentre. I knew that any job I got there would have to be on the books, and that I'd have to pay tax and insurance, but I couldn't even get one of those. I got a couple of weeks cash in hand on a demolition site in Southwark, but the Department of Social Security cunts got wind that some of the lads were signing on and working. The Gaffer's arse went and he binned us all.

In the scheme of things, life were looking pretty shitty. Tex ponied up my last 300 bar and told me he were off Tenerife and never coming back. He'd be promised a job selling these things called timeshare apartments to British holidaymakers. The bloke running the graft were called John Palmer. I'd never heard of him at the time.

One morning I gets up and goes down to where I parked my motorbike. I remember thinking at the time that I might have to sell it if things didn't improve. I pull the tarpaulin off it and there's an envelope stuck to the seat with a bit of Sellotape. I open it and it says: *give uncle a bell 01 ****** after 2 this aft. Memory.*

I were excited, flattered and anxious all rolled up. I did as instructed and memorized the number, went back up to the flat and flushed the envelope and note down the khazi. I sat on my bed thinking about whether or not I were really gonna call him. It had been ages, I thought he'd forgotten about me, didn't think I'd ever clap my eyes on him ever again. He'd been a blip. He'd come into my life and then he'd gone. We owed each other nothing. Which were a good job as it happens, because I were fucking potless.

I obviously knew what he were wanting to speak to me about. *How was I gonna break it to him that I'd retired after having only one hit with him? Was it comparable to The Beatles giving it to Brian Epstein, "ere, Brian. I know we've a had a fucking great smash hit with 'From Me to You' but we're throwing the towel in now"?*

All sorts were going through my mind. The thing is, I weren't thinking of my first kill for Uncle, or rather, I weren't thinking about the poor cunt I'd sent to his grave. I were thinking about me, and if I'd be able handle knowing I'd plugged someone else. It were totally selfish thinking. Would I be able to live with myself? Would I be able to justify another kill to myself? It weren't like I'd obsessed over Dennis and The Traffic Lights mark, barely gave them a thought. My mind had been elsewhere. There's nothing like being boracic – with no prospects on the horizon – to concentrate your mind.

I'd made the pledge to myself that I weren't doing anymore killing when I'd had that weird attack of empathy on holiday in Benidorm. A lot had happened since then. Having been stiffed for 30 large being the main thing. The very least I could do was hear him out.

THIRTEEN

If all the world hated you, and believed you wicked,
while your own conscience approved you, and absolved
you from guilt, you would not be without friends.

Charlotte Bronte

On the blower Uncle asked me to meet him on Westminster
Bridge. After a few pleasantries he asked straight out if I were up
for doing another piece of work for him. He said I'd get £40,000.
You could have KO'ed me with a duster, and I don't mean of the
knuckle variety. I can't remember if I actually said yes or whether
I just nodded my head. Probably nodded because I were gob-
smacked thinking about a 40 large payday. He then really threw
me by asking what size waist and feet I were and if I knew my
chest measurement.

Uncle said this hit were gonna be different. I didn't have
to do any stake outs, tailing or homework, didn't even need to
use my bike. Everything had already been meticulously planned
and it were a case of me simply being the trigger man. He gives
it, "The only way this job goes tits up is with the comin's n'
goin's".

He gave me an address to meet him at a week later. He told
me that if I even got a sniff of anyone following me to the meet

I were to turn around and go home. He added that I should take a circuitous route there, but he didn't need to. I knew the score.

The meet was above a dry cleaners near Clissold Park, North London. He told me to park up behind the parade of shops and take the stairs up to a flat. It were evening and all the shops were closed. I noticed a smart Jaguar parked up and assumed it were one of Uncle's motors. I knocked and Uncle opened the door with a wide smile on his mush. I weren't smiling though. There was somebody with him in the unfurnished flat and I froze.

Uncle locked the door as I stared at a smart middle-aged gent wearing a tailored whistle and a pair of *Two Ronnies* spectacles. He were a ringer for the playwright Harold Pinter circa late 60s. He looked really cool stood there sucking on a fag, leant against the wall, but it were still off putting. "This is your driver, son. We're all friends here. We don't need names."

The Driver held out his paw for me to go over and shake, which I did. A grip like fucking steel and eye contact that screamed: *serious man*. What followed was a set of instructions that wouldn't have sounded out of place in an M15 debrief.

Uncle paced and chained Rothman's and took swigs on his silver hip flask as he laid down the MO, "First things first son, you're gonna put on this whistle an' shirt n' tie n' shoes I've brought."

As I started to get changed, he got into it, "You get all this memorized, son. Word for word, it's really important … so, your driver's gonna take you over to Hampstead. He's gonna park up at the top of this avenue and you're gonna get out. You'll have a briefcase n' in the briefcase is your tool. It's loaded, six bullets, no silencer, no cunt's gonna hear you. You don't need it. Waste o' time. So, you gets out nice n' casual like and you walk down this avenue. You just walk down like you're meant to be there, right?"

I frown, "Uh…"

"Like you live on an avenue like this. See, this is a palatial avenue, fuckin' posh with knobs on. Different class. What I mean is, don't be put off by it. Don't be intimidated. Don't be gawpin' at the gaffs. Act like you're from round there. Don't stand out, yeah?"

"Yeah. I know what you mean, Uncle."

"Good, so you're there walking down this avenue minding your own business and you go past one, two, three, four of these detached houses and when you get to the fifth, *number five*, the gate's open and you just walk in and close it behind you. There's no numbers on these houses, son. They've all got different names, see."

Uncle shows me a polaroid photo of this mansion, "That's the one you're going in. Fifth house down. Fifth house from where you get out of the motor. Have a good butcher's … you got it?"

"Got it."

"Good," he says as he burns the photo, "Can't miss it can you?"

"No."

"No. That's what you call a pile that is. *Palatial* … anyway, you go through the gate and you walk right round to the back of the house. You'll come to some big patio doors, can't miss 'em, like the bleedin' Crystal Palace they are. You put your gloves on n' open the doors, they're already unlocked, and in you go, shutting the doors behind you. *Larry Grayson*. Don't worry about no alarm system, it's been turned off."

Uncle takes a deep breath, drops his fag on the floorboard and squashes it with the sole of his leather brogues. He has a nip from the hip flask and lights another fag, "So now you're inside this room and it'll look like it's been turned over, you know, some burglars have been in and been rifling through everything."

"Burglars"?

"Don't worry about it. They'll be gone by the time you get there. All's you need to know is that within the hour a bloke's gonna open the door o' that room and you're gonna shoot him. You just, just gotta be you know … what's the word? Uh, poised. You just gotta be poised … this is him."

Uncle hands me a photo of my mark clipped from a newspaper. If this mark is famous, I've certainly never seen him before. I *mentally* burn the image it into my memory. I hand it back to Uncle and he *physically* burns it.

Uncle continues, "You make sure his lights are out. Use the full clip if you gotta, yeah?"

"Yeah, right."

"There'll be a woman there, you might see her, you might not, I dunno, but you leave her alone, don't put one in her, in fact, don't touch a hair on this bird's head. You won't get any grief from her. You just put the piece back in the briefcase. You go out the way you came in. You'll see a Roller parked up in the drive. It's *his* Roller, the geezer you've just put out … so, nice n' cool remember? You walk back up the avenue and get in the motor. You sling the briefcase on the back seat and you're off. You'll be brought back here. I won't be here. You get changed back into your clobber and give him (the Driver) the whistle, everything you've been wearing. *Everything.* He'll get shut."

I'm nodding at Uncle as I slip on the suit jacket. It's lovely schmutter. Fits like a glove. He nods his head in approval, "When you've got changed you get back on your bike and you go home, right? He'll (the Driver) lock up."

"Yeah, yeah."

"When you get back to your gaff you burn the clobber you came here in as well."

"Right."

"Now, the only potential hiccups I can see, it's a long shot, not gonna happen, but it's the comin's n' goin's, either goin' there or comin' back. The motor's half inched and it's on moody plates, obviously, but if you *are* pulled over, you leave the talking to him (the Driver). Schtum. Not a dicky bird. I don't need to tell you that do I, son?"

"No, no."

"Now, if you get pinched between getting out of the motor and getting back into it, you're on your tod son, on your own, you know that, right? You understand?"

I'm nodding emphatically, "Definitely."

"He'll (the Driver) be on his toes if you get pinched. You got a choice to make at that point. You're gonna be tooled up, so you're gonna have the advantage on any plod before the heavy Old Bill get there. I can't tell you what to do, wouldn't even try, it's your shout. You might decide to do a Jimmy Cagney n' go out shootin', I dunno. All I'm sayin' is, you know the score … I can trust you not to drag anyone into it, eh, son?"

"Course you can, Uncle."

He really didn't need to say it. I could handle the thought of going out in a hail of bullets, but I couldn't handle the thought of what would happen to my Mum and Sis' if I grassed.

"Obviously, this is all … you know, what's the word … *academic*. Nothin's gonna go tits up. It's gonna be tidy."

Uncle then asked me to repeat everything he'd told me. *Twice.* The Driver kept glancing at his kettle and you could see he were getting a bit itchy, but Uncle weren't cutting no corners. Once satisfied I knew the MO backwards, Uncle bade us farewell and went outside. There were a Rover waiting for him and he were driven off. Me and The Driver waited a minute or two until we went and got in the Jag and headed over to Hampstead.

The radio were playing and he was singing along to 'Who Do You Think You Are?' by Candlewick Green. He never went over 25 mph and were constantly checking the wing and rear mirrors. I were calm and relaxed, Uncle's simple but important instructions ringing in my lugs. *I'm safe, nothing can go wrong, it's all been planned to perfection, simple case of bang bang you're dead! A fucking walk in the park!*

The suit were feeling a bit tight, but besides that I had nothing to grumble about. Obviously, some serious thought and time had gone in to this, and Uncle had made sure I knew exactly what I had to do. Also, I felt safe with The Driver at my side. He looked and sounded like he knew his way around this kind of caper. When I say 'sounded', that weren't really true. He hadn't said a fucking word and it were a bit of an awkward silence.

I broke the ice with, "Uh, anyone ever told you, you look like Harold Pinter?"

He frowns and thinks about it, "Pinter? ... there's a Pinter I know down Bethnal Green. Maurice, I think."

"No, *Harold*. He's a famous writer."

"Never heard of him."

And that was that. Not another peep out of either of us. Schtum. Professional.

The Driver had now slipped on a chauffeur's cap and he slowly parked at the top of the avenue. He pulled out a London A-Z and pretended to study it as I climbed out and walked casually down to the designated drum.

When I opened the patio doors, I were faced with a room that could have fit our council flat in it, *three times over*. It reeked of wealth. Not dough, *wealth*. There's a big difference. Like Uncle said, it had been rifled and did indeed look like a bit of burglary had gone down. I quickly but carefully pulled out the piece and aimed it at the only door leading into the room.

I'd never been in a gaff like this before. It were strange. Obviously, I knew people lived like this, but it felt like I'd walked on to the set of a film. The best way to describe the room is that it were like the room at the end of *2001 a Space Odyssey*, where the old astronaut pops his moonboots. It were a lot more cluttered with expensive ornaments and what not, and of course it didn't have that big bleeding monolith in it, but it had that classical look.

I still had the nerves at bay and were feeling confident and assured. I didn't feel alone, which I weren't in a way, but what I mean is this felt more like a joint enterprise than the first hit I'd done for Uncle. This felt a lot safer, but I knew there were a lot more skulduggery going down. This were an important cunt I were gonna snuff and it was gonna have some repercussions. I knew it were gonna make headlines. You don't off fuckers who live in a drum like this and it goes unreported. Still, I was cool as a cucumber.

My cue was raised voices. I heard 'em coming through outside of the room. Man and woman. All I could make out was the male voice giving it, *call the police*. Now that's when the arris started twitching and I broke sweat. I took a deep breath, said a prayer in my mind and steadied my aim at the door.

The poor bastard didn't stand a chance. He'd flung the door open and stomped in. It were a straight on hit. The first bullet ripped into his chest and he were spun around by the velocity of the slug and his own strident motion. The second caught him in the side midriff and he stumbled forward like he were drunk. The third and fourth knocked him to the lush white carpet and the last two went in his head.

I put the piece back in the briefcase and rushed out. I were breathless now and had to catch it. I counted to ten and told myself to fucking slow down before I strolled down the drive. I took a left and headed to the Jag. Nobody about. Not a lot of the mansions had lights on. Probably out having some delicious nosh or sunning themselves in exotic locations. Good on 'em. Long may they be ignorant that a contract killing had just gone down on their gilded manor.

The Driver didn't take his chauffeur's cap off until we were near Gospel Oak. When he did, I were expecting him to ask me how it had gone, but no, he gives it, "That Pinter mush you were on about ... wonder if he's related to that Maurice Pinter I know from Bethnal Green. Maurice ain't no writer, thick as two short planks, I reckon he'd have trouble writing his own name ... might be a relative of his though, eh? ... this Pinter *you're* on about. Got a few quid has he?"

FOURTEEN

Let other pens dwell on guilt and misery.

Jane Austen

I slept like a baby, no dreams or nightmares, no tossing and turning. I ate one of Mum's hearty full English breakfasts the next morning. The previous night's caper were playing over and over in my nut but it were like background TV. It were just there and I weren't paying attention to it. I couldn't turn it off but it didn't bother me too much. Didn't stop me thinking about the dough I'd just earned.

I nipped round to H's and asked him if he'd like to go swimming up the baths. He called me a 'homo' for even suggesting such a thing, "We're fully grown fuckin' men you cunt! Men don't go swimming with each other! Have a word with yourself."

We ended up going to a café instead, so H could tell me about his latest get rich quick scheme. I would have loved to have told him that I'd pulled down 40 large last night for a couple of hours work. Not in any gloating way, no. I just wanted him to share in my success. H, whatever he is, is not a jealous cunt. It would have been great to tell him, but I were a professional hitman now, and what he didn't know couldn't hurt him.

H gives it, "What you reckon those cunts who sell smack on the estate are raking in?"

I instantly knew where this was going, "I thought you were doing well flogging the motors?"

"You don't even know what I were gonna say."

"I think I do, H."

"Oh yeah, what's that then, clever bollocks?"

I leaned in, "You're obviously thinking of having 'em over."

H couldn't help but give me one of his one hundred guinea grins.

At least H weren't planning on robbing the dealers at the top of the smack chain. He were only going to target the two bob run-arounds who worked street level. It were still a very dodgy proposition though. The Big Boys weren't gonna wear suffer their joeys getting turned over. I told H this, obviously, but obviously he fucking ignored me.

"You could be up against some serious fuckers, H."

"What? Them Turks or Arabs or whatever they are? Leave it out. They're shitters. Mugs."

"Not from what I've heard, n' think about it: if they're *nothing*, how come the local firms ain't stepped on their toes?"

H just shrugged and guzzled his sweet tea, "It always takes *someone* to step up. There's always gotta be a first. *My* firm'll be the first."

"No disrespect, H, but you ain't got a firm."

I got on my toes, leaving H thinking about his new taxation scheme. I went back home and asked Mum about another scheme. Margaret Thatcher's government had brought in a new law that let council tenants buy their homes, and I wanted Mum to buy ours. I had to come up with something that weren't gonna make her suspicious though.

"Think about it, Mum. You'd be a property owner. A bit o'

security. No more rent, and you could do what you wanted with this place."

"Yeah, Sheila n' Norman are buying theirs. She told me about it."

"There you go."

"But where am I gonna get the money? I'd have to get a mortgage and I ain't working. The banks would laugh at me."

"Yeah, well, that's where I could help out, Mum."

"You ain't working either."

"I know, yeah, but what if I could get my hands on some cash?"

She snorted, "Sheila n' Norman had to pay 20 thousand pounds for theirs. Where *you* gonna get that kind o' money?"

I spieled Mum a massive amount of utter hairy bollocks and felt a bit bad about it, but needs must. I told her for the last couple o' years I'd been gambling: card schools, the horses, dogs, illegal dens, the lot. She gave me murderous looks initially, but when I hit her with the fact I'd managed to save up 40 large, well, she couldn't decide whether to faint, gimme a great big kiss or set about me with the frying pan. She were understandably confused. More than anything though, I think she were put out that I'd been keeping a whopping great secret from her.

"I knew you'd been up to something the way you was helping me out, but I thought it were just a bit o' grafting. Never occurred to me it were gambling you was up to."

"I didn't wanna tell you, Mum. I thought you'd gimme a bollocking. Tell me not to do it."

"I bleedin' well would … but …"

"So, see, I could buy the flat for us. *Cash.* We don't need no mortgage. You'd finally get to own something for once in your life."

It took a few more hours of persuasion but she finally accepted that it were the sensible thing to do, and agreed that it would be nice to be able leave the flat to me and my sister when she kicked the bucket, "It'll be worth a few bob more by then, eh?" *Not half! But none of us could imagine the insane rise in London property prices that were on the horizon back then.*

Mum rang the council and they sent us a figure to buy the flat outright. Because she'd rented for so long, the discount were fucking huge. They wanted £18750. She burst into tears when I told her I could easily get my hands on that kind of dough. I made her promise not to tell a soul and when people asked, she was to say she were buying the flat on a hooky mortgage. I like to think those tears were tears of joy and pride in her son, but maybe they were tears for the realization that her son was 'at it' big time. I'll never know because from that day on, Mum accepted – kidded herself – that I were something of a gambling wizard and we left it at that.

The 40 large that Uncle were paying me came in 4 instalments of fish suppers, spread over a month. With the legal fees and bumf, the flat cost me just over 21 grand. Mum had to get a cashier's cheque from the bank and go pay it in at the council offices. A few days later the paperwork dropped and she became the first person out of her large family that had ever owned property. She rang her Mum and sisters and brothers and cousins and any other cunt she could think of to tell them the good news. They all seemed genuinely happy for her, but I reckon a few of 'em were fucking green with envy, law of averages.

It were six weeks since I'd done the dirty in Hampstead for Uncle. The hit did make the headlines, but after a cursory look I ignored all the hullabaloo. I were now fully committed to the choice I'd made. No going back. If I were occasionally overwhelmed with feelings of guilt, I handled them by picking up a book to read and getting lost in other people's troubles.

I started seeing a bird around this time. Deirdre lived on the estate and I'd known her since infant school. She were pretty, in good shape and good fun to be around. Her Dad were away in the merchant navy and her Mum was hooked on Valium. Her older brother were severely disabled from birth and lived in a home in Southwark. I went on a few visits with her and on one of them, her brother waited until she'd nipped out for a slash to ask me if I could bring him some wank mags in. His body were fucked but his mind were firing on all cylinders. I dutifully obliged of course.

Mine and Deirdre's courting consisted of me going round to her drum every night at 9 and watching telly with her. Her Mum were always tucked up by 9, after guzzling her Valium, so we'd have the front room to ourselves for some how's yer father.

I'd always leave around 2 in the morning, could have slept with her, but never did. I think both of us preferred our own beds. Deirdre fucked me off one Monday night because she'd met a lad that weekend at a nightclub. He had a red XR3i motor and apparently this were enough to poach her from me. I weren't too bothered and I think this pissed her off. You really can't win sometimes. Fucked if you do, fucked if you don't. I missed the slap n' tickle but what can you do.

Incidentally, fast forward to 1998 and I see Deirdre in Finchley, North London, when I were stalking a mark, who was proving to be a major fucking headache, more about later. So yeah, Deirdre were driving a smart 4x4, had a couple of teapots in the back and pulled into the drive of a nice semi-detached. I were glad she'd done well for herself. It were always nice to see people from the old estate find their feet.

It would have been around this time that I first tried my hand at painting. GLC had opened this community drop-in centre on the estate for all the poor cunts having nothing better to do than sign on the dole every fortnight. They had art classes twice a week and I went along. You could use their paint, brushes and canvasses for a 50p donation and I really enjoyed it. It were very relaxing, and even though I couldn't draw or paint for toffee I did these colourful abstract pieces that weren't too unpleasant on the eye. The Tutor reckoned I 'understood Colour'.

H and the other lads from the estate swerved the drop-in centre, because, in H's inimitable words, "All them cunts that work in there are hippies, nonces, shirt lifters n' commie cunts. Wouldn't be seen dead in that shithole."

I carried on going for a few more weeks until I found out H weren't actually talking bollocks. The centre was indeed staffed by gays, socialists and 'alternative types', but I never had anything to do with them, just came in, fucked about with the paints for a bit and got on my toes, so it never bothered me. I never thought for a second nonces worked there, until one night I were shocked to discover that they did.

The drop-in centre were divided up into about a dozen classroom sized rooms. There were a café at the front and the rooms would lead off from it. One night by chance I was at a loose end and decided to nip in and 'borrow' a book about Mark Rothko from the art room, knowing that they never locked up when other stuff were going on in the evening.

I'm bowling down the corridor towards the art room when I hear a meeting taking place in one the rooms. The door's slightly ajar and I hear a couple of raised voices. I think, *sounds like a row going on*, so I start earwigging at the door.

What I heard was a meeting of about half dozen members

of the Paedophile information Exchange taking place. PIE for short. I were fucking flabbergasted and all ears as I stood there listening. I'd read about this secret group of scum in the papers and knew exactly what their game was: *advocating for the fucking legalisation of sex between kids and adults.* These cunts were notorious and had been infiltrating local Labour Parties all over London. I don't know why I were so surprised and shocked looking back, because these monsters were very active in the looney left circles of the 1970s and 80s.

So, there I am gawping at what I were hearing, and I couldn't help but have a peep at the kind of creeps that were meeting, bold as fucking brass, in *our* community centre. There's seven of them. A couple of middle-aged geography teacher types, an old cunt who might as well have had 'nonce' tattooed across his forehead, three 'normal' looking blokes and Godfrey, a raving lunatic lefty who worked at the centre. Godfrey would have been in his mid-thirties, had a plummy accent but dressed like a fucking oil lamp. As much as I detested the cunt I never had him down as a noncing slag though.

I carried on listening to the bastards jawing about pressure groups and media strategies and other nonsense pertaining to the furthering and acceptance of their fucking twisted sexual insanities. I were glued to that door and had completely forgotten I were there to half inch a book.

When I heard Godfrey bringing the perverted proceedings to an end I went and sat in the café to watch the monsters leave. I noticed each member was carrying a copy of a cheap little Xerox'd magazine. Godfrey goes and gets himself a coffee and starts gabbing with some of the other cunts that worked there. Cue some detective work.

I go in the room and head straight to a desk that's got a

shabby old leather bag on it. It must be Godfrey's. I opens it and inside are a few of the magazines the monsters had all walked out with copies of. I grab one, stuff it down my trousers and go home, forgetting all about swiping the book.

What I read were fucking sickening. Pure apologetics for the right to be able to molest kids. Turned my stomach. There were no graphic images but there didn't need to be. The words left nothing to the imagination. This were photocopied filth from minds of 'men' who were lower than a snake's cunt.

I nipped into the drop-in centre the next day and looked at the noticeboard. The nonce meeting was simply called Palaver and took place on the last Thursday of the month. There weren't any details about what the meeting was about, but *I* fucking knew, and it needed cancelling, and quick.

I did consider reporting the meeting to the council, but given that most of them were fucking loony leftists I didn't think they'd do anything about it. I could have gone to the press, but I didn't have a clue how you went about it. I didn't know any journalists and the only person I knew in the media was my sister. I don't know if delivering papers is classed as being 'in the media' mind.

I did know someone who would do something about it though. H had once bragged to me that if he were told he had terminal cancer or something, he'd get a shooter and go nonce hunting. All right-minded people hate child rapists, but H seemed to hate them more than anyone else, which he didn't, but he liked to say he did.

Not really thinking too much about it I showed H the grubby magazine and told him what I'd heard at the meeting. You could see him getting angrier and angrier as he read the vile thoughts of these abominable bastards. I were half expecting cartoon steam to come out of his ears. He paced about the room shaking his head and shoving his fist in his mouth and biting down on it every now and then.

"We've gotta do these cunts!"

"I agree, H."

"Do 'em proper."

"Proper, as in …?"

"Put their fuckin' lights out."

I knew that's what he were gonna say, "What? There's seven of 'em. We're gonna commit mass murder?"

When H calmed down, he agreed that we'd get Balaclava'd up and wait for them outside the drop-in centre after their next meeting. We'd give the cunts the kicking of their lives, disperse and disappear into the estate. I stressed, *nothing life threatening though. No stabbing or extra curriculum stomping on their nappers when they're laid out.*

H agreed and promised that we'd simply batter 'em and warn 'em not to ever step foot on our estate again with their sick, filthy, ideas. H said he'd set about recruiting soldiers for the good fight, and I told him to keep it tight. No more than three more lads I told him. H reckoned, and I agreed, that we could probably round up fifty lads to join in such a worthy crusade.

"That's what I mean, H. keep it tight, schtum, or we'll have the whole bleeding estate getting Balaclava'd up and wanting to join in."

Even though these fuckers were the scum of the earth and self-confessed destroyers of children – *if the law would only allow them to* be – it were still going to be a naughty attack, and I were wondering how Old Bill were going to react. Even though our faces would be smothered up and nobody on the estate would dare dob us in it, there were always the chance that one of us went a bit too far given the type of cunts we were attacking.

145

I have to admit that helping H plan this attack gave me something to do. I were itching for Uncle to give me another piece of work so's I was still regularly earning. It were actually me that came up with doing something about them, so I suppose I were actively looking for things to keep my mind occupied.

Mad as it sounds, I were more nervous about the nonce attack than I had been my last hit. I suppose it's because I'd be doing it with H and a few cowboys and ultimately, I had no control over what *they* did. On a piece of work I live and die by my own actions, and if I have to fall on my own pistol, so be it.

H, being the impatient fucker, couldn't wait a month before staging the nonce offensive though. One wintry night – a couple of days after we'd started the planning – him and a game little geezer called Vinny got tooled up with hammers, stuck on their Balaclavas and went and waited for Godfrey to leave the drop-in centre. As Godfrey were just about to get into his shitty old Citroen 2CV, they jumped out from behind a wall and let him have it.

Vinny were first off the bat with a hammer blow to Godfrey's mouth that knocked most of his top teeth out. Godfrey squeals and spits teeth and H is straight in with hammer blow to the back of his nut that knocks him arse over on to the icy asphalt. H and Vinny put the slippers in to his body and then finished off with choreographed hammer blows to his knees, hands and ribs. H said it took about 20 seconds to cabbage the cunt for life before they were on their toes and back into the maze-like safety of the estate.

Godfrey, the fucking oxygen thief, were on life support for 6 weeks at the taxpayer's expense. The hammer shot that H delivered were obviously the cause of the swelling and bleed on the cunt's diseased brain. It were reported as an extremely vicious mugging in the local paper. H and Vinny had cleverly swiped the cunt's wallet to make it look a common or garden financial crime rather than a nonce attack. Plod asked about a bit for a couple of days but turned up nish as usual.

H remarked he wished he'd killed the cunt seeing as how easy it'd been. I told H not to brag about it to anyone. There were still a chance Godfrey the fresh vegetable could pop it and plod would have to get a bit lively when it crossed over into murder. I doubt H listened to me, and I'll bet within hours half the villains on the estate knew it were H's handiwork. You can correct me if I'm wrong, H (wink).

Uncle told me on the blower that there'd be no more notes left for me, "I won't be sending anyone down the estate again, son. I've gotta start switching it up. You know Cyril's on the main road? The barbers?"

"Yeah, I get my barnet cut there, Uncle."

"Good for you. Well, above Cyril's is a bedsit, right? I want you to nip round every day. What is it, a minute or two from you?"

"Yeah, just round the corner."

"Well, you nip round there every day and you have a look up at the bedsit window. If the curtains are drawn it means you gimme a buzz straight away. I'll give you a new number to remember. Now, I reckon you should go have a shufty about one o clock every day. One, or thereabouts. You don't have to be cock-on, but let's say *one*, all right?"

"Weekends as well?"

"That's right. Weekend's as well. We got a fair bit o' work coming up, son. Now, remember this new number …"

My next piece of work was to be in a Maida Vale, West London. This were gonna be a tricky fucker to pull off. My mark lived in the basement flat of a large Edwardian three storey gaff, and after a full week of surveillance it became apparent that the only place I'd be able to do him was when he was either coming or going to his flat. This were furthered frustrated by the fact that he only ever left to go to the corner shop a couple of doors down the street. Add to this that there were never any free parking spaces on the road, and it were looking decidedly riskier every day.

I passed my concerns on to Uncle and he just said that if it weren't do-able it weren't do-able, but he gave me another day to think about it. I went back to Maida Vale, this time on the tube and foot. I timed it so I'd be there when my mark usually went to the shop. I watched him leave the basement, walk to the shop, stay in there for about two minutes and then return back to his flat with his groceries. This were the only opportunity I were gonna get.

There were no point going back on the motorbike to do the job, like I said, there weren't no parking spaces and the tube were just around the corner. Once down in the underground I could head in any direction I wanted. Doing it without the bike meant I wouldn't have the cover of my helmet, which were a bit scary, but I figured that there would be other times in the future when I'd have to be 'exposed' so to speak, so I might as well get some experience of it.

The beauty of this job were that the flat was in the basement. My mark would have to descend the steps with his groceries to get to the door and it were out of view of pedestrians. Another problem popped up though. There was really no space or recess to step back into and hide as he descended. This meant that I would have to either break into the flat and wait for him to get down the steps to pop him, or pop him when he's coming down the steps. Popping him as he's coming down the steps were a bit worrying. If any pedestrian were passing, they might see this poor cunt falling down or falling back on to the steps.

Getting on the tube at Maida Vale I were silently debating whether or not I should call Uncle. What would I say though? *Too difficult? Not in my league? I'm bottling it? Ain't you got something easier, Uncle?* No, my pride weren't gonna let me pull a sicky. This is what I were now and I had to take the shit with the smooth. If I didn't do it Uncle would just get somebody else to step in, and probably never offer me another piece of work. My career would be over before I'd really got into my stride.

The nerves kicked in by the time I got to Paddington. I climbed out of the underground and went for a walk. Two options: wait at the door exposed and run the risk of some pedestrian cunt getting an eyeful, or break in and do him when he opens the door and steps inside. The problem with breaking-in were the fact I'd never done it before and didn't know my capabilities or speed. Plus, I didn't know if the basement were wired up to the main gaff's security alarm or not. *Fuck!*

I got home and I were sat in the kitchen having a cuppa when H knocked. I were fretting over Maida Vale and not in a good mood. H had come to tell me that he were gonna start his taxation of the skag pushers that night. He had it all worked out, knew where they went and at roughly what times. He were doing it with Vinny. H was impressed with Vinny's performance in turning Godfrey into a vegetable. I were giving H short shrift and he knew it, "S'up with you, moody bollocks? You got a boat like a slapped arse you cunt!" I snapped, "Fuck off, H. I'm all right."

"Ooo," putting on a camp voice, "Get her! You got the painters in, love?"

"You don't wanna be taxing those smack rats you know. You could come a cropper."

"Leave it out. I know what I'm doing. I'm not having these skanky little fucks come round here selling their poison. Nah, fuck that! This is a respectable estate this is. If they think they can just bowl up here n' knock their shit out without paying a bit o' tax, well they can go take a running fucking jump!"

FIFTEEN

Do what you fear and fear disappears.

David Joseph Schwartz

As the tube train pulled into Maida Vale station I stood up, braced myself and stepped out on to the platform. I could feel the Glock with the silencer already screwed on rubbing against my chest. It were in the lining of my raincoat and I made sure not to brush up against anyone. My kettle said 2.15pm and I'd seen my mark go shopping four days on the trot at around 2.30. I were praying he was a consistent creature of habit when it came to timekeeping.

I took a left out of the station and headed to his street. It were drizzling, which was good, and it looked like it could start pissing it down soon, which was even better. I slowly, but not obviously slowly, started walking down his street. I kept my head down and pulled the collar up on my raincoat, not exactly Humphrey Bogart style, I weren't trying to look cool, I were trying to be fucking invisible.

I realized I might to be too early so I stopped, bent down and pretend to tie my shoelaces. Nobody were watching so I drew the charade out for as long as I could. As I stood up an Elderly Lady came up from one of the basement flats, looked at me and then looked up at the sky. I knew she were gonna try engage me with that Great British pastime of complaining about the fucking weather so I sped up a little bit.

I were about 4 doors away when he came out of the gate and headed down towards – what I hoped would be – the corner shop. This meant I had about five minutes to get in place. I darted down the steps to the basement flat and waited. He were definitely gonna see me when he started descending but there were nothing else I could do, having decided I weren't up to breaking and entering.

I took aim at the empty steps and waited. The heavens had opened up now and it were cats and dogs. I noticed he didn't have an umbrella when he left so he'd probably rush back trying not to get too soaked. I wondered what he'd buying. *Probably just the essentials: loaf, milk, maybe some butter and a packet of ham to make a sandwich with, or maybe some cheese – or maybe the cunt might stay in the shop until the shower ceased – fuck! How long am I gonna be here? What if he ain't gone to the corner shop and he's decided to venture out into the big wide world? He could have gone bleeding shopping on Oxford Street for all I know, and I could be stuck here like a fucking mug for hours!*

After what seemed like hours but were only a couple of minutes, or vice versa, I saw signs of life: his shoed plates of meat on the first step. By the second step I could see his legs, third, fourth, until finally he were in full frame and half way down. We caught eyes momentarily and he didn't even have to time to be shocked or horrified. Pfft pfft pfft! He's falls face down, belly flops and lands inches from me. I put the Glock back in my inner coat pocket, step over him and start to climb the steps.

By the 4th step it suddenly felt like I were half way up Mount Everest and my oxygen tank had run out. I stopped dead and greedily sucked in the moist air. Up until that moment I'd never really understood what the word *petrified* meant. I had turned to fucking stone, calcified. I really couldn't move. It felt like my mind was screaming at my body to obey it and get lively but my body were sticking the V's up at it and poking its tongue out, giving it, *"Make me, you cunt!"* like a sweary petulant child.

No, I weren't going anywhere. I were in deep schtuck! Panic burned through my *out of order* body and I started to think that maybe I would never move again. I were a piss drenched, graffiti smeared, broken elevator in the tower block from Hell. This was it; I were doomed to stay stuck on these steps for all eternity. Maida Vale, West London on a pissing down day and only the corpse – I'd created – for company, and company I couldn't even see because it were behind me and I couldn't turn my head.

I wanted to scream for help but couldn't even get my gob working properly. I could feel a big lump growing in my throat and I thought it were gonna choke me. Suddenly I were able to concentrate on something: *a fucking siren of all things*. It could have been fire, Old Bill or ambulance, but whatever it was it brought me back to function.

I got to the top of the steps and immediately crossed over the road. I'd forgotten which direction I had planned on taking and simply walked away directionless. It were *really* pissing it down now and I noticed people scurrying into their gaffs and cars for shelter. I kept striding forward hoping that my internal GPS would soon start kicking in.

Everything's a blur after that until I found myself sat in a Wimpy bar in Earls Court. I'm assuming I went into the underground and hopped trains going in every direction for a couple of hours, because that had been the plan, though I couldn't say whether I stuck to it or not though. I'd experienced lost time.

I remember sitting in that Wimpy bar staring at a burger and telling myself over and over that this were normal. Why *wouldn't* I be sat in a Wimpy in Earls Court, soaked to the fucking skin with a silenced Glock in my pocket, after having murdered a complete stranger in cold blood?

It were dark by the time I left the Wimpy. I descended back into the underground and headed down to see my old mate Mr. Thames, *he just keeps rollin', he keeps on rollin' along*. I don't know why I chose Blackfriars Bridge to let the silenced Glock fall from my hands, I must have exited the underground nearby. I do remember hearing it hit the water though, and I panicked because my fucked-up state of mind tricked me into thinking the splash it made were like a fucking great elephant had decided to dive in for a bit of a frolic. I knew nobody had heard it or seen me drop it or even given me a second glance whilst I stood there though.

I remembered to remember that I were invisible. I were Mr. fucking Nobody. I just kept telling myself that nobody knew me, nobody really knew anybody else and nobody really cared about nobody else. I were a nobody, and after meditating on the fact for a bit, I started to inhabit that *thing* we all agree on called reality again.

SIXTEEN

Have no fear of perfection – you'll never reach it.

Salvador Dali

It was the morning after the Maida Vale job and I were laid on my bed thinking how lucky I was, *blessed* even, because I had such a small circle of loved ones. Mum, Sis' and H. The holy trinity. I figured some people in my game would have a lot more people they *truly* loved and eventually that would become problematic. The more people you love, the more ammo your enemies have. You could say I were starting to think on a kind of 'war footing'.

The meltdown I'd had on those basement flat steps was, I reasoned, just another price I paid for the career I'd chosen. It rattled me, sure, but then don't *any* job come with occupational hazards? I suppose I were trying to convince myself that if moments of pure debilitating panic were the price I were gonna have to pay then so be it. I had handled it well. I'd gotten away from the scene of the crime without incident. I should be proud of myself.

What I needed to do now was create – as Uncle used to say- 'Distance' from my loved ones, so that if it ever came on top, they'd be protected. I weren't thinking about protecting them from the Old Bill, no, it went without saying that 'legally' I hadn't put my loved ones at risk, I were thinking about the risks that came from the kind of company I were keeping, or rather, working for.

Whoever Uncle were taking on these hits for, it were inarguable that they were seriously big players in the crime game. Even though I knew nothing and never asked about my marks, I were still the lynchpin that connected these clients of Uncle's to the murders. At what point would I become more strategically useful dead rather than alive? You've gotta believe me when I say that this weren't fear about losing my life, the fear was all about Mum and Sis' getting harmed because of what I'd been up to.

I think what I'm trying to say, is that it had really dawned on that I were so deep in the mix of it all now, I were a major ingredient and without me this fucking murder cake that Uncle were baking wouldn't be the same. Was I becoming a liability for him? Was I becoming so 'indispensable' to the point that would I need dispensing with? How could I go about asking my puppet master these kinds of questions without alarming him and sowing seeds of doubt? I were beginning to realize that the murder for hire industry was seriously lacking in the human resources department.

So yeah, foremost on my mind was this 'distancing' and protection. How I was gonna achieve it were a problem that I would have to solve on my tod. It would be lonely, but then I were a natural born loner and I'd had plenty of experience of solitary solutions, so it weren't impossible that I could come up with something.

Three days later I rode over to the chippy and picked up the first of my four 'fish suppers' worth 10 grand. The next day I went with Mum to a second-hand car lot and bought her a Ford Escort that were only a couple of plates old. She were thrilled and so was Sis', and we decided that we would start visiting the

Kent Seaside on weekends from now on, presuming the curtains weren't drawn at the window of the bedsit above Cyril's barbers on those days, and I'd have to call Uncle instead.

Not long after this, H rolled out his taxation scheme. Him, Vinny and a big bruiser called Bertie would simply approach smack pushers on the estate and demand cash from them in lieu of not dishing out a good hiding. It were very rudimentary. The pickings weren't exactly 'rich' either. Those low-level rats were mainly knocking out £5 bags of skag and one night H – *the tax inspector* – only managed to frighten out of them the sum total of 50 quid to be split between him, Vinny and Bertie. One of the rats had told H that they had already had 'protection' and that *his* weren't needed. H smashed one of those really heavy bottles of Lucozade – that they sold at the time -over his napper.

I give it, "The fuck are you doing it for, H?" It ain't worth it."

"It's a piece o' piss. They just hand it over. Fucking mugs."

"Yeah, but eventually the cunts that supply 'em are gonna do something about it, and you're right up in the frame."

"They don't scare me. I know who they are. They're fuck all! Couple o' Turks or something from over the river."

A few nights later H were leaving the local at chucking out time, a van pulls up, three goons jump out, bash him over the head, bundle him into the back and drive off at a fair clip. Vinny got a call at his flat early morning. It were H and he was being held prisoner until he could come up with 2 large they reckoned he'd 'taxed' their pusher of. They hadn't bashed him up too bad, *yet*, but if the dough weren't forthcoming sharpish, they were gonna get busy on him with baseball bats.

Vinny reckoned H didn't sound too worried on the blower, but I told him that obviously he wouldn't. H were a tough nut and he weren't gonna give his kidnappers the satisfaction of thinking they were gonna crack him easily.

H had told Vinny not to do anything and that they'd eventually let him go. On hearing this, his kidnappers grabbed the phone from H and assured Vinny that they would definitely *do summink* to him and they had no intention of letting him go until they were given their tax rebate. I were fucking seething. I felt like putting a couple of bullets in Vinny and Bertie for going along with H's fucking stupid caper in the first place.

Vinny kept looking at me with a fucking gormless, quizzical look on his boat. I didn't need this shit and couldn't think straight. I could obviously get hold of 2 large, but if H were insisting that the ransom was under no circumstances to be paid, well, rock and a fucking hard place without a paddle. Vinny were fucking useless and I were really beginning to resent him. Bertie bowled up and proposed we got tooled up, reckon we were coming over with the ransom, and then go in all guns blazing to free our fellow cowboy. There were no point even replying to this kind of stupidity.

We went to Vinny's flat and sat by the phone waiting for H and/or his kidnappers to call. I told Vinny and Bertie I'd take the call and that they were to keep fucking schtum. The last thing I wanted were those two pillocks in charge of hostage negotiations. I would willingly cough up 2 large to get my best mate back safe. It sounded like it weren't the kidnappers I had to convince though. I knew how stubborn H could be, and I were now in the strange position of thinking how I were gonna convince the hostage to let me pay the ransom to his kidnappers.

I were sat for hours in Vinny's flat staring at the phone, willing it to ring, while Vinny and Bertie were fantasising about freeing H in an *Iranian Embassy Siege* like rescue. I never opened my trap but I'm sure they twigged on that I thought they were cunts.

Vinny's Mum came home from work and asked Vinny, quite reasonably, why we were dossing about in her front room. Vinny told her to keep her schnoz out and they got into a right barney. This were giving me a fucking headache now and I were worrying that H were either gonna turn up dead or fucked for life. I think I might have piped up and told 'em to stop with agg, but I do know that even if H or the kidnappers had rung, we wouldn't have been able to hear it over the shouting and bawling.

Vinny's Mum finally fucked off to get ready for the bingo and we were still stuck in radio silence. Bertie had now jacked in the SAS fantasies at least, and were talking about the possibility that we might have to do the unthinkable and get Old Bill involved. Vinny flared up at this, and for a minute it looked him and Bertie were gonna go at it with each other.

A whole day of waiting for a dog to ring would send even the most mentally stable cunt over the edge. I were rattling and every time Vinny and Bertie opened their gobs I felt murderous. I genuinely believe that if I'd have been tooled up, they would have both got plugged. I'm not saying I would have offed 'em, but I think my nerves would have stretched to a kneecapping of 'em both.

H was, effectively, a Schrodinger's cat at that point. I didn't know if he were dead or alive and the suspense was fucking killing me. The thought of getting Old Bill involved weren't feeling too outlandish by this point.

There's a loud knock at the door and Vinny gives it, "I know who it is. Ignore it."

We ignore it and then the knocking starts up again. I give it, "You better answer it, Vinny. They're not going away."

"Nah, it'll be that cunt, Leonard. He'll be after the score I owe him."

Again, the fucking knocking, only this time accompanied by shouting we couldn't make out. Vinny sighs and shouts through as he heads to the door, "I'm coming Leonard, you cunt!"

Vinny opens the door and stood there beaming from ear to ear is a bashed-up H, "Who you calling a cunt, you cunt?" asks H.

I'm not casting aspersions on your account of what happened, H, but I only have your side of the story, so I don't whether it's what actually went down. What I will say, is that however you pulled it off, you pulled a fucking blinder mate.

According to H, when they nabbed him, they put a hood over his head and gave him a few digs in the back of the van. They then tied him to a chair in the back of a stinking Kebab shop somewhere over the river. They gave him a few more digs then started pulling out instruments, reckoning they were gonna torture him unless he arranged to have the 2 grand ransom handed over.

H said he told 'em to go fuck themselves and that they weren't getting a farthing out of him, which I don't doubt he would have said. They then told him to call someone to start arranging the payment. H said he resisted and got a few more digs and threats of plyers on his fingernails and stuff, but eventually gave them Vinny's phone number.

Vinny had already confirmed that H didn't want the ransom paying so that's where I got dragged into it.

H said he laughed in their faces and told 'em to do their worst because they were signing their own death certificates. He told 'em that they'd nabbed the wrong person, yes, he'd taxed their rats, but added that he were 'connected' and that they should have done their homework before plucking him. H told *them* to get on the blower and find out how fucked they were.

At first The Kidnappers told him he were talking shite, but as you've already seen, H is a persistent fucker and very persuasive. He got right in their ears and finally one of 'em decided to do a ring around to see if their hostage really was connected to a *someone.*

H told 'em that they were either gonna have to top him or let him go, because there were not a cat in hell's chance they were getting paid. He told 'em that if they let him go without any more digs, he'd give them his word his Uncle wouldn't have them buried alive.

When The Kidnappers were informed by someone on the blower that their hostage was indeed who he said he was, they only really had *one* decision to make; should they kill H to try cover up what they'd done or let him go and hope he didn't get his fearsome Uncle on the warpath. These weren't heavyweights. The drug business had yet to attract the really serious players, and these mugs were more opportunistic than organized.

They untied H and offered him their hands to shake, sealing a truce. They put the hood back on and dropped him at the edge of the estate. H said he could suss they were terrified of repercussions, but that they'd kept quiet on the journey to South London. H had seen their boats and weren't likely forget 'em. H said he too kept quiet and didn't rub their noses in the shit they'd done on the carpet, but I doubt that. I'm sure he would have been gloating on that trip back home, and unable to keep his cakehole shut.

This all reinforced to me how powerful and feared Uncle really was. His name did carry weight; fucking tonnes of it. H were very lucky he were related to him. I weren't going to dob H in it and tell Uncle that he'd put his name up to his captors. I remembered Uncle once telling me that he were sick of mugs using his name whenever they got in schtuck with other villains. I knew H wouldn't tell Uncle either for precisely the same reason. H still weren't aware of what I was doing for Uncle and I had to keep it like that for all our safety, so I pretend I didn't hear that H had used Uncle's name.

H still hadn't learned his lesson mind. No, he'd heard one of his abductors mention something about Whitechapel, so he were convinced that's where they were from, or based. He said he weren't gonna carry on with his skag taxation scheme, but he were definitely gonna get revenge for the kidnapping. I sighed and reminded H that he'd gotten off lightly, but he were having none of it. No, he were gonna get revenge and that was that. I told him he could count me out, it were fucking stupid. H didn't give a toss and replied that he'd be doing it himself anyway.

A few days later the curtains were drawn above the barbers so I got on the dog to Uncle. We met later that afternoon on Waterloo Bridge. I did wonder whether he'd got wind of his nephew's little kidnapping caper, but if he had he didn't bring it up.

"You're doing well, son. A natural."

"Cheers, Uncle."

"It's time to go international."

"International?"

"Abroad. France. You're gonna take out a frog. How'd you feel about that, eh?"

"Uh, yeah … no problem."

"You ever been to France?"

"Nah, just Spain."

"Been to Marseille a few times. It's more like Spain than France."

"I like Spain."

"Me too. Probably plot up there when I retire. You'll have to come n' stay."

"Yeah, thanks. I will."

"I'm not going that Puerto Banus. Too flashy if you ask me."

"Is it?"

"Oh yeah, full o' villains on the lam as well. I'll probably go somewhere quiet."

A week later I was stood at a bus stop in Deptford at 5.30 am with a big flask of tea and a Tupperware box full of cheese and pickle sarnies in my duffel bag, as I waited for my ride to Calais to turn up. An HGV hissed to a stop and I climbed up into the cabin. We'll call the driver Tommy. He were a black bloke in his late 40's and had been trucking for over twenty years. Tommy were one of those people it's hard not to take an instant shine to. He were originally from Canning Town but now lived in Camden. If there were an Olympic category for yapping, Tommy would have been a gold fucking medallist.

Tommy were really interesting though and the time flew as we headed down to Dover. He told me stories about growing up in Canning Town and some of the shit he had to put up with because of his skin colour, but he said he learned pretty quickly to befriend the local nasty bastards and managed to avoid the fate of a lot other black kids growing up there. He were the proud owner of seven HGV's and were in the process of buying his 8th. He had a good haulage business and he thought himself blessed.

Tommy never asked me what I were being smuggled into for France *for* and I never asked him if he knew *why* I were being smuggled in. It were just nice, pleasant conversation and it put me at ease.

Just before we got into Dover we pulled into services and Tommy told me it were time to get in the trailer. I climbed over ducting that was palleted up ready to be delivered on the other side. Tommy showed me a spot that had been prepared for me.

It were a gap surrounded by ducting with a few dust sheets laid down for me to park my arse on. I climbed over and sat down and Tommy said he'd see me in France.

I got comfortable, pulled out the torch I'd packed and read a book by its light. It were the best seller, 'Kane and Abel' by Jeffrey Archer and it were riveting. Two and a half hours later we pull up at services just outside Calais and the doors open. I climb out and Tommy tells me he'll see me later. As soon as he pulls away a tall biker wearing a one-piece leather suit pulls up on a Honda Nighthawk. I don't know what nationality he were because not one word passed between us. He handed me a full-face helmet, I put it on, climbed aboard and away we went. I pulled my gloves out of my duffel bag and slipped them on as we headed South.

He were a good rider and really throttling it. Uncle's instructions – which were very basic – played on a loop in my mind. So far everything were going to plan and I felt good. In fact, I remember thinking that I couldn't wait to get back into the HGV trailer so I could continue reading Jeffrey Archer's potboiler.

After about half an hour of him clocking around 60-70 we pull up at what can only be described as a large wooden warehouse in the middle of nowhere. It were built out of wide timber slats that had been painted matt black. I suppose it were like a mix between a large stable and a huge Scandinavian cabin, if that makes sense.

There's a gravel incline of about 60 meters that leads to a small, standalone office, built in the style of the main building, and this is where Uncle had told me my mark were gonna be. The mark's Audi convertible were parked up outside just as Uncle said it would be. I'd obviously let the photo of this geezer burn into my memory, but I weren't sure whether somebody else might be in the office when I entered.

Uncle had stressed that if there were, they'd have to go as well. I didn't have a problem with this, as long as it weren't a tea-pot lid I'd have to snuff. Uncle assured me it wouldn't be. The intelligence they had on this mark was that he were in that office alone 99 times out of a 100.

The biker pulls out a Walther PPK from inside his leather onesie and hands it me. Uncle had told me it weren't gonna be wearing a suppressor, *no need* he said. I prime it and let it hang by my side as I walk down towards the office. I notice to the left of me a couple of motors parked up by the entrance to this ware-house, but I don't hear or see nobody. There's a loud grinding noise coming from the warehouse and it clicks why I don't need a silencer on the PPK.

I'm about 10 paces from the office when I see my mark sat at a desk talking on the blower and flipping through some paper-work as he yaps. He's not looking up, engrossed in his call, and, fortunately this looks like a barney he's having. He's definitely not looking like a happy chappy, which means he distracted.

I open the office door and he's clearly bollocking some cunt on the other end of the line in French. I take five steps in and aim. He looks up and frowns as I fire. One shot, straight in the middle of his forehead that sends him flopping back in his chair. I take another step forward and put 2 more in his head. I turn and walk back up to the Honda Nighthawk. I hand the biker the Walther, climb aboard and we're off again.

I reckon it were 40 seconds from pulling up, doing the dirty, and getting back on our toes. Money for old rope really. All I was thinking about was what were gonna happen to Abel now that he were a waiter at The Hotel Plaza in New York. Couldn't wait to get back in that trailer and pick up where I'd left Jeffrey Archer's epic tale of sibling rivalry.

Tommy had unloaded his ducting, and on the way back over the channel I were hidden behind empty pallets, lost in the novel, thinking absolutely nish about the fact that I'd just executed some poor bastard.

I got back in the cab just outside Dover and Tommy continued telling me stories about the old days. He dropped me off at the same spot in Deptford he'd picked me up from just over 12 hours earlier. I got on the tube and were home in time to watch *Telly Addicts* with Noel Edmonds on the BBC. Me, Mum and Sis' considered ourselves experts and usually got all the questions right.

I were in bed by 11 and engrossed in the novel by the light of one of them Anglepoise lamps I'd recently bought from an hoister on the estate. Archer, I decided, were a fucking terrific writer and I would definitely go out and buy all his other books, or rather, I'd give the hoister who'd flogged me the lamp the list and she'd lift 'em for me for a third of the recommended retail price.

SEVENTEEN

A woman simply is, but a man must become.

Camille Paglia

I bought a few canvasses and acrylic paints and did some painting in my bedroom. I started experimenting by doing away with brushes and using my fingers to dab thick blotches on the canvas. I'd squeeze the paint straight out of the tubes on to the tip of my fingers and just randomly plop the acrylic down. It were very relaxing and – after taking ages to dry – the results weren't too bad. Chaotic but colourful.

I never showed them to anyone. These were just for me. It were my therapy I suppose. I'd done about a dozen of these 'painting's' and stacked them in my bedroom. Mum would see them when she'd change my bedsheets and every time she did she told me she'd never been able to understand *that modern art.* I told her I were just doodling, messing about. Which were true.

One night I grabbed them and took them down to the bins. I sprayed a couple of cans of lighter fuel on them and had a bonfire. An old bloke came and had a look. He asked me why I were burning them and I simply replied that I enjoyed watching 'em burn. He nodded his head like he knew exactly what I meant, lit a fag and stood there with me watching until the paintings were cremated. He then said he hoped I were gonna clean up the mess the bonfire had left. He went into his flat and returned with a yard brush and dustpan and I dutifully swept up and poured the ashes into one of the communal bins.

I now had just under one hundred and ten large in the peter under my bed and realized I needed to speak to the only person I could about this situation. I met Uncle on Westminster Bridge, "What do you wanna do with it, son?"

"I dunno, Uncle. I were hoping you might have a suggestion. I don't wanna put it in a bank."

'No, no, course not. I thought you might o' been spreading it about a bit to be honest."

"Spreading it about?"

"You know, putting it out of the street. Making it work for ya."

"No."

"So you just got it salted away, eh?"

"Yeah."

"Mmm ... not a *bad* problem to have though, eh?"

"I'm not complaining. I just want it somewhere safe, Uncle."

"Yeah, I got ya ... let me have a word with my accountant, though I reckon he'll just come back with 'buy some property'. S'all he ever says. Like a stuck bleedin' record he is."

I asked Mum again if she wanted to move somewhere nicer, but *again*, she weren't having any of it. She asked me if I were still gambling and I obviously had to reply that I was. She grilled me a bit and asked me if I were never scared about losing a big chunk. I lied and told her I were a good gambler and I had more than enough dough stashed to cover any big losses.

I can't honestly say that Mum *really* bought I were a successful gambler. A part of me likes to think she knew I were selling her a load of bollocks. I reckon, deep down, she knew I were bang at it. I think she might have probably thought I were grafting with H and his family, but she'd have never in a million years tippled to exactly what kind of grafting I were up to. If she *had* found out, I know she'd have been horrified and it would have probably killed her off.

When Uncle finally got back to me with some financial advice, he just parroted his accountant and told me to start going round property auctions, buying up cheap houses and flats with a view to the land they stood on one day being little goldmines. He gave it, "I'm talking toilets, son. Absolute shithouses. Snap 'em up. Trust me, one day they're gonna be worth summink."

I told him I weren't keen on having my name down on owners' registers and legal papers. He smiled at me and just said, "You put 'em in your Mum's name, you sausage."

When I explained to Mum that I were wanting to go into the property business and that I'd need her help, she didn't bat an eyelid. I didn't even have to spiel her about it were because I wanted to avoid tax or any other nonsense. She were game and over the next few weeks we were visiting property auctions all across London. She loved it.

I knew I'd have to keep a chunk back to see us right until the next piece of wetwork popped up, so I decided we were gonna have the hundred large down on the caper and keep 10 back to live on.

Over six weeks we bought 7 small gaffs from Barnard Marcus auctioneers. The gaffs were in desperate need of repair in shitty areas that might – fingers crossed – one day magically become 'redeveloped'.

It's hard to imagine nowadays how easy it were to get into the property game back then. Some people at the time reckoned they knew that property prices were gonna go through the fucking roof, but obviously they didn't or else a grafting little cunt like me would have never had the opportunity to become a landlord. This were all possible of course, because cash really was king back then, and you could literally get away with murder, get paid for it and invest your earnings with very few questions asked.

We never touched the properties, never even saw a couple of them, but Mum was made up that – more or less – overnight she'd become a fucking property mogul. O n *paper*, but still.

It weren't long after this that one morning I'm laid on my bed reading Stephen King's 'The Stand' when there's a knock at the door. Mum and Sis' were out shopping so I went and answered it.

There's a bloke in a scruffy suit and cheap raincoat stood there. My heart suddenly starts beating out my chest. You just know Old Bill instantly and my feet felt like they were dragging me down through the floorboards, through the roof below us right down into some concrete quicksand. He flashed his warrant card, told me his name then asked mine.

I must have answered because the next thing I remember he's stood in our kitchen and I'm making the cunt a cup of tea. The buzzing in my ear and the burning in my stomach and the almost debilitating sudden tiredness I were feeling started to fade, as I reasoned that if the cunt were here to pinch me for one of my pieces of work he would have come mob handed and tooled up. I handed him his tea and he asked me if I knew *so and so*.

What had happened were quite comical as it turned out. You remember that Chief cunt from the stone yard who had me over for 30 large and topped himself? Eighteen months after his expiration, his missus had found 1835 quid in used notes stashed in the garage. Instead of pocketing the dough the silly cow had called Old Bill and told 'em that this were proof of her suspicion that her dead hubby had been involved with some unsavoury characters before his demise.

When Old Bill matched up the serial numbers on the dough to a security van heist, they started thinking this silly moo might be on to something. Maybe her old fella's suicide had been made to look that way. Now, I'm stood there with this Old Bill cunt in my kitchen and I'm instantly cottoning on to what had happened. The dough I'd been paid for the hit, that I'd consequently lent to my stone yard Chief, had obviously been lifted in this security van heist. *Hats off, Uncle really did have his fingers in virtually every pie that were being baked in London.*

This D.I. tells me they are contacting ex-employees of the dead cunt to see if they knew anything about his possible links to people who could conceivably be involved in serious crime. I really wanted to laugh but remained stoney faced and faux shocked. I told the D.I. that as far as I knew, my old employer was a man of great integrity and a fine upstanding citizen and that I found it hard to imagine he could possibly be involved with the odious criminal fraternity. Or words to that effect.

I were more concerned about how the D.I. had located me. I weren't on the books at the stone yard, not that I told plod that. The D.I. told me one of my old work colleagues remembered I'd told him which estate I lived on. D.I. reckoned it were easy to find me. Which really got my goat to be honest.

The D.I. fucked off after about ten minutes, thanking me for my help and handing me his card in case I remembered anything in the future that might be of interest to him. *Yeah, right.*

I weren't rattled. I were covered. Nobody – to my knowledge – knew that I'd lent the dead cunt 30 large. I were instantly strategizing though.

If anyone *could* connect me to the 30 large loan and plod showed up again, I'd play it dumb; *Me? Lend some cunt 30 grand? You're having a laugh! Look at me! Do I look like I've got 30k lying about? I wish I had 30k I could lend some cunt! I worked at that yard cash in hand. The fuck were I doing if I had thirty thousand pound to lend out? Do me a favour! Leave it out! I don't even have a bleedin' bank account. Someone's pulling your pisser, officer.*

I also got the feeling this D.I. were just going through the motions, box ticking because the dead cunt's missus had given the station some earache. And in any case, even if they could prove I'd lent the dead cunt 30 large, they could never prove the security van dough his missus found were the same dough I'd lent him. I didn't give it another thought.

That afternoon I went to have a peep above the barbershop. The curtains were drawn so I gave Uncle a call and we arranged to meet on Blackfriars Bridge. I knew soon as I got a few paces away from him he weren't happy. He had a right fucking pus on his boat as he leaned over the railings looking down at the water. He were chaining Rothmans, which weren't unusual, but he had a certain aggression in the way he were puffing on 'em.

"You got summink to tell me?" He snapped.

"Eh?" I frowned.

"Old Bill at your drum this morning." He hissed, "You wanna fill me in or what?"

"How the ..."

"Never you mind *how* I know. What I *wanna* know is why the fuck they was there?"

I had never seen Uncle like this and it weren't very nice, in fact it were fucking scary and I quickly gave him the SP of what had gone down. I could see the mixture of anxiety, worry and anger slowly vanish off his face as I reeled off the embarrassing – *for me* – story.

Uncle gives it, all incredulous, "He had you over for 30 thousand?"

Sheepish, "Yeah."

"Fucksake, what *were* you thinkin', son?"

"Well, that's the problem, Uncle. I *weren't* thinkin'"

"Not half you weren't!"

I couldn't *not* ask Uncle how he knew Old Bill had paid me a visit. He told me he had people 'looking out for me' and not to worry about it and that it were beneficial for all our sakes and reminded me we were engaged in very heavy villainy and that it would be fucking stupid not to all have the bases covered. He were right of course, but I couldn't stop thinking about who it were on the estate that 'had my back'. It definitely weren't H or any of his family and it weren't my Mum or Sis'. Possibly one of the neighbours, but I wouldn't have had any of 'em down as spies or 'protectors'. I were now getting really fucking paranoid. Let's be honest. I were being spied on.

Around this time, H decided that he were now ready to take revenge against his kidnappers. He figured enough time had elapsed for them to think they'd gotten away with it, and their guard would have now dropped. I told him he were just asking for trouble, but I think you all know H by now, so I don't have to tell you how he replied.

H remembered that a lad on the estate called Bishop had once been courting a Richard from Whitechapel, and he told Bish that he needed his help in some reconnaissance he were gonna be doing on Jack The Ripper's old killing ground. Bish – who were a decent lad – found himself roped into the caper and he weren't exactly over the moon at the prospect of loitering around the East End looking for kidnappers with H.

H let slip to me that he were seriously gonna damage the first kidnapper he got his mitts on. He reckoned that a good beating wouldn't suffice because the cunt would eventually recover from it. H was planning on leaving a visible mark. Something really fucking nasty. He were gonna fill a Jif Lemon with ammonia and squirt it in their face.

There'd been a spate of these fucking horrible attacks in and around London at the time, and the damage they did to victims were severe and often face melting. The poor bastards that had been attacked spoke of being 'on fire' and praying for death so the agonizing pain would stop. Now, before you give it, *wait a fucking minute, how can this cunt get all moralistic all of a sudden? He murders people for money!* You're right of course, and in one respect it's pure fucking hypocrisy, but I'm telling you now, all the money in the world couldn't get me to squirt some cunt in the face with ammonia or acid.

There were a well-known story going around at the time that a Chelsea football hooligan had squirted a rival hooligan with ammonia when they were supposed to be having a straightener. This Chelsea hooligan's victim were so badly burned that he had to have years of reconstructive surgery on his boat. He were also left a shivering wreck mentally and became a terrified recluse.

Not long after his trial collapsed on a technicality this cowardly Chelsea cunt was allowed to walk free, but ended up being thrown off the top of a multi-storey carpark in an attempt to make it look like suicide. The geezers who did it weren't heavy, they were just allegedly a non-partisan group of football hooligans who had come together to mete out some real justice, appalled at what had happened. In fairness to Old Bill, they never delved too far into the case, they were just as sickened by the cowardly attack as everyone else.

I reminded H about this, but he said the circumstances were different. This weren't about silly football hooligans, it were about revenge for kidnapping; proper grown up stuff. H's plans would have to go on ice though. He got pinched for fencing stolen motor parts and because of previous was portioned off with 18 months in Wandsworth nick.

H took it in his stride and remarked that he were looking forward to a lie-down for a few months to recharge his batteries. He were instantly protected by virtue of who he was related to, but he really didn't need it. This were a Cat B nick and verging on Cat C status so it weren't exactly Alcatraz. H sent me regular VO's and I never missed a visit. I were hoping H were gonna forget about his little Jif Lemon and its ammonia content.

Uncle started mixing things up again. Instead of me having to nip round and see if the curtains were drawn above Cyril's barbershop, I were now to give Uncle a buzz religiously on Monday's, Wednesdays and Fridays at precisely 2pm, on a new number of course. If he wanted a meet he'd say "meet me at A" which meant Blackfriars, or "meet me at B" which meant Vauxhall, and so on. If he didn't need a meet he'd simply pick up the phone and put it straight back down, leaving me with an abrupt dead line and the knowledge that there were no work on the immediate horizon.

I'd had a fallow few months and my 10 large had now become 6. Truth be told, I couldn't wait to get back on the horse and start earning. It were becoming boring without H around, less stressful of course, but still boring. Vinny asked me if I'd be interested in some graft involving double glazing but I knocked him back.

When my next job came in from Uncle I were over the bleedin' moon, even though he reckoned it were gonna be a bit 'complicated'. He wanted me to do a disposal on top of the hit, and for this I were getting 50 grand. Uncle also explained that because of some cash flow agg he was having, the bounty would be spread out over a number of months. He asked I were OK with this. I told him it were fine. If I couldn't trust Uncle, well I mean, who could I trust?

The mark lived right up in Hertfordshire near a place called Childwickbury. It were proper out in the sticks and the first time in my life I'd ever really seen anything you could call 'country-side'. I used to take the M25 up there for reconnaissance and it would take me an hour up and and an hour and half back down. I bought a fourth hand Honda 250 Superdream from *Exchange and Mart* for the job. I paid cash and never changed the log book so the bike could never be traced to me.

I'd been back and forth to Hertfordshire for over two weeks trying to get my minces' on the mark. He lived in what could only be described as a cross between a cottage and a farm house. It even had one of those thatched roofs, which you never got to see in inner city London.

The gaff were sandwiched between a row of about a dozen small cottages that were bookended by two large detached houses. It looked to me like that this place were built by a farmer back in the day and him and his family lived in the big drums while their workers lived in the small cottages. My problem weren't the architecture or the living arrangements though, my problem was the fact that my mark only ever left the gaff to go for a jog a couple of times a week.

This bloke *absolutely* knew he were on a *to do list*, the first time I spied him jogging I knew this. He were a twitchy fucker, for-ever looking over his shoulders and had that haunted expression on his mug, that only comes from knowing you're on borrowed time. Why the cunt thought it necessary to keep fit were beyond me.

Now, under any other circumstances this hit wouldn't have been problematic. The thing is though, I had to dispose of the cunt as well, and that's where I had to get thinking creatively. I couldn't tell you why Uncle weren't recruiting a disposal expert to join me in the enterprise, he knew I preferred bikes rather than motors or vans for work, but obviously he had his reasons and he trusted me enough to think I could pull it off solo.

This were a piece of work where I would have to get my hands dirty, *literally*. The first thing I had to do was work out how I were gonna get a shovel up to the kill ground without it looking odd or suspicious. The answer came when I found a German army folding shovel in an *Army & Navy* surplus store. I could fit the shovel into a *Head* bag and put it over my shoulders. So, I knew I were gonna bury my mark, the problem now was finding a potential burial plot at a point right next to where I were gonna plug him. It had to be on the route that he jogged. Another fucking problem. He didn't always jog the same route.

I were pulling my hair out in trying to figure out which route he might take on any given day. Not only were this cunt not consistent, he were also prone to cutting his jogs short and heading back to his drum. None of this would have been a problem if I were simply clipping him, in fact it would have been perfect: hardly any traffic used the route he jogged, but seeing as I were 'disposing of' as well, it were a *big* fucking problem. I thought about telling Uncle I weren't confident this were gonna be a success, but I suppose professional pride stopped me. I figured if I could pull this piece of work off, I could pull off *any* piece of work that ever came my way in the future.

After many hours of calculating, I decided that I'd dig his

grave in a wooded area. X marks the spot was about 60 feet from the road and was quite soft ground. There was plenty of bush, weeds and a decent sized dead tree trunk that I could use to place over the mound as well. It took me two days to dig the grave and disguise the soil I'd dug up to fill the grave back in. If anyone had caught me, I'd come up with some fantastical tale that I thought treasure were buried there. As daft as it might sound, it's all I could fucking come up with.

There were woodland on the other side of the road and I scouted out the best position for me to lie in wait. There were plenty of cover, large thickets and overhanging trees. I parked the bike up about a hundred feet back from the road and, even though the Superdream didn't have a traction problem on the terrain, I still considered buying an off-road bike just in case it were pissing it down on the day of execution.

On the first day I got plotted up waiting for Jogger to reach the exact point I were gonna run out and pop him, I had to back down. A car overtook the Jogger just at the point I were ready to pounce. I suppose I could have simply jumped out and done him and then dragged him further than I had planned, but no, caution prevailed. Stick to the plan.

The next day the cunt didn't go for his jog so I were hiding in this woods for six hours. The third day came and again I were foiled by a van driving past just as Jogger were at the planned point of execution. I were beginning to think that this piece of work were never gonna happen.

On the fourth day the stars aligned and I were able to rush out of my hide. I were about twelve feet from the huffing and puffing Jogger when he noticed me. He had time to clock me momentarily and he knew his time were up. The pained expression on his boat was a mixture of shock, fear, fatigue and recognition that his jogging days were over. I steadied my aim and clipped him twice in the head. His body had barely hit the tarmac before I were dragging him into the woods where I'd dug the hole.

I had huge clumps of his barnet in my leather clad mitts and I heaved and heaved until I got him in place to push into the grave. I quickly pulled away the tree trunk and thickets that were covering the mound of soil. I'd dug it out at about six feet deep and 2 feet wide. I pushed dead Jogger in the grave and he plopped down nice and prostrate.

I went and grabbed the 2 bags of Calbux quicklime (CaO) I'd hidden a week back, opened them and poured them on Jogger's corpse. Once emptied I threw the empty bags in and got busy filling the grave in with the soil: *ashes to ashes, dust to dust, quicklime to quicklime.*

I were fucking knackered by the time I'd pulled the tree trunk, thickets and dead branches over to cover the freshly dug grave. I took about 30 paces back and stared at the now very well camouflaged resting place. Happy that I'd done the best I could, I ran over to my bike parked up in the woodland on the other side of the road and sped off.

I were out of breath and my limbs were aching, but I were pleased that I'd pulled off a great piece of work, that at one time had looked impossible. I knew there'd be a search for missing Jogger, but felt confident that his corpse wouldn't be found anytime soon. I imagined that the only time it'd turn up were if the woodland were to be excavated in the – hopefully – not too near future.

EIGHTEEN

We suffer more often in imagination than in reality.

Seneca

I picked up my fish suppers from the chippy over a six-month period, sometimes 5 large, sometimes 3, never less than 2 though. I just figured that even the murder industry were feeling the bite of the recession. In the six months I'd received just short of 30 large, but didn't have any doubt I'd eventually get parcelled off for the 20 large still owed me.

It were during this period that Mum started dating a bloke called Ray. He were the same age as her, mid 40's, and lived on the Isle of Dogs. He were a big fucker and looked like he could have a row. He were a carpet fitter by trade but hadn't been working for a few months because he reckoned his haystack were fucked from all the bending over he had to do laying the carpets, which made sense. Mum seemed to really like him and I didn't have much to do with him so it were sweet.

H were out of Wandsworth and now had all sorts of plans. He seemed to have forgotten about his Jif Lemon ammonia revenge attack in Whitechapel and were now concentrating on making it in the motor trade. He'd met a lad over the wall that were connected to a car ringing operation out of Essex. A 'ringer' or 'flopper' is a stolen motor that's had its identification numbers replaced with those from a legitimate motor that's been *written off* by an insurance company. Ringing were a big and very lucrative graft in the 1980s. The bird they were handing down for it weren't excessive, and some of the ringing operations were quite sophisticated and didn't leave the grafters too exposed for a pinching.

H said he needed a few quid to get into the operation so I slung him a monkey. Everyone needs a foot up after some porridge and H were grateful. He somehow managed to get hold of a second-hand Renault 5 GT turbo and he was back and forth to Essex on a regular basis. He asked me to go with him a few times but I weren't interested. He used to go to a disco over there and it sounded like a wild west saloon from his descriptions. He said the Richards over there were 'pure filth' and reckoned he were seeing 3 or 4 different ones at any given time.

Ray started coming over to the flat most days and nights. I didn't have a problem with it, but I knew my Sis' hadn't taken a shine to him. One night I were out at the pictures watching *Dead Ringers* starring Jeremy Irons, I think. Ray had turned up with some booze and him and Mum were having a night in. Sis' had come home from the youth club early and were in the kitchen making a pot noodle as this cunt Ray were pouring some drinks.

Sis' must have answered him back or something. Nothing too cheeky according to Sis', and this cunt, a bit pissed up, gives her a backhander, knocks her flying across the kitchen and cuts her lip. Mum rushes in wondering what the fuck's going on and this cunt Ray's on his toes, shouting abuse back at Mum and Sis' as she storms out.

When I gets home, Mum had Sis' sat on a chair and she's grilling her. They're both understandably upset but Mum's convinced that Sis' ain't telling her the whole truth. Mum's got it into her head that Ray must have been fiddling with Sis' or attempting to, because she couldn't believe he'd give her a backhand for being a bit lippy. I told Mum to leave it out. I'm fucking raging over what's happened and getting angry at Mum for trying to make it something more than it were. Sis' swore that Ray hadn't laid a finger on her and he gave her the dig because she'd answered him back. I ended up shouting at Mum and we had a barney.

The next morning, Sis' were sticking to the story and Mum had accepted that Ray were just a short fused cunt who'd lashed out at her little girl. I'd hardly slept thinking about what I were gonna do to the shithouse when I got hold of him. Mum rang Ray but he weren't remorseful, he were the fucking opposite. Mum said his exact words were, "You spoil that little cunt! It's about time she were put in her place."

When Mum told me this, out of earshot of Sis' of course, I were straight out the door and knocking at H's. My blood weren't so much 'up' as it were ready to burst out my nut like a fucking boiling red fountain. H were shocked and fuming. He'd known my Sis' since she were born and he thought the world of her. H also thought the world of violence as well, so I could see the bloodlust on his boat.

We didn't have an address for this cunt Ray on the Isle of Dogs so it meant driving over and seeking the cunt out. The first time we went over was during the day, just to get the lay of the land. I thought I saw him coming out of a bookie's but it weren't him when we got closer, and I were glad because we weren't prepared.

A couple of nights later, on the Friday, we grabbed a pair of Balaclavas and a couple of claw hammers and went to do some spying in the boozers on the island. We parked up, stuffed the Bally's and hammers in our jackets and started the rounds. It were about 9, two hours before chucking out time, so we figured the cunt would probably be half tanked up by now.

We nipped in the North Pole for a look. No cigar. Then on to the Anchor & Hope and the Ferry House. Still no sign. Just as we were about to go into the Lord Nelson, I spot the cunt through the window. He's sat at a table with two other big bastards: all cauliflower lugs and off kilter hooters. I took a deep breath and asked H if we should call it off and return with reinforcements the night after. H called me a *bottling cunt* and said we'd just wait until they headed out and steam in with the hammers, straight at their boats, fast and hard, no quarter.

I felt sick. I weren't sure we'd be able to handle 3 Oggers even with hammers, but H were confident and told me stop worrying. Fortunately, we weren't gonna have to deal with 3 of the cunts, because through the window we saw Ray kill his pint, stand up, pat backs and head out. We stepped back round a corner as Ray heads out and starts walking in the direction of the water.

We started following him and kept a good distance. H whispered that we should smother up, get the hammers out and run at him. *Do him right in the middle of the road.* I told him to wait a minute. We carried on following him for a few hundred yards. There were a few pissed up pedestrians about so we needed to wait until he got to somewhere we weren't gonna get seen attacking him.

Ray slings a left down a side street stops and puts one of his arms out against a wall. Bingo! He whips his old man out and starts pissing. We smother up and take our hammers out. H springs forward and pushes Ray's face into the wall. Crack. Ray staggers back, stunned but lights still on. He gives it, "The fuck …"

H swings the hammer and catches Ray on his cheekbone. Ray's knocked back with the impact and he instinctively puts his mitts up. Queensberry Rules aren't on the menu tonight though. I jump in and catch Ray on the arms as H hits him on the side of the nut with a brutal hammer blow. He's out. Sparko on the pavement. H instantly puts the slipper in and hisses urgently at me, "Do his fuckin' hands!"

I lean over and rain blows down on the Ray's digits while H nicks his wallet, kettle and gold chain to make it look like a violent mugging. H were now a dab hand at this if you remember?

I couldn't tell you how many times I struck Ray's hands but they were pulped. The sound of metal on bone was hideous. I could handle seeing his mitts turn to mush but hearing it were another thing. I stand up straight and take a deep breath and we hear merry voices approaching. We got on our toes doublequick, barging past a sozzled couple and nearly knocking 'em over. We headed down to where we'd parked up, our Bally's still on and hammers still in hands. We heard a scream ring out and speeded up. We reached the motor winded but jacked up on adrenaline.

H spun the motor around, pulled the Bally off and gives it, "That'll teach the cunt not to slap little girls."

"You see the state of his mitts?" I asked.

"Yeah, you done good."

H sped right up to the water and I got out, wrapped the Bally's around the hammers and slung 'em in. Splash. We were headed off back to the estate and a quick visit to our local boozer just in time for last orders.

We changed our clobber round the back of the pub and burned the incriminating garments. We went inside, washed our hands and faces in the gents and then went to the bar. H puffed up his chest, looked around, pointed at me and shouted, "Me n' him have been in here since early doors, all right?" He mentally calculated how many punters were in and grinned at me, "Thirty alibis. You can't go wrong."

H ordered himself a pint of lager and an orange juice for me. We went and sat in the middle of the pub and H winked and nodded at the people who would be kindly giving us alibi's if it came on top. I were starting to worry we might have gone too far with Ray, but H didn't have didn't give a monkey's. I didn't think for a minute we'd killed the cunt, but I knew he were gonna be seriously fucked, especially if he ever fancied becoming a concert pianist.

I really wanted to know how bad he were. When you snuff someone there's no doubt, but this were torture not knowing the damage I'd done. H could see I were fretting. He leant across and whispered, "What you worried about? You killed that mug, Dennis."

I panicked a little, "What? You think we *killed* Ray?

"Nah, I'm just winding you up, you cunt. He's a big lump, he'll be fine."

"You reckon, H?"

"Yeah. Cunt got what he deserved that's all. He won't be laying his hands on any little girls now."

On the walk back home, I couldn't resist nipping in a phone box and calling around a few hospitals. I finally found Ray at Mile End Infirmary. The bird on the line gave me the usual about not being able to give any information out. I did some acting and told her I was his son and I were out of town and worried sick to my stomach. I finally got it out of her, "He's in a stable condition but he has multiple injuries. Actually, can you just hold on a second? There's a police officer that would like to talk to …"

The Painter

Dial tone and away to my kip in the knowledge that the cunt were still drawing breath, and worst-case scenario, if pinched, we'd only be up a GBH. Ray didn't strike me as the type who'd go running to Old Bill though, but he did strike me as someone who might come looking for revenge, and that meant I'd have to be even more careful than I already were.

Mum later found out at Bingo that Ray had been 'savagely mugged' and that he'd been in hospital a month because the muggers had smashed his hands to bits. When she told me, it were obvious she knew I'd been involved in some way. I don't think she thought it were me that had actually hammered him, but I think she thought I'd put H up to do it. I could live with that.

NINETEEN

*Only crime and the criminal, it is true, confront
us with the perplexity of radical evil; but only
the hypocrite is really rotten to the core.*

Hannah Arendt

I hadn't heard from Uncle in ages. I were still owed 20 large but
weren't worried about it. I had 18 large stashed in the little peter and were hardly spending anything. I'd bought a Suzuki 750
Slabside on an 85 plate and were enjoying taking it out for runs. I
was getting a bit bored though. H was hardly ever about because
he were now running his own motor ringing operation in Essex.
Mum now had a job working at a launderette on the high street
and Sis' had started to the rites of passage ritual of hanging out
with her mates outside the shopping precinct.

I can't remember whether I were happy or not that Uncle
hadn't thrown any more wetwork my way. I suppose I just didn't
think about it too much. If it came it came, but I started thinking
about what I would do for a living if I weren't gonna be a professional killer. What did I like? Riding motorbikes, watching telly,
reading and a spot of painting when the mood took me ... oh
yeah, and killing people.

The flat were paid for and I had nearly 100 large invested in shithole properties, so I were a relatively wealthy young man, no money worries, but the idea of being idle for the rest of my life panicked me. I thought about maybe buying a business, maybe going into the skip hire business or scrap, something cash based.

I just decided one day that I were gonna get away for a bit. I didn't know how long for or where I were gonna go, other than it would be in the UK, not having or wanting a passport since my last one had run out. And, if Uncle did have some graft for me, I wanted to get back for it lively.

I made contact with Uncle and told him I were fucking off for a bit. He gave me a number to check in with him weekly, that I memorized, and he apologized that the 20 large still hadn't landed. He said there were a lot of changes happening in his business but left it at that. I obviously knew that he were referring to a move by him and his associates to get right up into the drug smuggling caper.

This were 1988 and Europe – especially the UK – were about to see drug consumption go through the fucking roof, and all the smart, serious criminal money had moved into the supply of gear. There weren't a decent firm in the UK that weren't dipping their toes into the narcotics pool. The potential profits were just too fucking huge not to get involved. I knew Uncle had more irons in the fire than British Steel, but I suppose he'd have looked like a dinosaur if he hadn't jumped on board. Who knows though, really? Just pure greed maybe?

I packed my duffle bag: seven pairs of boxer shorts, seven pairs of socks, 2 jumpers, a pair of jeans, three t-shirts and some toiletries. Travel light. I then went and bought a clean driving license from Gary, a smackhead on the estate, who were around the same age as me. This would be my identity on my travels. Remember, driving licenses didn't have photo id in the 80s. You really could be any cunt you wanted to be back then. *Tonight, Matthew I'm gonna be Gary Mirren.*

It were 2 days after my 25th birthday. I gave Mum 3 large to live off, put 5 in my bag and left 10 in the peter for when I got back. I filled up the Suzuki Slabside and off I went. I headed down to Kent first and spent my first night in a bed and breakfast above a boozer in Dungeness. I'd always wanted to see this strange, alien landscape. From there I went to Hastings, Eastbourne, Brighton, Bracklesham Bay and then over to Southampton. I'd been on the road a week and the average price of a bed n' breakfast for the night were working out at fifteen quid. I worked out that at this rate I could stay on the road for 280 days when I factored in food, petrol and oil. I really liked that I now had a regime. A regime that made me feel totally free, which to some people might sound like a contradiction, but to me it were logical.

I get on the blower to Mum and Sis' once a week and checked in with Uncle at the same time. Uncle would pick up, here me say "All right, Uncle?" and then put the dog down. No work. I weren't too bothered though, I were enjoying my 'escape' into the beautiful country I'd never got to see before, and when I say 'beautiful', I mean it. You don't appreciate what a wonderful country England is until you get on your toes and have a good look at it. For probably the first time in my life I started feeling very patriotic.

The North were probably my biggest surprise. In between all the once heavy industrial northern cities were countryside that looked like it had been painted by one of The Old Masters. After spending a night in Manchester, I popped over the M62 to Bradford and from there I were straight into the Yorkshire Dales and from there I hit The Lake District. There really is no sight like that of heading up the approach road and seeing Lake Windermere come into view. Breath-taking.

I instantly knew that I were gonna stay for a bit in Cumbria. Besides the mountains and lakes, it just felt like a place you could lose yourself in. I plotted up in a small market town called Kendal, just below the great lakes. I found a one up one down cottage for rent. 35 bar a week with electric and gas bills covered. Fucking bargain.

It were quite spacious for a cottage and was fully furnished. The telly were a bit temperamental and the bath took forever to fill up, but besides that everything were sweet. There was even a decent radio cassette player that I fully utilised. The landlord were quite happy to rent to 'Gary Mirren' and only wanted a month's wedge in advance.

I moved in and Gary Mirren went and joined the well-stocked local library. I were half expecting the locals to be a bit wary of a cockney cunt loner plotting up, but it were nothing like that. Everyone was friendly and minded their own business. There was a Co-Op supermarket just round the corner from me, and I couldn't believe how cheap everything were compared to London prices. I even had a phone box at the end of the street, that weren't perfumed with piss and regularly out of order because the coin tray had been jemmied open.

I were probably reading about 3 books a week, all sorts: novels, history, biographies, even a bit of psychology and philosophy. Every other day I'd get on the Suzuki and go site-seeing. Some of the roads were so quiet I could really open it up and go for miles never dropping below 100 mph. The weather could change really quickly though, one minute dazzling sunshine, the next pissing down rain, so I had to keep my wits about me, which actually honed my riding my skills.

There were a clay pigeon shooting club just outside of Kendall and Gary Mirren went and joined. It worked out that if I paid the yearly subscription rather than coughing up for individual sessions, I'd save quite a few bob. I fucking loved it and were turning up three days a week sometimes. I were getting so good at it that one of the geezers there asked me if I'd like to join their team and start competing. I thanked him but KB'd the idea.

Most nights I either read or watched some telly. One day I sees a documentary advertised called 'The Men Who Killed Kennedy'. I'd read the *Crossfire* book about JFK's assassination on Uncle's tip and thought the documentary looked interesting. I didn't have a clue *how* interesting it would turn out to be.

Writers Note* The Author told me about the incident but he also advised me to look it up on the internet, which I did. I'm putting up the official, thoroughly researched, and to this day, still not discredited account of who the assassin(s) of JFK were. What follows is basically the transcript of what The Author watched that night. This is an important piece of the jigsaw that makes up the puzzle of Uncle's involvement in the international crime world.

"Antoine Guerini was born in Marseilles, France. As a young man Guerini associated with gangsters from Marseilles. During the Second World War the Second World War He joined the French Resistance and was responsible for smuggling arms into the city for the Mouvements Unis de la Résistance (MUR). After the war Guerini, became the dominant crime boss in Marseilles. It was later claimed by the journalist Stephen Rivele, that Guerini organized the assassination of JFK. President. According to his contact, Christian David, the killing was carried out by Lucien Sarti and two other members of the Marseilles mob."

"In the 1960s Marcel Francisci, the owner of a lucrative international gambling syndicate, began to threaten Guerini's control of Marseilles. On 23rd June, 1967, two hired assassins fired eleven bullets into Antoine Guerini while he was in a gas station."

"Lucien Sarti worked for the French-Corsican heroin trafficker and convicted Nazi collaborator, Auguste Joseph Ricord. It was claimed by the journalist Stephen Rivel that Antoine organized the assassination of President John F. Kennedy. According to his contact, Christian David, the killing was carried out by Sarti and two other members of the Marseilles mob. It is believed Sarti fired from behind the wooden fence on the grassy knoll. The first shot was fired from behind and hit Kennedy in the back. The second shot was fired from behind, and hit John Connally. The third shot was fired from in front, and hit Kennedy in the head. The fourth shot was from behind and missed."

"Lucien Sarti was officially killed by Mexican police in Mexico City on 27th April, 1972. His death was not reported in the United States at the time. However, it was in France's leading newspaper, *Le Monde*. It reported that the killing of Sarti was the result of a "close Mafia-police-Narcotics Bureau collaboration" in the United States to 'shatter Corsican influence in the worldwide narcotics traffic, and create a virtual monopoly for the U.S.-Italian Mafia connection, whose key figure was Santo Trafficante.'"

"The initial turning point was the first meeting that I had with the French narcotics trafficker at Leavenworth Penitentiary. His name was Christian David. He had been a member of the old French Connection heroin network. He had then been a leader of the Corsican drug trafficking network in South America known as the Latin Connection. And he had also been an intelligence agent for a number of intelligence services around the world. In exchange for my help in finding him an attorney to represent him against the possibility of his deportation to France after he finished his sentence at Leavenworth, he agreed to give me a certain amount of information concerning the assassination based upon his own knowledge. The first thing that he told me, very reluctantly and only after four or five hours of my arguing with him, was that he was aware that there had been a conspiracy to murder the president, and indeed in May or June of 1963 in Marseilles, he had been offered the contract to kill President Kennedy.

"That was the initial breakthrough, if you will. He was eventually deported to France. I remained in contact with him. I went to Paris to interview him in two prisons in Paris. And in the fear that he would be either committed to an asylum or that he would be convicted of an old murder charge, he gradually gave me additional information about the assassination."

"David's position was that there were three killers, and that they had been hired on a contract which had been placed with the leader of the Corsican Mafia at Marseilles, a man named Antoine Guerini. Guerini, he said, was asked to supply three assassins of high quality, experienced killers to murder the President, and that Guerini did so. In the course of one of the first significant conversations I had with David on this subject, he told me that he had been in Marseilles in May or June of 1963, and that every evening he went to Antoine Guerini's club on the old Port of Marseilles to meet people who owed him money. And one evening, Guerini sent for him, asked him to come to the office which was above the club."

"Guerini told him that he had an important contract, and he asked David if he were interested. David said, "Who's the contract on?" Guerini said, 'an American politician.' David asked, "Well is it a congressman, a senator?" And Guerini said, "higher than that... The highest vegetable." At that point of course David knew who he was talking about. David asked him where was the contract to be carried out. And when Guerini said it would be done inside the United States, David refused on the grounds that that was much too dangerous."

"About two weeks before the assassination, Sarti flew from France to Mexico City, from where he drove or was driven to the US border at Brownsville, Texas. Sarti crossed at Brownsville where he was picked up by someone from the Chicago mafia. This person drove him to a private house in Dallas. He did not stay at a hotel, as not to leave records.

"David believes that Sarti was traveling on an Italian passport. David said the assassins cased Dealey Plaza, took photographs and worked out mathematically how to set up a crossfire. Sarti wanted to fire from the triple underpass bridge, but when he arrived in Dealey Plaza the day of the assassination, there were people there, so he fired from a little hill next to the bridge. There was a wooden fence on that hill, and Sarti fired from behind the wooden fence. He said Sarti only fired once, and used an explosive bullet. He said Kennedy was shot in a crossfire, two shots from behind, and Sarti's shot from the front."

"Of the two assassins behind, one was high, and one was low. He said you can't understand the wounds if you don't realize that one gun was low, "almost on the horizontal." The first shot was fired from behind and hit Kennedy in the back. The second shot was fired from behind, and hit "the other person in the car." The third shot was fired from in front, and hit Kennedy in the head. The fourth shot was from behind and missed "because the car was too far away." He said that two shots were almost simultaneous."

"David said that Kennedy was killed for revenge and money. He said the CIA was incapable of killing Kennedy, but did cover it up. He said the gunmen stayed at the private house in Dallas for approximately two weeks following the assassination, then believes they went to Canada, that there were people in Canada who had the ability *to fly them out of North America."*

Writer's Note* back to The Author's words.

So, I'm sat there in this little cottage in Cumbria watching this documentary and my fucking jaw's hitting the floor. This 'new, hot off the press, revelatory evidence' they were talking about in the documentary had already been told to me years back by Uncle. How the fuck did Uncle know all this? There'd been nothing mentioned about these cunts up until this broadcast! No newspaper articles, books or other documentaries.

Now, the way I were seeing it, Uncle were either psychic or he was *in the know* about the most famous assassination in history! He definitely weren't mystic fucking Meg as far as I were concerned, so that meant he were *in the know,* and if he were *in the know,* had he been involved the assassination somewhere along the line?

My nut were racing. I obviously knew Uncle was big league, but this were fucking World Cup level stuff. Kennedy's assassination changed America forever. This weren't some dodgy cockney cunt getting plugged for having his hands in the cash register. It were history making murder.

I were shocked, excited and dying to speak to Uncle about it. All sorts of scenarios and questions went through my mind, the chief one being: if Uncle were involved in the JFK job, *how* involved were he?

It sounds fucking doolally, don't it? Thing is, this is where I were at and there were no escaping. Here's a South London council estate Herbert doing hits for a big-time villain, who may or may not have been involved in the snuffing of one of the most famous men in history, but the fact he had told me something years back that had only just come to light, meant he were a lot more important than I'd had him down as being, and *I* worked for him.

It got me thinking about all the other assassinations he might have been involved with over the years. I'd recently read book about the Israeli intelligence agency MOSSAD, who were known to have offed loads of cunts who gave Israel agg. Were Uncle part of the UK intelligence services? Were he IRA? Were he Baader Meinhof? The Red Brigade? CIA? If you'll pardon the fucking awful pun, were Uncle the actual fucking *Man From U.N.C.L.E?*

Reason eventually turned up with its sleeves rolled and started putting my flights of imagination straight: *just because he knew the frog cunts who'd offed JFK don't mean he were involved, you pillock! Some cunt could have just told him. All this stuff could have been common knowledge in the crime underworld since it happened. It don't mean Uncle were involved, you prat!*

I did feel a bit of a cunt for imagining Uncle as this fucking secret supervillain, but it still don't change the fact that he were cock-on knowledgeable about JFK's assassination. Evidently more knowledgable than the media, governments, and all the powerful agencies that were supposed to have found this stuff out before a London villain.

I spent the next few weeks rifling through the crime and history sections of Kendal Library looking for Uncle's fingerprints in all kinds of famous capers, but found fuck all. I can't remember whether I were happy or pissed off I didn't find anything on him. And, truth be told, I don't know what difference it would have made even if I'd worked out Uncle had been involved in the disappearance of Lord Lucan, knew where Shergar was stabled, or had been the brains behind the Brighton Bombing after he'd arranged for JFK to get clipped.

I started painting again after I'd overdosed on crime and

espionage books. I'd bought twelve blank canvasses and a couple of boxes of acrylic paints. The style were chaotic but colorful again, and *again* it relaxed me. Reading relaxed me, but painting were definitely more mediative. I could lose all sense of time when I painted – or rather daubed – and because of the layered style I were doing I could keep going over and over the daubing's until I were satisfied. I'd pull many an all-nighter fucking around like this. I'd listened to The Smiths cassettes I'd bought – coincidentally – from the local WH Smith's as I daubed away. I became obsessed with their *'Strangeways Here We Come'* album and it became the official soundtrack to my life at that point.

After I'd finished the paintings, I had this fucking garrity idea to leave a couple outside the door of the local art gallery. I were only gonna end up burning them all anyway, so I figured I'd just leave them lying there to see what happened. I would have never had the bottle to walk into the gallery with 'em under my arm and ask whether they thought my paintings were any good. The thought of actually asking some cunt to even look at them filled me with dread.

The gallery weren't a big place and not like these fucking pretentious holes you find in London. They had a few abstract pieces on the walls but it were mainly landscapes they was flogging. I dumped the couple of canvasses there about 4 one morning. It didn't care whether the postie or milkman half inched 'em.

I were regularly tear-arsing around beautiful Cumbria on the bike and Lake Windermere were my go-to place. I used to enjoy feeding the ducks and swans with ground up stale bread. They were bold as fucking brass; they'd come out the soup and toddle right up to you giving it, *come on you cunt! Feed me!* They might have been Cumbrian cunts but they had South London council estate attitude. H would have got on famously with 'em.

I'd be in Kendal five months and Mum were giving it, *you ever coming home again or what, son? We miss ya.* I missed her and Sis' but I didn't miss the city and its ever-present reminder that I were a murderer for hire. My killings weren't haunting me or anything, because up there in Cumbria I were anonymous and getting used to being called Gary Mirren and, in a way, I'd never done any killings. I did know that soon as I stepped foot back in London, I were tempting the ghosts to come out and haunt me though. It's not like I didn't think I could handle that, but why stick about someplace that weren't relaxing if you had the means not to? That's what fucking holidays are all about aren't they?

TWENTY

*My friendly advice is this: do it or do
not do it – you will regret both.*

Soren Kierkegaard

It'd been nearly a month since I'd left my paintings at the door
of the art gallery, like some abandoned Victorian child doomed
for the workhouse. I'd walked past a few times to see if they'd
hung them up. Not that I were expecting them to. Why would
they? They probably thought one of the village idiots had
dumped them there. They wouldn't have been too far off the
mark. Anyway, they hadn't hung them.

I called Mum one day and got the distinct feeling something were wrong. She assured me everything were all right, but
I couldn't shake the suspicion she were holding back on me. It
started getting my goat and I couldn't rest. I got on the blower
again the next day and told her to tell me the truth. She gives it, *it's
nothing, don't worry about it.* I asked her to put Sis' on the dog but
she claimed she were out, which didn't sound too convincing. *The
fuck were going on!*

All right, I thought, I'll ride home and find out for myself.
I could do it in a day, 5 hours there, 5 back, and it'd be nice to
see Mum and Sis' even if everything were kosher and I were just

being paranoid. Call it intuition, but somehow, I knew I weren't gonna be returning to Kendal.

Just before I set off, I went and looked through the art gallery window, and, stone *me!* One of my paintings were hung in quite a prominent position. I thought I were fucking hallucinating or something, but no, there it was. One of *my* paintings hanging in a fucking art gallery of all places! I think I blushed as I stared at it.

I tried to get a better look. The gallery were open but there weren't a cat in hell's chance I could muster up the bottle to go inside. As I squinted, I zeroed in on the card underneath it. It read: *untitled, unsigned, anonymous. £25. Proceeds to National Trust.* I don't know how long I stood there drinking it in because I were transfixed. The words *untitled, unsigned, anonymous* were ringing in my nut like they were some fucking epic poem. In the scheme of things, it were nothing, but to me it were everything. I know this don't make sense, but it felt like my anonymous life had been vindicated. I had finally achieved anonymity and here, hanging in a legit art gallery, there were proof of it.

I'm sure some psychoanalyst would have had a fucking field day trying to work out what state my mind were in at that time, but I just felt what I felt and knew what I knew. Someone had decided that my painting were good enough to show other people. The fact nobody knew who'd painted it and there were no explanation of what it were trying to express filled me with excitement.

Over the years I've tried to find a word that describes somebody who takes great pleasure in being anonymous, but there ain't one. Nowadays I suppose it'd come under the huge fucking umbrella of obsessive-compulsive disorder and they'd shovel a load of pills down my Gregory.

As I were speeding down the M6 those three beautiful words: *untitled, unsigned, anonymous* were ringing in my ears. I felt that they perfectly captured who I were and what I were about. I were a fucking enigma and the handful of people who visited that gallery in Kendal knew I were an enigma. This is a good six years before Banksy became the ultimate anonymous artist. Not that I'd ever compare myself to Banksy, he's actually got something to say, and I very much doubt he moonlights as a contract killer between throwing up his artworks, but when he did come along, I immediately understood the satisfaction he got from no cunt knowing who he really was.

When I walked in the flat it were obvious Mum had been worrying. She looked haggard and weak and her voice trembled a little as she told me how good it were to see me. It certainly didn't look like it. *What's wrong, Mum?* She really didn't want to tell, "Promise ... promise you won't get mad."

What followed were a couple of hours of me listening to her crying and self-blame and pathetic apologies and sobbing and looking through official papers that might as well have been written in fucking Latin for as much as I could understand them. It were frustrating and confusing and I couldn't get my nut round it. I kept telling her to slow down and calm down and take a breath, but she were breaking into bouts of hysteria and it got to the point where I were gonna nip out and buy a bottle of whiskey to sling down her Gregory just to calm her down.

What she was trying to tell me is that she'd made a big mistake. *A very fucking costly mistake!* She'd seen an ad in some paper from a city financial firm that were offering huge dividends on property portfolios. *Fucking portfolios!* And using the equity in homes you owned they invested it for you and returned a fuck load of dough. It were a classic scam going down in London at the time, part of it aimed at fleecing mugs out of the profits they'd made out of the buying of their council gaffs, and part of it aimed at anyone who found they were sitting on equity in their gaffs after the recent property price boom.

This were the 1980s remember and the Fraud Act that might have helped us didn't come into law until 2006. So, yeah, these shyster cunts were slick and knew exactly what they were doing, and like a lot of the white-collar graft that were happening at the time, a blind eye were being turned to it from the powers that be. These cunts were having it right off and leaving these poor mugs fucking destitute. The bottom line is they were getting homeowners to sign their properties over to them, on what they claimed was a 'temporary basis'. This firm then claimed they were gonna free up the equity in the drums and use it to invest for their clients. They were coming out all with all sorts of slather about high yields and incredible dividends. Fortunately for this firm of cunts, quite a few gullible people fell for it without engaging the help of a brief.

At the end of the day, all these swindling cunts were doing is robbing people out of their properties. People who found they were now 'property owners' and getting a stake in society. The firm weren't forcing any cunt to sign over their homes. They were just banking on these mugs *not* to read the small print or show the contract to someone in their right mind who weren't blinded by greed.

I dare say a lot of people tore up the contract when they realized these confident cunts were trying to have their trousers down, but many didn't. It's got to be said that the graft were quite ingenious, in a diabolic sense. Once this firm had the properties signed over to them, they quickly liquidated the gaffs, diversified the cash they'd hooked, declared bankruptcy and got on their toes to go live the life of fucking Riley abroad somewhere. It were a 'long firm' on an industrial scale.

Initially I thought Mum had just signed over our flat, but no. She'd gone full fucking Gordon Gecko and signed over the seven shithole gaffs we'd bought at the auctions. On hearing this I had this image of my Dad stood pissing against a wall laughing demonically, giving it, *100 large! What a cunt, ha ha ha.* I tried to remain calm and asked Mum if she were sure it were a long firm she'd fallen for. She went and got a copy of The Evening Standard and it were there in black and white. These poor mugs who'd been had over were telling their tales of woe and calling on the government to do something about it. The firm's response was simple: *read your contract you fucking mugs!* Less brutal than that of course, but you get the gist.

It turns out that there weren't any law in place that protected fucking idiots from signing over their drum's deeds to suited and booted-fancy letter headed-well-appointed scamming cunts to sell and do what they liked with the dough. *Quelle fucking surprise!* At the time it felt like half of London were suffering a recession, while the other half were sat in the Square Mile concocting schemes to rip every cunt and his dog off.

I were stunned when it sank in. We'd not only lost our home, but I'd lost the loot I'd invested, that I'd earned risking doing a life sentence of porridge for. All the emotions ran through me like mental diarrhoea. Mum went to bed piping and left me sat staring at the telly as it played the BBC's closing ritual of 'God Save The Queen'.

The next morning, I were furiously flipping through the Yellow Pages trying to find a brief that would look over these contracts Mum had signed. Something that my gullible wannabe Gordon Gecko Mum should have done 2 months back. *Gordon was my new name for Mum from that day on and she hated it.* I found a brief in Chancery Lane. It knew it weren't gonna be cheap but there was a lot at stake. I explained a bit to the Richard on the dog and she told me I'd have to bring Mum in with me as it were her whose name were on the contracts. I were hoping Mum weren't gonna start piping at the meeting.

We sat down with a brief called Clement Green. He were an elderly gent and you could tell he'd been around the block. We handed over all the contracts and bumf and sat with him for an hour while Mum tearfully explained everything. He didn't quote us a price for his services, probably thought that if we were in the habit of spunking one hundred and twenty large we were probably poked up and wouldn't squabble.

The bottom line was that Mum hadn't been coerced into signing, she weren't given fraudulent papers to sign, no fraudulent information had been given to her and she had been shown that she should engage a lawyer to look through the offer. It were just a simple case of crafty cunts taking advantage of simple people.

Clement laid it out brutal for Mum, "I'm afraid, the chance of this 'company' selling your properties, investing the profits and giving you the return after taking their commission is extremely unlikely Mrs, **********. I will do everything in my power to try and challenge this transferal of deeds though."

On the tube going back home, Mum just shook her head and sighed. I told her to stop worrying and tried geein' her up by telling her that old Clement wouldn't see us wrong. I didn't believe this of course. I thought we were fucked and that even having a sniff of getting the properties back would cost us an arm n' a leg in legal fees.

I'd been fucked by the suicidal, gambling degenerate, fucking stone yard Chief out of 30 large and now Mum had topped it three times over. It felt unreal. Like all the murdering I'd done hadn't really happened and I'd imagined it all. This was my life and it were reading like a fucking comedy of errors. Surely, I were gonna wake up soon.

All the stress I'd got shut of in Kendal were now back on my shoulders like a 10-tonne weight. I needed to see H. The last thing he'd ever be would be a shoulder to cry on so it didn't really matter that I couldn't tell him Mum had been had over on such a fuck-off scale. If he'd known I'd had 100 large to play with in the first place he'd have tried roping me in to one of his grafts. Which, looking back, would have been a lot safer investment.

H said he'd missed me and that I were a cunt for going away so long. He told me he were doing well with the car ringing in Essex and that he'd also got involved with some truck jackings.

"I were grafting with this ronker Jo Jo from Billericay n' his cousin. We'd knocked off a couple of lorries coming out of Felixstowe and we'd had a right fucking score. We get the nod about this lorry on its way to Holland and we stick it up about ten miles from the port. Bish bosh, piece o' piss! We arrange to meet at the slaughter a couple of days later, but the next day this fucking Jo Jo mug gets pinched for wounding some cunt in a boozer. He's got previous so they remand him. The cunt's looking at a four stretch. So, I'm thinking where's the slaughter, where's my swag ain't I. I can't get hold o' this fucking cousin mug n' I'm trying to get word to this cunt Jo Jo over the wall. Cunt's fucking ignoring me! Blanking me he is! There were 65 Cambridge leather two-seater sofas we nabbed, n' we had a buyer for 300 apiece. That's 19 large. 9 for me and 9 split for them two cunts and a grand for the tipster. It were my contact see, so I weren't cutting 'em fifty fifty, but I'm in schtuck now. I don't know where these fucking melts have hid the lorry."

H went on to explain that on the previous heist they'd off loaded the lorry in a derelict airfield hanger in deepest Essex, but he's been scouring everywhere and he's turned up nothing. He's now thinking that this Jo Jo's set it up for his cousin to slaughter the leather sofa's and keep all the lucre for themselves. H had found out that Jo Jo were definitely on remand in Chelmsford nick and he were getting word out in there for Jo Jo to make contact with him. H goes on to explain that if Jo Jo kept ignoring him, he were gonna arrange to have him chibbed to ribbons in the nick. Some things never change in the wonderful land of H.

I actually sympathised with H. I'd now been properly stitched up twice – *once with my Mum's fucking naïve cooperation* – and it's a horrible feeling. I'd gone from the high of seeing one of my paintings hung in an actual art gallery to the low of coming home and finding out I were on the verge of being boracic again. If I'd been a drinker I'd have put my liver through its paces that night I can tell you.

I still had 10 large in my little peter, but I were thinking a chunk of that were gonna have to go Clement the brief as he tried to get my gaffs back. I were still owed 20 grand off Uncle, but I still didn't know when it were gonna land, so, against all better judgement, when H offered up some graft I actually listened.

"These Mancs I've been put on to have got a lorry full o' *Snap on Tools. Full fucking cabinets!* They can't dish it up North because no cunt wants to pay for the quality. They want 40 thou' for it, but I've got a buyer lined up who'll have it for 60. It's just a straight pass over. 20 large profit for fuck all. Couple of hours work. I've gotta come up with the 40 though. I'm fifteen lagging. Ringo reckons he can do me 6, but I still need 9."

The 'Ringo' H were talking about weren't somebody who resembled Ringo Starr from The Beatles, no. Ringo were called Ringo because as a kid he suffered something rotten with ringworm. He now owned a pool hall and amusement arcade just off the estate and were doing all right for himself. He had kindly agreed to lend H the 6 without any vig for a couple of weeks. I say 'kindly', it were a well known fact Ringo were wary of H and his family, and probably thought the loan were an insurance to keep in their good books. H had helped Ringo out with rowdy customers in the past without putting the bite on him, so in all fairness it were the right thing to do for Ringo.

Call it loyalty to a mate, call it idiocy, call it never looking a gift horse in the kisser, call it not learning from your mistakes, or call it what it were really were: good old fashioned opportunistic greed, but I asked the question, "Just say, for instance, I could get hold of the nine large …"

Before I could finish, H snaps, "2! 2 grand! Tell whoever you can get it off they'll get 2 grand for borrowing me the 9."

I thought about it as H studied my boat expectantly, "And this is good as gold, H? No fucking about? It's a straight hand over?"

Crossing his heart, "On my mother's eyes. It's just a meet up and then straight on to the buyer. No monkey business. These Mancs are vouched for."

"Who's vouched for 'em?"

"Good lads over Essex way."

The thought of 2 grand for doing absolutely fuck all sounded tasty after swallowing all the shit of recent days. This were H though, and even though he'd had many a good score in the past, doing graft with him always came with the caveat that it could turn garrity at the flick of a switch. I'd asked the question now though. He knew I could possibly get hold of the shortfall dough and he weren't gonna rest until I'd handed it over to him.

I asked him to explain the graft in detail. He gives it, "We meet these Mancs at a spot in Essex, I have a gander inside the lorry, make sure the Snap's On's are all there, I hand over the dough and then we all go this industrial estate and off load into a warehouse."

I gives it, "What if they decide to just fuck off with the dough?"

"They won't 'cos we'll have one of 'em in the motor with us when we go to the industrial estate. Insurance."

"Why not just meet 'em at the industrial estate, off load and hand over the dough?"

"Because I don't want the cunt I'm passing 'em on to knowing I'm making 20 large on it."

"Won't these Mancs just tipple?"

"I'll be telling 'em that they keep their trap's shut when we get to the off-load. And that goes for the cunt who's buying the haul off me as well. Look, they all know I'm not to be fucked with. The Mancs get their 40, this other cunt gets his Snap On's and I walk away with 20 profit, minus the 2 for whoever's lending you the 9. It's a fucking doddle."

"So, you're gonna risk fucking off both these Mancs *and* the geezer who's buying?"

"Fucksake! Course I am! It's called supply and demand, you cunt. I ain't a fucking charity! Do I look like a charity? Have I got *Do They Know It's Fucking Christmas* tattooed across my napper? These cunts ain't gonna get saucy. Don't worry. They know the score. So, when can you get me this 9 large?"

I could piss and moan again at this point but I don't wanna bore you, so here we go. The great Snap On Tools caper. H picks me up in an Escort XR3i ringer and we head over to Essex. H has got the 40 large in used notes stuffed into a Woolworth's plastic carrier bag on the back seat and decides to tell me he's tooled up. He pulls out a deactivated Radom VIS p.35 pistol. He said, *it's from the war* and I replied, *yeah, the fucking Napoleonic war!*

"Why the fuck have you brought a deactivated piece with you, H?"

"It's for just in case."

"Just in case, what?"

"You know, in case it goes wobbly."

"You said these cunts were vouched for?"

"They are!"

"So, what's with the fucking Antiques Roadshow?"

"You never really know with these Northern mugs."

"H, if you think that, what the fuck are you doing bringing a dud pistol?"

"I couldn't get hold of a live one. Stop fucking whinging. It's all gonna be sweet."

TWENTY- ONE

It is the bungled crime that brings remorse.

P.G. Wodehouse

I came to in St. Peters Hospital in Maldon, Essex. They were about halfway through putting 50 stitches in the back of my crust. I had an oxygen mask on and were wired up to the monitors.

We'd pulled up at this remote beauty spot. I remember thinking something were off. There were no way these Mancs were gonna get a fucking HGV down this lane. H just said if there were any nonsense from these Mancs we'd just drive away and forget about the deal.

The next thing I remember is seeing three big gorillas surround the motor. A baseball bat came smashing through H's side window and his door was yanked open. I was watching what were happening to H and heard *my* side window go through. A second later I could feel the back of my head suddenly become like wet ice. I turned and saw my attacker holding a bloody crowbar in his hand. Lights out.

H told me he'd held on to the steering wheel with one hand and with the other tried getting the toy pistol out of his jacket. They smashed him in the temple with the bat and he ended up sparko like me. The Manc cunts – or whoever they'd laid it on for

– grabbed the Woolworth's bag full of dough *and* the toy pistol and were on their toes. I'm assuming someone driving past saw us both KO'd in the motor and called 999.

The doctors and nurses were addressing me as Mr. Mirren. They'd found my moody driving licence and I were a bit confused at first. The concussion had disorientated me and I had a shooting pain from my shoulder right up to the big fucking gash in my head. I asked for some pain relief and they told me I'd already had some. The needlework didn't hurt because the throbbing from the wound grabbed all my attention.

One side of H's face looked like the Elephant Man's. It were swollen like a balloon and his eye were the size of a pea. We were told that we'd have to stay in and were put in beds opposite each other. Essex plod wandered in and H told me to just say I couldn't remember anything. *Can't remember, don't know, haven't got a clue, didn't see anyone, must have got jumped, can't remember can't remember can't remember.*

They knew me and H were giving them the mind your own business treatment but there were fuck all they could do about it. I were loving it that they were calling me *Mr. Mirren* and *Gary*, but the joy wore off when it dawned on me that once again I'd been fucked over. *What the fuck is wrong with me?*

H were already plotting his revenge from the hospital bed. It didn't matter who had actually turned us over, H were blaming *every* cunt. The lads from Essex who'd vouched for the Mancs were gonna get it and the Mancs were gonna get it and anyone else who'd had anything to do with it were gonna get it.

It should have been me that were foaming at the mouth. I'd just been fucked for 9 large. H told me to tell whoever I'd lent the 9 grand off that they would get it back. H hadn't lost fuck all though! All the dough he'd put in had been borrowed anyway, and none of his creditors were gonna get heavy. Yeah, his credit rating might have hit the skids but he weren't worried about that. H were only worried that he'd been mugged off and took a hiding in the process.

I were now laid in an hospital bed stitched up like a fucking baseball with no job, no drum, no properties, no prospects and exactly £1700 to my name. That night I had a dream that I were living in a house with all the marks I'd offed, including Dennis. This drum were on fire and we all kept scurrying around from room to room pointing at these fires and telling the others to put it out. Not one of us were willing to fight the flames, instead we just bollocked each other as the fires started spreading.

We signed ourselves out the next day, despite the doctors and nurses telling us not to, and H arranged for a mate of his, Vernon, to come up and pick us up and take us back home. H had contacted someone in Essex to pick up his XR3i and take it somewhere safe. As Vernon dropped us off, H gave him orders to start getting lively, do some gumshoe work and find out who'd been behind the attack on us. I didn't know this Vernon but it were obvious he were a joey for H, who would have probably jumped in a grave if he'd asked him to.

Mum were verging on the hysterical again when I walked in. They'd shaved my barnet around the wound so there were no hiding it. I told her it were nothing to worry about and that I'd just got into a bit of agg with H, and we'd had a tussle with some idiots who were tooled up. To be honest, at this point I don't know why I were sugar coating shit for Mum. She clearly knew by this time that I were bang at it.

I'd been impressed that the hospital and plod had called me Gary Mirren. I went round to the *real* Gary Mirren's gaff and asked him if he'd ever been pinched and had his fingerprints taken. He just nodded negative. I then asked him to sell me his national insurance number and birth certificate. Gary were by now a full time junkie and happy to flog me his life for a score, no questions asked. It did, however, take the cunt over an hour to find the documents amongst the squalor he were living in.

Mum started deteriorating even faster from this point on. She were glugging cheap Lambrini wine every day and chasing it with Valium. I told her straight that she had to get off the jack n' jills but she wouldn't listen. I even went to her doctor and told him to stop prescribing them to her, but he told me he couldn't betray doctor patient confidentiality and, essentially, it were none of my business. Me and Sis' started nicking her pills and flushing 'em down the khazi but it were pointless. She just got repeat prescriptions and became a master at salting 'em away so we couldn't find 'em.

She were obviously still gutted about handing over our flat and the shithole properties. No matter how many times I told her to stop worrying about it and that she were just one of the many victims of a very elaborate scam it didn't matter. I tried to assure her that Clement the Brief would see us right, but I didn't believe this and she knew I didn't.

I had to get a job, and because I were now – to all intents and purposes – Gary Mirren, it didn't have to be cash in hand. I went an opened a post office bank account in my new name and deposited 250 quid. I went round dozens of businesses and factories on my bike with a moody CV I'd knocked up, but no cunt got back to me.

Clement called me and Mum up to Chancery Lane one day and basically told us were fucked. Although 'very immoral', what the scamming cunts had done to Mum weren't illegal. Clement showed us the wording in the contracts stating that before signing and entering into the contract, legal advice should be sought, blah, blah, blah. Black n' fucking white! The fucking devil ain't in the detail. The devil is in the small print. Clement then went on to tell us something I already knew. This firm of scammers were likely going to close up shop at some point and move on to their next graft. Chasing them through the courts would be eye wateringly expensive and there'd be no guarantee of getting the property deeds back.

Mum lost it at this point, and I thought she were gonna have a stroke when Clement got on to the subject of our flat. I don't know why, but Mum thought that because we lived in it, we'd somehow be all right to keep it and carrying on as normal. Nope. *Not on your fucking Nelly!* Clement said that this company now owned the property and could evict us at any time. He told us we should start making plans to find somewhere else to live.

When we were waiting for the tube back home, I actually thought, at one point, that Mum were gonna throw herself down on to the tracks and end it all there and then. For the next two weeks me and Sis' took it in turns to be with her all the time. Sis' even started sleeping in Mum's bed to keep an eye on her. It were fucking horrible and heart-breaking and I didn't know what the fuck to do to try make it better.

I got on the dog to the Mum's doctor and told the cunt straight that I thought she might be suicidal. He gave me an appointment that day for me and Mum to go in and see him. It were a waste of fucking time. Mum put on a front and lied through her teeth. She assured the quack that she weren't suicidal and that, yeah, she were feeling a bit low, but suicide had – and never would – cross her mind. She had two kids who she thought the world of and she were horrified that me and Sis' could think she'd ever top herself. It were a good performance. The doctor sent us on our way.

I, or rather Gary Mirren, managed to get a job at Batley & Hutchinson builders merchants in Rotherhithe. I drove the forklifts and it were decent pay and conditions. It had recently been bought out by a corporation and they were laying on subsidised meals for the workers. For 75p you could get a huge all-day breakfast or fish, chips and peas or shepherd's pie and veg or pie n' mash, as much tea and coffee as your bladder could hold and spotted dick to top it all off.

I were pulling down 310 bar a week after they'd deducted Gary Mirren's tax and insurance and there were plenty of overtime if you were up for it. I didn't give the scamming cunt firm the opportunity to evict us from our beloved flat. I got us a two up, one down little terrace house to rent just off the estate. I had my own room and Sis' shared with Mum. Mum hated moving off the estate. She were now eating very little and had jacked in her job at the launderette. She'd even stopped going to the bingo, which were actually more worrying than everything else.

One day I'm at work loading timber on to the back of a flat bed when this nondescript geezer walks up to me, hands me a slip of paper on the sly and walks off. It just said *fish supper ready. Call me after 6* and then the number. I were excited, and not just because I knew some dough were incoming, I really wanted to connect with Uncle. I memorized the number, popped the piece of paper in my gob and swallowed it.

We met on Tower Bridge a couple of days later and it were like only yesterday we'd seen each other. Uncle apologized for the cash flow hold up and said I'd have my full remaining 20 large over the next couple of weeks. I were a bit hacked off he didn't have any wetwork for me but he did say we'd started connecting again regular. He gave me another number to remember and said to call once a week on Wednesday evenings. He knew we'd moved off the estate and probably knew I'd lost the properties as well, but I weren't gonna offer it up if he didn't mention it. I were dying to ask him about his JFK hitman knowledge but bottled out. I were thinking he might have thought I were digging and it might make him suspicious of me.

On the way home I recalled the conversation that had just happened and realized that absolutely nothing Uncle had said could implicate him in contract killings. Even if It'd been wired up, nothing passed from his lips that would give him or me away. I had to admire him, he were a real professional and I felt lucky to know someone like him. His professionalism did make me feel like a mug though. Uncle would have never let any cunt have his trousers down like that. I were too fucking soft and trusting to ever become a proper businessman.

I picked up 20 large in Fish Suppers over the next three weeks. I put 5 of it in my Mr. Mirren account, 10 in my little peter and used the remaining 5 to have a good blowout. I redecorated the gaff we were renting, top to bottom, bought my Sis' her very first motor, a Mini Cooper and then paid for Mum and Sis' to go to Benidorm for a whole month. I were thinking it might get Mum out of her depression, and Sis' agreed so I packed 'em off. On the very same day I got a bill from Clement the Brief. I owed him nearly two large for basically reading the contracts and laughing at Mum's gullibility. *Fucking Brief's! They give villains a bad name.*

TWENTY-TWO

The art of living is the art of knowing how to believe lies.

Cesare Pavese

The funeral were really well attended, over 300 showed up, and we had the wake at the working men's club on the estate. Sis' had found a good caterer from Peckham and she put on a beautiful spread. I slung 600 behind the bar and Sis' gave me loads of earache for it, even the Steward of the club told me that people would take advantage but I didn't care.

Uncle even showed his face at the church for 10 minutes. I knew he'd never come to the wake but I were happy he'd paid his respects. H were there for me every step of the way. What a fucking man! He proved to me that you only really ever need *one* friend in life.

Mum died three weeks after coming home from Benidorm. They couldn't decide whether she'd accidentally or deliberately died of a Valium overdose. Her death were put down as 'misadventure', I'd say her life had been a fucking misadventure as well, because she'd ended up lumbered with my cunt of a Dad.

Me and Sis' were obviously distraught but what could we do? It looked like Mum wanted out at any cost and I kind of had to respect that. Me and Sis' went over it again and again and ended

up agreeing we couldn't have done anything differently. We'd
tried to help her but it didn't wash. I sort of consoled myself that
she'd slipped away rather than going in agony or fear. Sis'
went through a period of calling Mum a selfish cow for taking the easy
way out. I disagreed with her. Suicide ain't fucking 'easy' and I
don't subscribe to it being the cowards way out.

H gave me a recent plated Golf GTi for Sis', in lieu of the
9 thousand I'd lost on his ill-fated Snap On Tool's graft over in
Essex. I told him he didn't have to but he insisted. Sis' were over
the moon and the envy of all her mates.

Uncle gives it, "It's only 30 large, son. Up to you if you want
it. No pressure."

"Definitely, Uncle."

"Good. Glad to hear it."

"Geezer called Billy's gonna give you the details."

"Billy?"

"I'm moving things around a bit. Gonna be spending a bit
more time abroad. Billy's solid. Trust him with my life. Remember
this number."

I called Billy later that day and we met up outside the Angel
tube station. 'Billy" would have been about 40 at the time. No
words, he slipped me a piece of paper and walked off. I'd memorized the details by the time I'd descended the stairs back down
to the tube. There were no photo or image of the mark but there
were a detailed description. I ripped the piece of paper into really tiny pieces as I sat on the train. I got off at Elephant & Castle
and walked to where the old Bedlam nuthouse used to be and
then turned back on myself to make sure I weren't being followed. I put the details, which were now confetti, in a bin and
went back down to the tube.

I called the builders yard and told 'em I had the lurgy. If I needed more time for reconnaissance, I'd have to go blag a sick note from the doctor, but I arrogantly went against all my better judgement and thought I'd be able to pull it off in a few days. *What a cunt!*

The hit were gonna be in Russel Square in Bloomsbury; one of the large townhouses that overlooked the park. I went up on the bike a couple of times just to get a feeling for the area. There were plenty of side streets to slip down but I decided once I'd done the job, I'd shoot up the A4200 swing a left and head west on the A501.

It soon became apparent that my mark hardly ever left the gaff. What I did notice though was that motorcycle and van couriers were back and forth to the address. I watched two bikes and a van turn up at intervals in one day alone. One of the vans was from a photography developing company, and the bike couriers I'd seen were handing over large bound envelopes at the door. This gaff definitely had something to do with photography, not that I were bothered, but it gave me an idea.

I went and bought a large top box and stuck it on the bike to make it look like I were a courier. I then went and bought a large brown envelope and put it in the box. I picked up the piece from the fish & chip shop that evening. It were an Heckler & Koch P9S with a moderator. I'd never fired one before and should have fucking practiced, but didn't.

I were surprised and even a bit shocked to get a call at home from Billy. He sounded a bit flustered asked me to meet him that night outside Kings Cross station. I went along and we walked up York Way. Change of plan. He told me that the mark now needed to disposed of once I'd snuffed him. The disposal would be arranged by him but he said that I'd have to kill the mark in the house. I told him I didn't have a problem with this. I'd step inside when I made the delivery, do him, lock the door and bring the key with me.

He thought about and gives it, "Do you reckon there's a plant pot outside the front door? If there is you could leave the key under it for the cleaners."

I told him I didn't know if there were a plant pot but I had my bike with me and could nip around and have a look. Billy said he'd wait in Mabel's Tavern for me. I were back 15 minutes later and simply popped my head round the door and gave him the thumbs up. He nodded and I were off. I were back in business and looking forward to it. The only reservation I had was with the pistol, not knowing my way around an HK P9S. Again, arrogance on my behalf, thinking it would be fine.

I pulled up at Russel Square right outside the gaff. I made sure when my mark answered he'd see the bike and be assured I were just a courier. There were a gate and then a dozen paces to the eight steps leading up to the front door. I've got my full-face helmet on, leather gloves, the envelope in in hand and my other hand free to whip out the piece. I take a deep breath, press the door bell and wait.

The door opens and it's my mark. I immediately step inside saying that he's got to sign for the delivery. He frowns and stepping back gives it, "Excuse me?" I push him in the chest, immediately pull out the shooter and aim. He panics and puts his hands up in defence. I fire but the bullet just grazes the side of his forehead. He screams and lunges at me. I kick the door shut with my heel as he flops into me screaming.

He's right up against me and he bows his head. It's like he's trying to be so on top of me I can't fire again. I manage to get him in an overarm headlock and I'm pushing down on him. He's screaming blue murder now so I stick the snoz of the silencer right up behind his ear and fire. Ping! He folds and lands at my feet in a praying position. I push him away with my foot onto his back and see that there's blood all down the front of my jeans. It's from the first shot that scraped his nut. I'm fucking panicking now. He's jam and I only have to drag him a couple of feet back to make sure that the cleaner is able to open the door, but the claret down my Levi's is driving me fucking potty. It's messy. A fucking mess and I'm working myself up into a right two n' eight. There's no way I'm leaving that gaff with blood on me.

I start pacing and cursing myself and banging my hand against my helmet. *Look at you! You're supposed to be a pro you mug!* My vision starts narrowing and I'm feeling like I'm gonna throw up. The watery acid in my mouth is choking me and everything starts slowing down. I look around the hall, for what, I don't know, and then I force myself to look down at my bloody jeans. I can't, I refuse to leave with the blood of my mark on me.

I take off my jeans and place them on top of the corpse. Why? I don't fucking know; panic makes you do all kinds of fucking stupid. I shoot up the stairs and see like a photo studio. I run straight past it into another room. I open the wardrobe and see a tracksuit folded up. I grab the bottoms and quickly put 'em on. They're far too big for me. I. AM. A. FUCKING. CLOWN. I fly back down the stairs and stand over the corpse, my bloody Levi's draped over his chest. Now, if I'd have been thinking right, I would have grabbed the jeans and stuffed them inside my jacket.

I weren't thinking right though. My thoughts were like little bubbles that kept popping every time I tried to grab hold of one. At least the nausea had subsided but it were now replaced with like a clenched fist in my throat. I were having trouble breathing and I thought that I were gonna pass out.

I had to crouch down and take deep breaths. The dead mark turned his head and started laughing at me. I closed my eyes and tried to remember how to summon up reality. I started talking out loud, probably gibberish and then I remember counting. My motor neurons finally kicked up and I dropped the shooter on top of my bloody jeans that were on top of my dead mark that were on top of a pool of blood that were on top of an expensive Parque floor and I … I stood up. I stood up and I went to the door and I opened it and then locked it from the outside and put the key under the plant pot.

I couldn't tell you if anyone saw me leave and get on my bike because I were blinded by self-loathing. I don't know which route I took and I don't know how long I were riding. I were on auto-pilot and certain I were gonna crash. I finally pulled up somewhere and could feel tears of anger rolling down my cheeks. I took my helmet off and walked down a street. It were night and I went and sat on a bench and replayed what I'd done back in Russel Square.

I were a fucking pretender. A mug playing at being a contract killer. Who the fuck did I think I were? I'd jeopardized everything by not planning properly. I were a lazy, arrogant cunt that didn't deserve to work for people like Uncle. I were a liability that deserved to be taken out for fucking things up so badly.

Uncle asked me to meet him on Waterloo Bridge a couple of days later. I were shitting myself, expecting him to tell me that he never wanted to work with me or ever see me again. I were expecting him to tell me I were dead to him and to wipe from my mind that I'd ever even met him.

Before Uncle could say anything, I gives it, "I'm sorry, Uncle. I know I fucked up. I should have practised with the piece. I were being fucking lazy."

Uncle frowned at me, "What you on about, son?"

"The job. The jeans. I missed him with the first shot and he –"

"- woah, wait a minute. Billy said it were a good job. Said it were sweet. I don't know what you're rabbiting on about, son."

I explained to him what had happened. He thought about it and then simply shrugged and smiled, "So you got a bit of claret on your strides and left 'em for the cleaner to get rid of? Is that what you've been worrying about? … You did what you had to do, like old Blue Eyes, stop fretting. No cunt's perfect."

TWENTY-THREE

We are in a world that is quite extremist and extremism
makes more noise. Normality does not sell.

Vicente del Bosque

I worked at the builder's merchants from 88 to 97 and only took
three contracts in those 9 years. It weren't that Uncle had fucked
me off over the Russel Square job, it's just that he were busy
in the drugs trade and he'd slacked off a little on the contract
killing side of his business. 'Billy' seemed to be his right-hand
man now and it were him that contacted me whenever anything
needed to be discussed.

So yeah, I were laid off from the builder's merchants in 97.
They laid about five of us off because the timber side had fallen
off due to competition from another merchant nearby. I were
now living in the flat where I'm still at. I'd paid for Sis' to go
to university in Birmingham, and when she graduated, I bought
her a nice drum in Bexleyheath out of the dough I'd earned on
the three contracts. I were so proud of her. She was the first person in our family ever to go to university, and I know Mum would
have been over the moon.

I'd took up painting again but still just for my own enjoy-
ment. I weren't showing them to any cunt and I were fine with it.

I didn't look for another 'day job' because I were enjoying just staying in the flat reading, watching films, avoiding the neighbours and occasionally painting. I had a routine and I liked it.

It were around this time that I started taking stock, thinking about my future. I were still young, 35, but I felt old, ancient sometimes. Not physically but mentally. I felt liked I'd crammed a lot into my years. This were obviously down to the killings I'd done. They had definitely aged me. It's like old Freddy Nietzsche said, "Battle not with monsters, lest ye become a monster, and if you gaze into the abyss, the abyss gazes also into you."

I had enough to pay my rent, food and bills for two years but if the contract work dried up after that I didn't know what I were gonna do. I'm not gonna apologize for saying this, but I only ever truly felt alive when I were engaged to kill some poor cunt. I suppose it were at this point I realized I were a proper psychopath, which might sound odd after reading about all the previous skullduggery I'd done, but now I'd read enough to realize that I were a fucking headcase. A functioning headcase, but a bleeding headcase none the less.

I decided I finally wanted to find out about the corpses I'd created. It weren't pretty reading, some of them were venal cunts, but even if it had been saints I'd offed I don't think it would have rattled me. I'd done what I'd done and that was that. No point crying over spilt claret, and even taking into account having my trousers down a couple of times, I'd managed to set Sis' up for life, and that were an achievement.

H had now moved to Essex and settled down with his long-suffering missus (wink) and they had two lovely teapots who they doted on. H had done really well for himself and had three legit' car lots and were importing high end car parts from the continent. He hadn't changed though and were prone to fly off the handle at any given moment. He had never go to the bottom of who had us over on the great Snap On Tools graft, and this had made him even more suspicious of people.

I used to go over to Essex once a month for a visit and it weren't long after arriving before he'd be filling me in on the all the agg he'd been dealing with. Why he moved to Essex is beyond me. He seemed to hate every cunt that lived there and he weren't bothered about telling 'em. H were in clover because of his family connections, but even if he hadn't been connected, I don't think it would have stopped him putting it on the toes of the good people of Essex.

H told me about a young Muscle Mary who'd tried to take advantage of his good nature by pulling a stunt on the sale of a Porsche 911. This juiced up whippersnapper fancied himself as a tough guy and when H laid the law down he more or less laughed in H's face. This Muscle Mary were supposed to be the new hotshot on the block serving up gear, and had a few joeys running around with him. Him and his firm had taken over a pub and used to lord it there most nights.

H went in one night when he knew it would be packed, tooled up with only a smelly old sock. Mary and his boys were peacocking at the bar as H went straight over to the pool table and interrupted the game by grabbing two of the balls and slipping them inside the smelly sock. A few seconds later and Mary's on the floor screaming like a little girl, begging H to stop battering him with the offensive sock. One of Mary's joey's steps up and H gives him it as well. The others had a collective prolapse.

It were quite tame by H's standards, but I could see the love in his eyes as he told me the story. H said Mary coughed up the 2 large he owed him that very night. Mary were apparently paying a respected Essex villain to use his name, but when the villain found out he'd tried having H over he gave him an hiding as well.

I missed having H on the doorstep. I even considered that I might move over to Essex one day. I love London but I fucking detest the gentrification. Where I were living at the time – and still am – hadn't yet succumb to the creeping, characterless shit-ness of it all, but it were in the post and, unfortunately, as of today it's being delivered.

I met Uncle *and* Billy on Westminster Bridge on a very cold November late afternoon in 98. We went for a cup of tea, which felt weird. It were getting dark and we sat outside a café. Uncle looked like he had a lot on his plate but Billy were cool.

Uncle were right into me, whispering, "This one's a biggie. A lot – and I mean, fuck loads o' dough at stake. There's no time for fucking about, son. We've had a snoop and he only goes back n' forth to the office. Billy don't reckon you'll be able to clip him on his way to work n' back, tell him, Billy."

Billy closed in, "I doubt you'll be able to do it without getting seen. Tail to tail traffic. Jammed."

Uncle sighed, "It'll have to be another doorstepping. No time for planning."

I didn't see a problem, "That's all right."

"You sure? That thing in Russel Square. I remember you were a bit flummoxed."

"That were 'cos of the piece. I prefer Glocks."

"All right ... you get 40 straight if you pull it off, son. How's that sound?"

I nodded, "Sounds good, Uncle. Sweet."

Billy leaned in even further, "Thing is. We're up against the clock. It's gotta be done yesterday, day before if possible. I know it's impossible but you know what I mean." "Yeah, sure."

Uncle looked at Billy and Billy looked back at Uncle. There were a few seconds where I could tell they were telepathically debating whether I were getting the contract. Uncle finally patted me on the back as he stood up to dissapear into the brass monkeys' night, "It's yours, son. Do us proud."

I didn't have a bike at the time so I went to the auctions the next morning and bought a Kawasaki KE 125 with cash and a moody name. I didn't wait for them to get me the logbook. I figured that this caper, because I were doorstepping, could possibly end with me being chased and I needed something that I could go off road with. I thought about getting something bigger, engine wise, but in my experience bigger engines weren't as good on the rough.

That afternoon I went up North London for a recce. Under any other circumstances I would have never took a contract on that were so obviously risky, but I could tell this were a VIP job for Uncle. The street were pretty quiet. It had these nice semi and detached houses that were painted white and the road were lined with these strange looking trees, like massive Bonsai trees. Down at the end of the street were an A road where I could fly down to on the getaway. Just off the A road were some land with a stream running through it. That's where I'd be heading if it came on top. Billy told me my mark would be arriving home between 5.15 and 5.25 so it would be dark. At least *that* were a positive.

I went back to my flat and changed the license plates on the bike. I had two hours to kill before I could kill some poor cunt in North London. As I sat down with a cup of rosy, the gravity of what I were about to do landed on my shoulders. There were a song out at the time called 'Wide Open Space' by a band called Mansun. I had it on CD single and I played it on repeat as I psyched myself up. There were something about it that inspired me, inspired me in that indescribable way only music can do. I must have played it 20 times. There's a line in the song that gives it, *you'll never get to heaven with a smile on your face from me,* so I suppose I were acting the cunt a bit and romanticizing what I were about to do.

I rode on to the street just as my mark were pulling up outside his drum. I parked the bike and climbed off. He were heading to the side door at the rear of the house. I pulled out the piece and took aim. He sensed me and looked over his shoulder just as I put three into his back. He fell forward and crawled a little. I stepped forward, put another one into the back of his head and he were jam. He never let go of the briefcase with his left hand.

I walked backwards for a few paces, staring at his corpse, put the piece back in my jacket, turned and walked to my bike. I stayed steely calm, turned the key and rode off. I never opened up the throttle, I knew I weren't being followed. When I got to the A road I slung a right and headed east. I threw the piece in the spot where the River Lea and Pudding Mill River meet.

There'd been no splashback so I didn't have to ditch any of my clobber. I thought about pushing the bike into the river, I don't though, sixth sense. I just had a feeling I should get shut. I got home and changed the plates back over and put the plates I'd used on the hit in a black bin bag with a dumbbell. I threw the bag in the Thames later that night.

My wetwork were in the papers and on the news the next day, and someone had given Old Bill a description of the bike that were seen leaving the scene. My spider senses had been right and I should have ditched the bike when I ditched the shooter. I changed the plates back over again and set off for Bedfordshire.

I'd remembered H telling me about a place where he'd burnt out a few stolen motors in the past.

I bought a plastic jerry can and filled it with petrol at a station just outside Luton, then rode to a quarry at Sundon just as night were falling. H were right. There were loads of burnt-out vehicles scattered about. I put my helmet on the seat of the Kawasaki, poured the petrol over, light a match, stepped back and watched it burn. I walked into Luton and caught a train back to London.

I were feeling good on the train. Uncle would be happy with how smooth the hit had gone. This were an important one for him and I knew why. Not that I'd have ever told him I knew why, or that I'd even spill the beans today, but I'd worked out from the newspaper reports that were a hit that would massive repercussions, some good, some bad.

The payments came in four installments of 10 large 'fish suppers'. I'd started to get a bit paranoid having wedges of cash in the flat. The dough were in my little peter but if I'd ever been burgled, some cunt were gonna have a beano. There were no way I was gonna open a bank account in my real name, and I didn't exactly have a good track record with lending and investing, getting a safe deposit box would mean answering questions I didn't want to, so I weren't left with any option other than to keep it stashed in the flat.

I went and got a chippy to put an expensive fortified door on the flat. I were even a bit paranoid about this, thinking this chippy would be wondering why I were turning my modest flat into Fort Knox. I pretended to him I were worried about the rising crime levels in the area. Part of me fucking hated being paranoid, but another part of me knew I needed to be in the job I did.

I'd finally settled on a painting style. You might have seen some of my paintings but you wouldn't know they're mine, so I suppose the best way to describe them is to imagine symmetrical blocks that have been daubed with bright colors. This won't help, but here's a poncy review of my paintings by some art critic cunt. It'll give you a giggle at least.

He provides the viewer with the ethereal experience of finding images and shapes within and behind other shapes and providing the viewer with a "safe passage" through the canvas. His work is full of motion, inquiry and adventure, but it also brings one a sense of comforting direction. He subconsciously guides the viewer and holds their hand as they manoeuvre through life and find their way despite the emotional roadblocks encountered in the uncaring, alienating and often suffocating cultural capitalism that tries desperately to negate his and their creativity.

Absolute fucking bollocks of course. It's like this: I paint because it relaxes me and seeing the end product makes me feel like I've achieved something. I also like painting because, as you're gonna find out, it means I can wash the dough I make from murdering people. There's also the fact that I'm making these pseudo cunts look like fucking mugs. I don't care that they don't know this. *I* know it, and that's all that matters.

TWENTY-FOUR

I exist as I am, that is enough.

Walt Whitman

Uncle told me it *had* to be a two-man job. He said my mark –
The Rat – could be tooled up, adding that if *he* were The Rat,
he'd definitely be tooled up. Uncle weren't even trying to pretend this hit weren't personal. Whoever this Rat were, he'd really
yanked Uncle's chain, and the anger was etched into his boat. I
knew fuck all about this Rat but it were clear that he was either
an employee or partner of Uncle's and something had gone seriously tits up.

The personal aspect didn't bother me. What bothered me
were the fact I'd be doing the hit with someone else. It just felt
wrong and Uncle sussed I were feeling uneasy. He told me not
to worry. I'd be working with the driver who looked like Harold
Pinter and chauffeured me to the job in North London, donkeys
back. Still, there's a big difference between getting a lift off some
cunt and actually executing someone with 'em. I'm a lone wolf
and I like it that way. Like I've said before, I live or die by my own
performance.

Uncle assured me that 'Harold Pinter' weren't actually gonna
be doing any shooting. He were gonna be there as a kind of

decoy and then he were gonna be disposing of the body. It were a relief but I still couldn't picture what the plot were. Uncle's deep-seated hatred of this Rat cunt was clouding his professionalism. Uncle were all over the shop when he was giving me the SP.

"I can only stretch to 10 large. Are you all right with that, son? This ain't a contract. It's a favour."

"Yeah, I understand. I don't need paying."

"Don't be daft, son. Course you do. We've all gotta earn a crust."

"No, honestly, Uncle. S'all right."

"No, I insist … at least take five. I wouldn't feel good about it."

Dough was the last fucking thing on my mind. This didn't sound like an assassination. It sounded like a fucking ambush of this Rat. It sounded like there were gonna be some chicanery involved instead of simply stalking and executing. This Rat might be tooled up and the thought of an actual gunfight worried me. Would I have the arse to be 'stand up' when a piece were actually pointing back at me? This thing weren't my style, but I kept schtum. I didn't want Uncle thinking I were a one trick pony or, more truthfully, that I were a bottling cunt.

Uncle was airyated, had the right fucking hump and I didn't like seeing him like this. I looked up to him like a soldier looks up to his general and Uncle weren't exactly giving off General Patton vibes. I were witnessing something I doubt any of Uncle's other minions had ever seen: he were frightened. It was quite shocking.

I told Uncle I'd want to meet up with 'Harold' to go through the MO. Uncle were fine with this and I met Harold the next day at Waterloo Station concourse. He hadn't changed much and he still had those dead eyes and carried himself well. He blinked at me through his thick specs and just said, "Oh. It's you."

Harold laid it all out: he picks me up in a van. We drive down to the West Country. The mark's holed up in a gaff and we call on him. The mark's gonna ask what I'm doing there and Harold tells him I'm gonna drive him in to the port and then drive his motor back to the hidey hole. Harold lulls the mark into a false sense of security, asks him some questions that need answering and then I clip the cunt. I stay with Harold while he disposes of the body.

"Where you gonna dispose of the body?" I ask.

"There."

"There? What do you mean, *there?*"

"In the drum. I'm gonna give him an acid bath. Well, sodium hydroxide and lye, actually."

Harold explains he were no novice when it came to dissolving bodies. I'm sure he must have clocked that my jaw had dropped, but carried on assuring me that everything would be hunky dory. *A piece of piss.* He explained that all the chemicals and equipment he needed would be in the van we were driving down in. He'd turn the body into slush – that could be washed down the drain – in little under 24 hours, and then we'd be on our toes back to London.

Now, before I continue, my problem here weren't that Harold were gonna dissolve this mark's corpse, my problem was that I were gonna be around while he did it. It went against everything I'd learned as a hitman. It felt ridiculous and rushed and desperate and not thought through and totally fucking unprofessional.

I asked him why I couldn't just follow him down there on my bike, clip the cunt and ride home whilst he turned the body into a slush puppy. He just replied that Uncle wanted it that way. I asked why, but he just shrugged.

I said, "I don't like it, to be fair. It sounds messy."

He snorted, half smiling, "Oh yeah, it's messy all right, but I know what I'm doing."

"I don't mean the acid n' stuff. I mean the whole thing. I don't wanna sound like a cunt but ... well, it sounds a bit rushed."

Harold told me if I had reservations, I should go and tell Uncle and then he could find someone else for him to do it with. I bristled at this and explained that it weren't that I didn't wanna do it, I just thought it were unnecessary to have us both there during the disposal. The cunt actually asked me if I didn't have the arse for seeing the mark dissolved. I told him it had fuck all to do with that, and reiterated that it weren't how I usually operated, and that I had a certain way of doing things.

I reminded Harold that I worked for Uncle and that we'd been pretty successful so far. Harold weren't wearing it though, he kept giving it, *orders are orders*. I asked what difference it would make if I just followed him down on my bike. *Who'd know?* This riled him up, "Do me a favour! *I'd* fucking know and if anything goes pear, how do I explain to the gaffer we'd just ignored him and done what the bleedin' 'ell we liked?"

Harold did have a point, but it were the arbitrariness of it all that were putting the willies up me, and I started thinking this job were gonna be a fucking suicide mission. I asked Harold what sort of piece I'd be using. He gives it, "Beretta M9A3."

I replied, "I don't like Luger's."

"I'm not a fuckin' armorer! You use what we have."

"I don't like this. It's not right."

He leaned into me, "Right, get on the fuckin' blower and tell him you're not up for it."

"I didn't say that. I just think … I think we need to think about this."

"There's nothing to think about. All the thinkin's been done. Now … you in or what?"

I sighed and nodded positive. He picked me up in a van the next morning at 8 near Stockwell tube. I hadn't slept a fucking wink and felt like shit. There were a fucking great boulder in my stomach and I felt nothing but dread and impending doom. All I wanted to do were sleep and wake up after the job had been done. Me and Harold didn't exchange *one* word for about half an hour. He were listening to an oldies radio station and singing along without a care in the world. He got particularly excited when 'What Are You Doing Sunday?' by Tony Orlando and Dawn started playing. The way he were acting, it were like we were off to have a lovely little picnic in the countryside.

I really wanted to like this cunt but I couldn't. I just intuitively knew he were gonna be a hindrance and the whole plot were fucking topsy turvy. I couldn't believe Uncle had sanctioned this kind of hit. It were rank fucking amateur and I couldn't believe it were gonna go down without a cock up.

He finally started talking to me when we got on the A303, but that were only to ask me if I'd had any grub and whether I were feeling a bit peckish. We stopped at a *Little Chef* and Harold remarked, "They should call these places the little fuckin' extortionists."

I weren't interested in his Egon Ronay restaurant criticism, my mind were already focusing on what were gonna happen when we got to our destination. Harold said he knew this Rat really well and, yeah, he probably would be armed, but we had fuck all to worry about. It were simply a case of us going in and Harold speaking to him. Once that were done, I'd then snuff the cunt. This Rat clearly weren't expecting to be popped so I asks why he'd be tooled up. Harold explained that this Rat had a bounty on his head the size of the national fucking debt, and that he were already hiding out from a firm out of North London. Harold reminded me – as if I needed reminding – that we were doing this job as a big favour to Uncle.

See, I didn't want to hear any of this. Uncle had always been careful to give me just the right amount of information I needed to do my hits. This were just fucking wrong. I couldn't get the image of Uncle being nervous out my nut. *Had he been playing at operating like a professional cool cunt? Were he a phony? Were he really just an amateur who'd manged to get lucky and avoid being pinched all these years? Had I been sold a fucking pup? Were I really part of a two-bob murder outfit instead of an outfit who I'd thought were on a par with Murder Inc.?*

By the time we got to Wincanton, this cunt Harold were singing along to John Paul Young's 'Love is in The Air' at the top of his voice. He didn't give a fucking monkeys. I just stared ahead at the road and seethed. *This* was my life and I just had to accept that *every* choice I'd ever made had led me to this point.

Good old Reason bowled up with his sleeves rolled; *nobody's perfect, in fact there's no such thing as perfection! And so what if Uncle's dropped a bollock on this one? The cunt's only human! You don't know what he's going through! The poor cunt might have his reasons! This could be the only way he can think of to get rid of this Rat! Uncle's never let you down before, you cunt! Why you acting like a prima donna? Who the fuck do you think you are? Billy big bollocks! Have a little faith, you pillock!*

Reason was bang on the money as per usual. I started to relax a bit. What point were there resisting an irresistible force? This was *it*, and I were in *it*. Simple.

236

Supertramp's 'Take The Long Way Home' came on the radio and I hummed along to it. Harold didn't know it, but he didn't slag it. *If* he had slagged it I would have pointed out that genius mouth organ solo. Next up were 'Happy Heart' by Andy Williams and the cunt were singing along like a bastard. Harold *really* did live in the moment, and he didn't learn to do that at one of them poncy, fucking expensive Buddhist retreats. Harold lived in the moment because in Harold's world he had no choice. His past was an alibi and his future would probably be curtailed by some cunt like me snuffing him. Harold only had *the now*.

We got to the very picturesque Penzance around 2pm and immediately got lost. Harold reckoned he'd memorized the directions but clearly hadn't. It's not advisable to ask some cunt on the street for directions to a gaff you're gonna murder and dissolve some cunt in, so Harold got on the blower. Mobile phones were around at this time but they always used phone boxes if possible. Pagers were a big thing with Uncle's firm for quite a long time as well. I watched Harold on the phone in the box and he were nodding his head like an obedient dog. As he climbed back in he gives it, "It's just round the corner. All these places look the fuckin' same. The fuck would you wanna live in a shithole like this for? Back o' beyond."

I give it, "I thought you'd like Penzance. It's full o' pirates."

It were lost on him and he just frowned at me. We drove off and he started giving me the MO. I listened and pulled out the Beretta from under the seat and inspected it. It were already cocked which I found a bit dangerous, but kept schtum. We went down a winding road and arrived at a large detached cottage. Harold swung the van around the back and parked up next to nice new BMW 3 series coupe.

The Rat were stood at the door, looking more like a rabbit in the headlights than a rodent. He were about 40, tall, handsome and very fucking posh. He were also sweating like a cunt and looked like he hadn't slept for days. He looked at Harold as if to say, *what's that cunt doing here?* But in a posh accent.

Harold waffled him about me being there to drive him to the port once the chinwag were over. The Rat didn't seem too convinced and he paused before he let us in and bolted the door. Me and Harold sat at the kitchen table as The Rat went and put the kettle on. We both clocked the Ruger P series pistol tucked into his waistband. I recognized it by the silver trigger. You don't see too many yank pistols over here and I'd heard it were a decent tool.

The Rat were probably the poshest berk I'd ever met. He reeked of 'old money'. You know the kind who robbed all the peasants centuries back, when villains were called lords and lairds and gentlemen. I couldn't help wondering what the fuck he were doing getting in the mix with the likes of Uncle and Harold. He made us coffees and Harold weren't happy, *ain't you got any fucking rosy?* The Rat actually offered to nip out and buy some teabags, and for a minute I thought Harold were going to let him. The Rat poured our coffees down the sink. Harold settled on a tumbler of whiskey and I had a can of lukewarm Tizer.

The Rat sat down with us and he were shitting it in a way I'd never seen before. You don't often get cunts of his stature and breeding so lacking in confidence. He had a few ticks and a bit of a stutter going on and sounded not unlike that cunt Hugh Grant in that 4 Weddings film. He called Harold by his real name and they certainly knew each other. It became clear that it weren't me and Harold The Rat were shitting it about, so by that reckoning, it can't have been Uncle either. It were this firm from North London making his sphincter open and shut like a muppets mouth, and mine would have been as well, knowing what this outfit did to people who crossed 'em.

I didn't have a fucking dolly what they were yapping about and I didn't want to know. The bottom line were that this Rat had grassed some cunt up or were about to or he'd been touted to do some grassing. Harold were pressing him for names and dates and this, that and the other. The Rat's spilling like a broken pipeline and Harold tells me to go wait in the living room.

I thought about flicking the telly on but noticed that there was a well-stocked bookcase, so I had a gander. Lots of history books, a few political biographies and one on the actor Peter Sellers that I pulled out and sat down with. I were feeling a bit shagged but it wouldn't have looked good having a kip on a contract killing. I focused and really started getting into the book. Sellers were a right fucking mummy's boy but there were no denying his talent and he were obviously a bit of an headcase, but you've got to hand it to him, he were smart and didn't take any shit off producers and directors.

I were about 70 pages in when Harold and The Rat joined me. They were both on the whiskey now. Harold asked me what I was reading *for*. Not *what*. I just told him there were nothing on the telly but this sparked him to turn it on to see if there actually was *nothing* on the box. The Rat had calmed down a bit now and slumped on the sofa. We caught each other's eyes and he asked me what I were called. I gave him a moody name. You could tell that whatever Harold had said to him had alleviated the weight he were carrying.

Harold were looking at the telly and flicking through the channels when The Rat asked me where I were from. I just said *London* and he said *me too*. Harold said he were gonna have to nip out and make a call and did either of us any coins. The Rat reached into his pocket and pulled out a handful of pound coins. Harold just grabbed the lot and said, *ta.*

I were hoping Uncle wouldn't be too long with the phone call. I really didn't want to start having a chat with The Rat. Whatever he'd done he were very polite and seemed like a nice bloke. Besides Dennis, The Rat were gonna be the first cunt I'd snuffed that I'd conversed with. I didn't like the idea of it. When I asked Harold if he were gonna be long on the blower, the cheeky cunt said, *why? You got summink better to do?*

Soon as Harold were out the door, The Rat asked me if I worked with him a lot. I just said, *sometimes.* The Rat starts off loading about how he can't wait to get out of the country and tells me he's never coming back. He says he'll miss his family and friends and I can see him getting a bit teary eyed. I'm thinking, this poor cunt don't have a clue about where he's *really* going, and it's only gonna be a toss-up between two destinations: the grave or the crematorium ... I then remembered he were actually destined for the plug hole or drain.

Just as I've started to feel a tiny bit of empathy for him, The Rat starts blaming every cunt and his dog for the schtuck he's in. All these names, one after the other, he were singing like fucking Pavarotti, and it's dawning on me that this cunt can't help himself put names up, like he had some form of fucking Tourette's syndrome, only instead of effing and jeffing he were spouting on about the biggest names in the London serious crime game. More than that though, this Rat cunt weren't taking any responsibility for *his* choices. None of it were his fault. Typical fucking narcissist.

He shut his cakehole sharpish when Harold came back. The Rat were asking Harold if everything had been 'smoothed out'. Harold told him it had, but he couldn't guarantee that the North

Londoners were gonna buy it. Whatever 'it' was. The Rat said he weren't concerned about that. He reckoned they'd never get to him where he was going, a bit too smugly for my liking. The Rat then started slagging off this North London firm and I could see Harold thought the same as me: *this cunt can't keep his gob shut. He's a fucking liability.* The Rat nipped for a piss, and Harold whispered that the time had come for me to do him. Harold wanted him doing in the kitchen because it would be easier to clean the claret off the linoleum floor.

Harold manoeuvred us all into the kitchen under the pretence that we were Hank Marvin, and The Rat should make us something to eat. The Rat started looking through the cupboards as I pulled out the tool and crept up behind him. Just as he were telling us he didn't have much in besides soup, I closed in and put one straight into the back of his head. There were no silencer on the Beretta and the report rang out something rotten.

The Rat shot forward into the door of the cupboard and collapsed to the floor face up. I put another one in his heart for good measure. Harold stood up and rubbed his hands together, "Right. Let's get cracking."

Me and Harold brought in all the equipment from the van: gallons of various chemicals, a huge empty copper-bottomed metal barrel, a stove contraption, five bottles of Calorgas, dozens of bottles of bleach and Vim and disinfectant, a bag of cleaning cloths, various tools, a gas mask, rubber gloves, a crate of bottled water, a first aid kit, a full protective rubber suit, a portable radio and a couple of bags of Asda groceries.

Harold set up his stall in the bathroom, it were quite spacious and Harold were clearly pleased with his work environment. The empty metal barrel was placed on top of the big stove that were connected to the gas bottles. We dragged the dead Rat up into the bathroom and Harold undressed him. When he were bollock naked we lifted him into the empty barrel. He were in a crouched position and there were plenty of room still left for Harold to pour his corrosive chemicals in. Harold told me there were a couple of Cottage pies in the Asda bags and that I should warm 'em up in the oven in about an hour. He added that there were a couple of tins of peas and potatoes as well.

I laid out on the sofa and got back into reading the Peter Sellers biography. I could hear Harold upstairs, stomping about, doing his business and singing along to the radio. He obviously didn't have his gasmask on yet. I were wondering how much more assistance he were gonna need from me. I'm not squeamish and were intrigued as to how Harold were gonna turn a corpse into soup, so I suppose I were hoping he'd ask for my help.

About an hour and a half later me and Harold sat down for Cottage pie, peas and potatoes in the kitchen. Harold wolfed his down in a breath and went back upstairs to continue chemically boiling the Rat. I went up a bit later and stood on the landing watching Harold perform in the bathroom. He were wearing the rubber suit, the gasmask and gloves and were taking a peek inside the barrel. He saw me and then gave the 'thumbs up'. He shouted through the gasmask, "I reckon another 20 hours and he's good."

I laid on the sofa but couldn't concentrate on the biography. I had a sudden attack of nihilistic thought. I started thinking about all of mankind's achievements down the ages and how all of them would one day mean fuck-all in the scheme of things, and how all the smart cunts who'd pulled off all these achievements would be forgotten and then I started thinking about what happens when … I had to stop myself. It didn't matter. Nothing really mattered, but nothing *could* matter because there's no matter in nothing. *Fucking stupid invasive thoughts.*

I put the telly on and caught the arse end of a documentary about the state of the NHS. I were feeling really knackered now and went and laid down again. There were a kind of metallic smell in the air so I pulled my jumper up over my mouth and nose and started to nod off. I were picturing what would happen if Old Bill unexpectedly turned up. *Could I shoot a plod? No problem. Could I shoot a bird plod? Yeah. Would I leave Harold if I had to get on my toes? Absolutely. Would I put one in Harold's nut before leaving in case he turned over? In a breath.*

I don't remember having any dreams. Harold shook me awake about 8 in the morning. He were stood over me in the gas-mask and I nearly jumped out my fucking skin. He were talking to me but I couldn't make out what he were saying. He took the gasmask off, "I reckon about another ten hours. Ten or twelve hours I reckon, 'fore we get him down the drain. Fancy a bacon sarnie n' a cup o' rosy?"

By noon I were fucking rattling with boredom. I wrapped a tea towel around my mouth and hooter and went up to the bathroom. Harold were sat on a chair staring out of the bed-room window, his back to me, singing along to 'Hold Me Close' by David Essex on the radio. I didn't interrupt him. I grabbed a bottle of bleach and some clothes and went down to the kitchen and started cleaning up the claret The Rat had spilled when I clipped him.

Harold's estimate were out by a few hours. It were 2 am by the time the goose were cooked. That meant The Rat had been stewing for 31 hours. Me and Harold carried the barrel downstairs. It were heavy as fuck and we kept having to stop for breathers. There were a jubilee ring lid on the barrel and I sud-denly tried to imagine what would happen if it came unstuck and spilled out. *Would we be burned to death and our bodies dissolved into The Rat's slush like some fucking unholy trinity of gloop?* We could hear the radio playing in the bathroom. The strange, spooky and very fucking annoying 'Cinderella Rockefella' by Esther and Abi Ofarim were playing, and this cunt Harold were singing along to it, even singing the bird's part of the song. He were really getting on my tits now.

I pulled the grate off the drain. Harold put his gasmask back on and I smothered up in the tea towel again. We slowly and carefully tilted the barrel and poured the creamy reddish slush The Rat had been reduced to down the drain. It took fucking ages, but it didn't smell too obnoxious. Harold reached into the barrel and pulled out the dregs, he were wearing the gloves, obviously, and then we poured about a dozen 4 litre bottles of bleach and drain cleaner down to chase away The Rat sludge. I went to the kitchen, turned both taps on and let the water drain down the sink while we grabbed all the equipment we'd brought and loaded it into the van. We then scrubbed everything we'd touched with soapy clothes and diluted bleach.

Two hour's later and Harold's shining a torch down the drain with a satisfied grin on his mush. There's no trace that The Rat ever existed in the corporeal form. It were about 7 am by the time we drove away. Harold were only bothered about finding somewhere 'nice n reasonable' to have our breakfasts. He was vehement that we wouldn't be stopping at a Little fucking Chef. I were just happy to be heading back to London. I were like that Dorothy in The Wizard of Oz: *there's no place like home.*

TWENTY- FIVE

A large income is the best recipe for happiness I ever heard of.

Jane Austen

It just came to me when I were coming back from doing some wetwork in Holland. I suppose it were just one of those fucking eureka lightbulb moments, although having just visited the Van Gogh Museum, after popping some poor Dutch cunt, might have had something to do with it. Anyway, it were March 2001 and I were still living in the flat and taking contracts from Uncle. I figured that if I sold this idea to him properly we could both really benefit.

I really did have to start thinking about my future. I'd resigned myself to the fact that I were never gonna get wed and have a family, so I suppose I were a bit like Fagan in the film *Oliver!* You know, where he starts singing about who's gonna look after him when he's an old codger and worrying about whether he's salted enough dough away to see him right with a nurse or something when he's dribbling n' pissing n' shitting his self. As old David Bowie said, *time is the sniper in the brain,* and there's no escaping its sights.

Now, don't get me wrong, as I've said, it's not like I'm afraid of popping my clogs, but I'm not gonna top myself either, I enjoy reading books and watching films too much and I wouldn't do that to Sis' after what Mum did. So, at this point I'm thinking that simply shoving my wages in the peter weren't such a good idea. I still needed to stay completely under the fucking radar, but I also needed something in place to legitimize me to a certain extent as well. What if I got pinched doing a contract? What if some villainous cunt had *me* snuffed? What if I died with a massive wedge in the peter? Where would it go? All kinds of what ifs.

I could have just started handing my dough to Sis' – she would be the only beneficiary when I kicked the bucket anyway – but then I were getting a bit para about that too. Giving her big fuck-off wads of used notes were, in effect, making her complicit in my murderous lifestyle.

Me and Uncle met on Tower Bridge. I told him what I wanted to do were find an art gallery in London and persuade them to put my paintings up for sale in there. Instead of Uncle paying me in cash for my hits, he would simply send someone into the gallery to buy one of the paintings for the price we'd agreed for the hit, in cash. The gallery owner would take their percentage for flogging the painting, and then the rest would be transferred by the gallery owner into a company account I would have access to.

Uncle thought about it and then started slowly nodding his head, he liked it. He liked it a lot. He asked me if there would be anything stopping us from doing it on a bigger scale, as I knew he would. I were honest with him and admitted that I weren't no expert in the art market. I told him that I couldn't see any problems in him opening an art gallery of his own and washing *his* money through it.

It were a relatively straight forward graft: open an art gallery, sell any old shit paintings for as much cash as you want and

Bob's yer uncle. Uncle suddenly changed his mind and said that it were too simple to be able to work.

He gives it, "Where would you get these pictures?"

"Anywhere, *I* could knock 'em up. It's modern art. A teapot could do it."

Uncle gives it, "Nah, nah, let's think about this ... we're missing summink."

"What we missing?"

"I dunno ... it sounds too fuckin' easy."

"That's cos it is, Uncle. All good ideas *are* simple. Look, you fill this gallery with a load of so-called art, it don't have to be any good, any old fuckin' tat'll do. You get some cunts going in n' buying it with the cash you need washing and, well, there you go. Instant laundry service. You don't actually need anyone going in come to think about it. You just run your dirty cash through there and any tax and VAT men coming sniffing about you just tell 'em all your sales have been in cash. How they gonna prove they weren't? Think about it."

I thought Uncle were gonna plant a big kiss on my lips. It were the first time I'd ever seen him so excited. His eyes were lit up with very clean £ signs. Anyone who knows anything knows that making dough from villainy's quite easy compared cleaning that dough. I had just handed Uncle a big fucking cure for his headache.

We were on that bridge for over an hour and half as I went over it again and again. Uncle were desperately trying to find holes in it but couldn't. I went one further as well, "Look, Uncle, you don't even have to sell the paintings most o' the time. They don't even need to exist. You just put the sales through your books. You tell me how the authorities are gonna prove anything? You do it for a year, shut up shop and go an open another gallery if you want. The last place the taxman's gonna look for laundering is the artworld. Plus, it's all silly money! You can say you've sold some of these paintings for six figures. Just imagine how much dirty dough you could wash through there."

Uncle were fucking ecstatic. I told him we should rope some cunt in who were in the artworld or knew how it operated. I could see his mind racing. It were going like one of them rolodex's, hundreds of contacts flicking past his eyes, and him trying to think if any of them had anything to do with art. The working mind of a master grafter is a wonderful thing to witness.

I said to Uncle that it were gonna be best if we found an art gallery where I could start putting my paintings in first, and have people come in and buy my 'art' in payment of my hits. Uncle replied that we could just put my paintings in the laundry gallery and have people come in and buy them in cash. I told him this wouldn't work, because if anything came on top there, Old Bill would be able to connect me and Uncle and that's the last thing on earth we needed after all the shenanigans we'd been up to. Uncle nodded, "Good thinking, son."

Uncle saw me in a new light after that night. He already knew I weren't no fucking mug or he'd have never worked with me in the first place, but after handing him the new plot on that bridge, he started rating me as smart cunt rather than just a cold-blooded killer.

It took Uncle just under two weeks to find our 'in' on this new graft. I don't know how the connections lined up but he managed to serve up someone who we'll call 'Daisy'. Daisy were in her late 20's, naturally beautiful, very posh and as daft as a fucking brush. Daisy were the daughter of some cunt or cunts who had plenty of coin, because there's no way a girl of her limited intelligence could have opened an art gallery in Mayfair off her own graft.

The gallery weren't large but she had some expensive pieces in there: a Rothko, some Warhol's, Hirst and Basquiat prints, some of Jeff Koons' balloon dogs and some Tracey Emin neon. Uncle arranged for me to go see Daisy at her gallery, and it were clear from the kick off that she were only hanging my painting under duress. I had it delivered there and went down the day after she'd received it.

She were a bit off with me and asked what price tag I wanted on it. I told her I didn't know yet. I mean, I genuinely didn't know because I didn't know how much Uncle would be paying me for my next hit. I told her to stick on 50 large. She sighed and gave me a disproving glance but agreed she would. I told her that the price might change and she just shrugged. She never commented on what she thought about my painting.

As I headed to the tube I started to feel a bit sorry for Daisy. Here she was trying to run a legit art gallery, and because somewhere along the line her family or someone she knew had become indebted to Uncle or one of his associates, she were now having to stick my shit in there amongst the genuine art. The more I thought about it though, most of the gear she were flogging in there *was* shit, besides the Warhol's in my opinion, so fuck her. She knew she were getting into a shitty business when she opened the gallery; a business just as bent and full of confidence tricksters as any pavement graft.

I went back to Mayfair a couple of nights later. I had a peek through the window and saw that my painting were now hanging between a Georgina Starr print and a fucking grotesque Chapman Brothers sculpture. I had a chuckle to myself. *What a fucking swindle this art caper were!*

About 4 months later Uncle – or whoever's name he'd put up for it – was now the proud leaseholder of a small, trendy, art gallery in Shoreditch that were gonna wash his dirty dough. He had managed to rope in the son of a Chap from Bromley, who we'll call Gene. Gene were perfect. He were a grafter and also fancied himself as a 'proper artist'. Gene and his team quickly knocked up over 200 paintings in the space of three months. They were basically ripping off Warhol's style but adding a few poncy touches.

What happened, as it so often does in the wacky world of art, is some dozy cunts with more dough than sense actually started legitimately buying these 'paintings', so now Uncle, as well as washing his dirty cash, were making money on top of it as well. Fucking Charles Saatchi couldn't lace Uncle's daisy roots up.

Uncle knew it were best not to push it and told me he were only gonna keep the gallery open for a year. Of course, as we've already well established, greed reared its head and Uncle started looking for some other premises' where he could continue carrying on the graft.

I can tell you that Uncle had his fingers in all kinds of 'art' grafts from the late 90's to the late 2000s, and he were literally 'cleaning up'. He obviously always used people to front the capers and nobody had a clue Uncle were the head honcho behind it all, but believe me, Uncle were probably the biggest player in the UK art market scam for well over a decade. It were my idea that set the ball rolling, and he saw that I got a big drink out of it, but to be honest, without his contacts and dough it could never have worked.

I figure that Uncle washed somewhere between 7 and 8 million when he were a 'patron' of the arts. I could have hung up my Glock, stopped being a hitman, and gone to work for him in the art graft at the time, but I didn't. I still saw myself as a professional killer who did a bit of painting as a hobby, and besides, nothing could give me the same life affirming thrill and masochistic panic as clipping people could.

On the first foray, Uncle arranged for someone to go in to Daisy's gallery and buy my painting for 40 large, *cash*. Daisy got her 20% cut, a nice 8 large, and she seemed happy. I were now her biggest selling client because the most she'd flogged a piece for before mine were 35 grand. One of Uncle's accountants set up a legit tax and VAT compliant business for me, that means I'm pretty much sorted for life. When I eventually retire – or *get* retired – I should be worth about a million and a half, depending on how many hits I do between now and then of course. If anything does happen to me the dough goes to Sis' and her lovely little family.

So yeah, like I said, getting involved in the art racket were a smart move, and just like Uncle's gallery opening in Shoreditch, it had unintended consequences. Because Daisy were selling my paintings, a buzz started that I were a 'hot property'. You genuinely can't make this shit up, but *I* became a 'collectable' and relatively 'valued' painter. Some of you with your beak in the world of art might have already worked out, or have a good suspicion of who I actually am now, but believe me, you'll never be able to prove it. I know, because some stupid cunts have already tried and failed miserably.

Little old murderous *me* started getting some press and attention from the cunts in the avant-garde, under a moody name obviously, and I played it cool. Like I said at the beginning, I played the 'tortured, publicity hating' artist and milked it. I'm very proud of how I've managed to remain totally fucking anonymous but 'well known' at the same time.

The art game, in my experience, is far more fraudulent than the murder for hire game. Any cunt can fake being an artist, but nobody can fake being a hitman. Well, they can try, but they'd soon get sussed out. Look at all the so called 'contract killers' that have been pinched after only doing one job.

Do I regret killing people? *Absofuckinglutely!* I found out years after the fact that I'd snuffed a cunt who were involved in child abuse pornography. My *regret* is that I didn't shoot the fucking scumbag in his groin and watch him bleed out in agony.

I suppose the biggest hit I've ever carried out were the most famous one. When Uncle and Billy gave me the name of the mark, I'd have had to have been living under a fucking rock for decades not to know who he was. I didn't give it a second thought though. He were gonna get snuffed whether I did it or not. The order had come down from 'upon high', and it weren't just the UK organized crime hierarchy that sanctioned it. This were a 'joint enterprise' with shadowy powers to make sure that things that are buried, *stay* buried.

This piece of wetwork was my highest paid, and one of the easiest I've ever carried out. I spent a lot of time on surveillance, but beside that, it were simply a case of climbing over a fence, running up to my mark in broad daylight and firing.

Uncle's knocking on nowadays and spends most of his time living between sunny Limassol in Cyprus and a big country pile in The Cotswold's. I wouldn't even try to guess how much coin he's raked in over his long and varied criminal career, but I'd be surprised if it weren't in the tens of millions, at the very least.

Billy, who Uncle were apprenticing to take over the operations, unfortunately went missing over a dispute about the murder of an hotelier's son. Billy were in Florida at the time trying to sort out some kind of 'life insurance' payment when he vanished. According to reports, Billy were last seen in a shithole area of Miami called Liberty City. He were doing the graft for Uncle and allegedly Uncle took it really hard when Billy turned up missing. I don't know whether it's true, but there were a rumor going around that Billy were Uncle's son from an affair he'd had with a Richard who served in one of his Soho clip joints in the early sixties.

Life has a habit of picking you up and plonking you down in all kinds of situations and relationships that you could never imagine. I don't buy that nonsense about people becoming criminals because of poverty and lack of opportunities. I know people heavily involved in crime who were born into wealth and had every opportunity available to them, and I know people who were born into families that didn't have a fucking pot to piss in and no opportunities whatsoever, and they're as straight as the day's long and have got the cleanest snouts around.

If I hadn't chosen to be a hitman I'm sure I would still have become involved in crime, and it's got fuck all to with the circumstances of my upbringing. You see, truth be told, crime excites me. Commiting crimes makes me feel alive. There's something in my nature, or psychological make up, that gives me an overwhelming satisfaction knowing I've gotten away with something, evaded capture and consequently punishment. There's a truth in criminality that you don't get in the legit employment market.

Now, you might put this down to the fact you believe I'm a fucking psychopath, and that may well be the case, I wouldn't argue with you, but whatever diagnosis or labels are put on me, I've still got free will and I know I could choose *not* to murder people for dough. I don't hate people. I hate the choices they make and I particularly hate that they don't take responsibility for those choices. I believe the world's plagued by cunts who don't take life seriously enough to stop and think about the impact their choices have on other people.

I know the impact my choices make on people, but more importantly, I know the impact my choices make on *me*. Let's be honest here, we're all selfish when you really get down to it.

Nobody really gives a fuck about war, disease, famine, disaster and death unless it impacts them, or the ones they really love, directly. Yeah, sure, we might stop and think it's horrible when shit happens, but how many of us would swap places with these poor cunts? We can get upset at the injustice of it all and think ourselves lucky and maybe do a bit of charity work or throw a few quid in a collection tin, stick a red nose on once a year and post some bollocks on social media, but it's all just a gesture.

I dare say there are people who've convinced themselves they genuinely fuck a give about others that they don't personally know, but the only way I'll really believe them is if they put their own lives on the line to help others, and I don't just mean being soldiers or emergency workers, I mean doing it without the guarantee of pay or prestige or being able to convince yourself and everyone else you're a 'good' person.

I wouldn't piss on most people I know if they were on fire, and in many cases I'd only piss on them if I were pissing petrol, and I don't have a problem admitting this. I don't wish harm on anyone, I just don't really care that much, and I don't feel responsible for them. Obviously, if there were a starving kid on my doorstep or some old age pensioner being mugged I'd do something about it, but I'm not gonna go out of my way looking for people to help so I can make myself feel better. Call me a cynical cunt but I'm very suspicious of so-called heroes and people who claim they're altruists.

The only person I know in history who *really* walked it like he talked it were Jesus Christ. He *chose* to be crucified to settle our debts for sinning – now that's what you call a fucking social justice warrior – and he were the only bloke in history who went and turned over the tables of the money-lenders, violently I might add, and, let's be honest again, it's because of the tear-up with the banker's the real reason why he were tortured and crucified. JC *chose* to be a victim and had the bottle to take it on the chin. A proper martyr. How many of these so called 'idealists' nowadays would put themselves through the hell JC did?

Do you know who the most oppressed, smallest minority on the earth is? It's the individual. I'm an individual and there's no collective sympathy for me and I'm happy with that. I don't want it and I don't want to be told I have to have sympathy for other individuals. It should be up to me who I have sympathy for. When you try and *make* people care, you're forcing them to act against their true instinct of self-preservation. What really gets on my tits about these cunts who try forcing you to care, is that they're usually atheists who believe we evolved from a cosmic slush. If that's the case, why do we *need* to care? If we weren't created by a God who gave us free will to choose to be good or evil, and we're just evolved slush, what the fuck does it matter if we just *don't* care?

I like proper Christians. In proper Christianity you're not claiming or trying to be a God. You admit you're a fallen cunt. You don't claim to have power over anything and you don't want any. You're basically admitting you can do fuck all about the state of the world. Proper Christians don't ram shit down people's throats if they don't wanna hear it. They're quite happy to let you carry on being a nasty cunt because they believe you're gonna get your comeuppance one day. Proper Christians admit they've got very little virtue and they'll admit that they're sinful and in need of saving. All I ever hear from these atheist woke cunts is *do this, do that, think this, don't think that, say that, don't say that, feel guilty for this, feel guilty for that.* Fuck. Off. You fascist cunts!

In my opinion, we're living in a really dangerous time. We've got a shitload of weak cunts around and weak cunts are far more dangerous than strong cunts. You've got all these hysterical fuckers crying out about oppression and inequality and *ism* this and *ist* that and how we've all got to apologize for the 'sins' of our forefathers. I've got news for these mugs: there'll always be oppression and inequality 'til the world ends. We chose to listen to that grassing cunt snake in the garden of Eden. We're fallen creatures. We're self-centered. End of.

What these berks are creating is a society full of hypocritical cunts who live in fear of offending *any* cunt, and end up bowing down to the weak fuckers who've made terrible choices in their lives. When *every* cunt's a victim. *No* cunt's a victim! And talk about human rights. I'm a human and I want the right to *not* give a fuck about every self-identifying victim of whatever they've decided is offensive this month.

It's getting to the fucking point where if people can't feel sorry for you, and don't see you as a victim, they hate you.

Well, let me tell you this, I'm *never* gonna be a victim ... I *create* victims.

PERFORMERS

Irvine Welsh and Dean Cavanagh revisit the dying days of the 1960s to reimagine what happened during the making of the first true British cult film.

They Don't Think They're Gonna Let You Stay in the Film Business.

Performers deals with masculinity at the point when the sexual revolution was saturating culture. For many working-class men, it was confusing and threatening. As secularism started to replace traditional Judaeo-Christian attitudes, a lot of men found themselves torn between embracing the liberation and clinging to the simpler, more morally binary past.

In the swinging and hallucinogenic London of 1968, visionary Scottish filmmaker Donald Cammell joined forces with cinematographer Nicolas Roeg to make "Performance". The film would star James Fox, Mick Jagger, and Anita Pallenberg, but the casting process was frustrating for Cammell because he insisted on bringing "real villains" into the roles that supported the lead character of South London gangster Chas Devlin.

What Welsh and Cavanagh identify is that strange cultural moment in 1960's London when bohemian intelligentsia flirted with the world of organised crime

VARIETY

A CRAFTY CIGARETTE
TALES OF A TEENAGE MOD

Foreword by John Cooper Clarke.
'I couldn't put it down because I couldn't put it down.'

'Crafty Cigarette, all things Mod and a dash of anarchy. Want to remember what it was like to be young and angry? Buy this book. A great read.'
Phil Davis (Actor Chalky in Quadrophenia)

'A Great Debut That Deals With The Joys and Pains of Growing Up.'
Irvine Welsh

'A coming of age story, 'A Crafty Cigarette' maybe Matteo Sedazzari's debut novel but it's an impressive story.'
Vive Le Rock

'It's a good book and an easy read. That's pretty much what most pulp fiction needs to be.'
Mod Culture

'A work of genius.'
Alan McGee (Creation Records)

'Like a good Paul Weller concert the novel leaves you wanting more. I'll be very interested in reading whatever Matteo Sedazzari writes next.'
Louder Than War

A mischievous youth prone to naughtiness, he takes to mod like a moth to a flame, which in turn gives him a voice, confidence and a fresh new outlook towards life, his family, his school friends, girls and the world in general. Growing up in Sunbury–on–Thames where he finds life rather dull and hard to make friends, he moves across the river with his family to Walton–on–Thames in 1979, the year of the Mod Revival, where to his delight he finds many other Mods his age and older, and slowly but surely he starts to become accepted...."

A Crafty Cigarette is the powerful story of a teenager coming of age in the 70s as seen through his eyes, who on the cusp of adulthood, discovers a band that is new to him, which leads him into becoming a Mod.

ISBN-13 : 978-1526203564

THE MAGNIFICENT SIX IN TALES OF AGGRO

Foreword by Drummer Steve White (The Style Council, Paul Weller, Trio Valore,)
'A vivid and enjoyable slice of London life in the 80s, with a wealth of detail and characters,'

'Tales of Aggro is a kind of time machine that takes one back to the days of 'Scrubbers'. Very redolent of those atmospherics.'
Jonathan Holloway – Theatre Director and Playwright

The **MagNiFiceNt** in tales of aggro

Matteo Sedazzari

Foreword by Steve White – Drummer – The Style Council, Paul Weller, Trio Valore. A vivid and enjoyable slice of the 60s with a wealth of detail and characters.

The Magnificent 6 in tales of aggro

Matteo Sedazzari

'Tales of Aggro has got the feel of 'Green Street' and a touch of 'Lock Stock and Two Smoking Barrels'. This is fiction for realists.'
Vive Le Rock

'A real slice of life told in the vernacular of the streets'
Irvine Welsh

'Laugh out loud funny, exciting and above all, written with real warmth and passion for London and the Character's making their way through this tale and life itself.'
Gents of London

'It's A Treat to Read, Just Like A Crafty Cigarette'
John Cooper Clarke

'Tales of Aggro is lively and funny'
Phil Davis (British Actor - Quadrophenia, Silk, The Firm)

'Tales of Aggro is a kind of time machine that takes one back to the days of 'Scrubbers', 'Scum' and 'Get Carter'. Very redolent of those atmospherics.'
Jonathan Holloway – Theatre Director and Playwright

Meet Oscar De Paul, Eddie the Casual, Dino, Quicksilver, Jamie Joe and Honest Ron, collectively known around the streets of West London as The Magnificent Six. This gang of working-class lovable rogues have claimed Shepherds Bush and White City as their playground and are not going to let anyone spoil the fun.

Meet Stephanie, a wannabe pop star who is determined to knock spots off the Spice Girls, with her girl group. Above all though, meet West London and hear the stories of ordinary people getting up to extraordinary adventures.

Please note that Tales of Aggro is a work of fiction.

ISBN-13 : 978-1527235823

TALES FROM THE FOXES OF FOXHAM

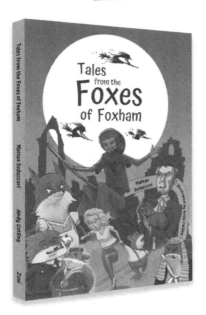

It is the late fifties and the Witches of Benevento are determined to plunge the world into darkness by kidnapping and sacrificing the jolly and young Neapolitan fox, Alberto Bandito, in a sinister ritual.

Yet, fortunately for Alberto, he is rescued, then guarded, by his loving mother Silvia and mob boss father Mario with his troops, a good witch Carlotta with an uncanny resemblance to Marilyn Monroe, the Bears of Campania, the boxing wolves' brothers Francesco and Leonardo, and other good folks of Naples and beyond.

However, their protection is not enough, for Alberto has been cursed. So, the young fox, along with his family, has to travel to the village of Foxham in Norfolk, the spiritual home of foxes across the world, to rid himself of this spell. The ritual has to be performed by a good fox witch, Trudi Milanese, but there is a problem, Trudi doesn't know she is a witch....

Tales from The Foxes of Foxham is a magical adventure story, packed with colourful characters and exciting situations, in a battle of good versus evil.

ISBN-13 : 978-1-8384624-0-6

COLA BOY

A brutal but hilarious semi-autobiographical account of Dubai in the 90s told by a young Scottish hack. A sobering story of excess and corruption with a mix of zippy dialogue, Tarantino violence and Trainspotting honesty about drugs and addiction. A must read.
Eva Pascoe (Entrepreneur and Writer)

A fast paced, kinetic debut from a writer with his finger on the pulse of the working class culture. Endearing, exciting and authentic.
Dean Cavanagh
(Author & Screen Writer)

The characters and story are as vivid and bright as the 49 degrees sun! Get involved with Cola Boy - it's the real thing!
Leo Gregory (Actor)

The year is 1996. 24-year-old Jimmy Irvine quits the tombstone grey skies of Scotland for the sun-kissed beaches of Dubai. A news reporter and small-time club DJ, Jimmy soon becomes exposed to the city's underbelly of organised crime - a seedy world which has infiltrated the cabin crew of an Arabian airline.

Out Now on Amazon

THE DESIRED ARTICLE

J.L. DISLEY

The Desired Article is like a stylish wardrobe lovingly arranged into the finest sartorial editorial.
Jason Brummell, Author

If you love your clobber, then this is the book for you. Your bookshelf will be underdressed without it, and we can't have that can we?
Mark Baxter, producer of of the film, John Simons: A Modernist

It is a wonderful book written by a guy whose attention to detail is obviously paramount.
Dr John Cooper Clarke

Writer and Poet Jason Disley, with zeal and attention to detail, like any good connoisseur, embarks upon a journey with his latest work, a book that delves into the origins and history of men's fashion.

Out Now on Amazon

MORE BOOKS FROM
www.zani.co.uk

Feltham Made Me – Paolo Sedazzari

Foreword by Mark Savage (Grange Hill)

The poet Richard F. Burton likened the truth to a large mirror, shattered into millions upon millions of pieces. Each of us owns a piece of that mirror, believing our one piece to be the whole truth. But you only get to see the whole truth when we put all the pieces together. This is the concept behind Feltham Made Me. It is the story of three lads growing up together in the suburbs of London, put together from the transcripts of many hours of interview.

ISBN-13 : 978-1527210608

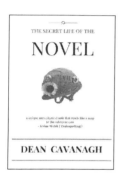

The Secret Life Of The Novel: Faking Your Death is Illegal, Faking Your Life is Celebrated - Dean Cavanagh

"A unique metaphysical noir that reads like a map to the subconscious." **Irvine Welsh**

A militant atheist Scientist working at the CERN laboratory in Switzerland tries to make the flesh into Word whilst a Scotland Yard Detective is sent to Ibiza to investigate a ritual mass murder that never took place. Time is shown to be fragmenting before our very eyes as Unreliable Narrators, Homicidal Wannabe Authors, Metaphysical Tricksters & Lost Souls haunt the near life experiences of an Ampersand who is trying to collect memories to finish a novel nobody will ever read. Goat Killers, Apocalyptic Pirate Radio DJ's, Dead Pop Stars, Social Engineers and Cartoon Characters populate a twilight landscape that may or may not exist depending on who's narrating at the time.

ISBN-13 : 978-1527201538

7P'S Paperback – A.G.R

The 7 P's. An unusual title you may think, but its meaning will become as apparent to you as it did for four friends and comrades who, in a desperate move of self-preservation, escaped the troubles of 1980s Northern Ireland, and their hometown of Belfast, only to find themselves just as deep, if not deeper, in trouble of a different kind on the treacherous streets of London.

ISBN-13 : 978-1527258365

ZANI ON SOCIAL MEDIA

///////////////////////////////

After enjoying *Tales from The Foxes of Foxham,* please follow ZANI on Social Media.

ZANI is a passionate and quirky entertaining online magazine covering contemporary, counter and popular culture.

Follow ZANI on Twitter
twitter.com/ZANIEzine

Follow ZANI on FaceBook
www.facebook.com/zanionline?fref=ts

Follow ZANI on Instagram
www.instagram.com/zanionline/